STATUTE LAW IN COLONIAL VIRGINIA

EARLY AMERICAN HISTORIES

Douglas Bradburn, John C. Coombs, and S. Max Edelson, Editors

THE

Statutes at Large;

BEING

A COLLECTION

OF ALL THE

LAWS OF VIRGINIA,

FROM THE

FIRST SESSION OF THE LEGISLATURE,

IN THE YEAR 1619.

PUBLISHED PURSUANT TO AN ACT OF THE GENERAL ASSEMBLY OF
VIRGINIA, PASSED ON THE FIFTH DAY OF FEBRUARY,
ONE THOUSAND EIGHT HUNDRED AND EIGHT.

VOLUME I.

By WILLIAM WALLER HENING.

"The *Laws* of a country are necessarily connected with every thing belonging to the people of it; so that a thorough knowledge of *them*, and of their progress would inform us of every thing that was most useful to be known about them; and one of the greatest imperfections of historians in general, is owing to their ignorance of law."

PRIESTLEY'S LECT. ON HIST. pa. 149.

RICHMOND:
PRINTED BY AND FOR SAMUEL PLEASANTS, JUNIOR, PRINTER
TO THE COMMONWEALTH.
1809.

Statute Law in Colonial Virginia

*Governors, Assemblymen, and the
Revisals That Forged the Old Dominion*

Warren M. Billings

University of Virginia Press
Charlottesville and London

University of Virginia Press
© 2021 by the Rector and Visitors of the University of Virginia
All rights reserved
Printed in the United States of America on acid-free paper

First published 2021

9 8 7 6 5 4 3 2 1

Library of Congress Cataloging-in-Publication Data
Names: Billings, Warren M., author.
Title: Statute law in colonial Virginia : governors, assemblymen, and the revisals that forged the Old Dominion / by Warren M. Billings.
Description: Charlottesville : University of Virginia Press, [2021] | Includes bibliographical references and index.
Identifiers: LCCN 2020024741 (print) | LCCN 2020024742 (ebook) | ISBN 9780813945644 (hardcover) | ISBN 9780813945651 (epub)
Subjects: LCSH: Virginia. General Assembly—History—17th century. | Virginia. General Assembly—History—18th century. | Statutes—Virginia—History—17th century. | Statutes—Virginia—History—18th century. | Legislation—Virginia—History—17th century. | Legislation—Virginia—History—18th century. | Virginia—History—Colonial period, ca. 1600–1775.
Classification: LCC KFV2478 .B55 2021 (print) | LCC KFV2478 (ebook) | DDC 349.75509/032—dc23
LC record available at https://lccn.loc.gov/2020024741
LC ebook record available at https://lccn.loc.gov/2020024742

Frontispiece: Title page to Hening's *Statutes at Large* (Wolf Law Library, William & Mary Law School)

Cover art: Elizabeth O'Neill Verner, "The governor's palace Williamsburg," pencil drawing, 1936.
Prints & Photographs Division, Library of Congress
© 2020 Estate of Elizabeth O'Neill Verner
Licensed by VAGA at Artists Rights Society (ARS), NY

For Charlotte Warren Schafer

❦ CONTENTS ❦

Acknowledgments	xi
Preface	xiii
Author's Note	xix
1. Beginnings and the Acts of 1623/24	1
2. Sir John Harvey and the Revisal of 1632	17
3. Sir William Berkeley and the Revisal of 1643	26
4. A New Constitutional Order: The Revisals of 1652 and 1658	39
5. Safeguarding Virginia's Autonomy: Sir William Berkeley, Francis Moryson, Henry Randolph, and the Revisal of 1662	55
6. The Long Road to the Revisal of 1705	70
7. Sir William Gooch's Gift: The Revisal of 1748	101
8. Endings	118
Notes	121
Bibliographic Essay	155
Index	159

ACKNOWLEDGMENTS

Richard Holway and the late E. Lee Shepard offered encouragement at an early stage of my research. Mary Sara Bilder, Carol Dunlap Billings, W. Hamilton Bryson, Marilyn Campbell, Carl Childs, Mark K. Greenough, John Ruston Pagan, Brent Tarter, Linda K. Tesar, and Nadine Zimmerli commented on various iterations of the manuscript. The Colonial Williamsburg Foundation awarded me a Jack Miller Fellowship, which enabled the research that I undertook in the John D. Rockefeller Jr. Library in 2018 and 2019. The library staff were most welcoming and uncommonly helpful while I was in residence. Thanks to John McClure at the Virginia Museum of History and Culture and to Sandra Gioia Treadway, Trenton Hizer, and Audrey McElinney at the Library of Virginia for their assistance. Thanks as well to the Wolf Law Library at the William & Mary Law School for permission to reprint the title page to William Waller Hening's *Statutes at Large* as the frontispiece to the book.

I dedicate the book to my granddaughter Charlotte Warren Schafer.

❧ PREFACE ❧

An idea for this book came to me some years ago when I wrote an article about southern colonial legal culture for the *Journal of Southern History*.[1] I made the point in that article that statutes constituted a vital element in the legal cultures of the settler societies that sprang up between the 1560s and the 1750s from the Chesapeake Bay to Florida and the Gulf Coast. Their inspirations, their designs, and their relationships to the laws of the mother countries figured prominently, if differently, in the development of each colony. They were, I argued, obscure subjects that ought to be studied more methodically than had been the case heretofore. The idea stuck, and this book is the realization of how I worked it out. Virginia seemed an appropriate place to test the premise. Its General Assembly was the first representative legislature in the Western Hemisphere whose members were the first legislators to begin routines for enacting statutes that defined their colony and regulated its people.

❧ ❧

Acts of the colonial Virginia General Assembly are compelling in themselves for an understanding of a legal environment that was always in stages of being and becoming. When first fashioned they were few, but as the Old Dominion grew from a tiny outpost to the largest province in British North America, the number of statutes expanded until they regulated most facets of the colony's internal affairs. Products of the times and social conditions that brought them into being, they arose from a blend of necessity with memory, borrowing, and inventiveness. They spoke to their creators' outlook on the right order of things, which was upheld through the good, the bad, and the ugly applications of an extraordinary legislative power.

Historians have written copiously about these matters in relation to the adaptation of English law to a Virginia setting, although none of them ever attempted a comprehensive enquiry into how the acts came to be during colonial times.[2] Arguably that is because the long arc of the colony's statutory evolution has always been difficult to re-create. Much about the origins of the acts—political upheavals, royal intervention, settler petitions, gubernatorial communications, legislative journals, draft bills, higher court records—was lost to carelessness or burned to smoke and ash in the Richmond fire of April 1865. Thanks to William Waller Hening (1767–1828) the acts themselves escaped a similar fate.

Hening identified most of the acts and compiled them into *The Statutes at Large; Being a Collection of all the Laws of Virginia, From the First Session of the Legislature in the Year 1619,* which he published in a thirteen-volume set between 1809 and 1823. The importance he ascribed to the statutes as a guide to understanding colonial Virginia underscored the observation of his contemporary, the English polymath Dr. Joseph Priestley, that "The laws of a country are necessarily connected with every thing belonging to the people of it; so that a thorough knowledge of them, and of their progress, would inform us of everything that was useful to be known about them."[3] Hening went far to reconcile his sources. He incorporated supplementary documents that no longer exist elsewhere, and he annotated everything without editorial extravagance. A purist when it came to textual fidelity, nothing was more inappropriate to him than changing "the spelling of the words, to suit the fluctuations of a living language." That approach, he insisted, would be as improper as an artist who copied the likeness of a hirsute Turk with "his mustachoes, [but gave] him the beardless face of a modern American Indian." Constraints of time, difficulties of travel, and shortages of money stymied his quest for thoroughness and frustrated his goal of producing "at the end of the work . . . a correct history of our several laws from the earliest period to the present time." Those limitations do not minimize his achievement, which remains a model of documentary editing. Hening's great work stands as the major compilation of the acts of the Assembly adopted between 1619 and 1792, although it has been repeatedly augmented by finds that have been unearthed since the 1820s.[4]

The Statutes at Large and its supplements provide a fund of documentary evidence about the colony's legal order that is not to be found elsewhere. These collections share an attribute that can act as an avenue around the stumbling block created by the 1865 fire: they are the sole record of seven occasions when the General Assembly overhauled the written *corpus juris*. The first revisal happened in 1632; the last in 1748. Each was undertaken at a particular moment. Each was linked to the singular circumstances that begot it. Each affords an insight into legislative proceedings that built on prior written law. Each embodied the Assembly members' legal knowledge and statutory craftsmanship. Each shows the members' use of their unbridled discretion to further the interests of "the grandees of government" they represented.[5] Each notes reactions of the home government. Collectively, they resemble a series of snapshots that depict the ongoing construction of "Just laws for the happy guiding and governing of the people."[6] Each revisal resulted from a legislative process that abolished the existing statutes in force and replaced them. These replacements then constituted a new *corpus juris,* and so it continued until the next revisal annulled it. In other words, Virginia legislators came to equate revisals with codes, which is an equation that endures to this day.[7]

Losses of personal papers bar deep analyses of the various hands that members were dealt and played in the process. In those instances where journals of the House of Burgesses and the Council of State exist in quantity, it is possible to follow the course of the revisals from beginning to end, but only in a general way. They disclose the introduction of the draft acts, their referrals to committees of the whole, and their eventual passage. Occasionally they even contain limited indications of the political alignments of the members in both houses. The destruction of virtually all the higher court archives prevents exploring how the revisals were interpreted and how those interpretations promoted statutory revisions.

The very first overhaul, the Revisal of 1632, grew out of the uncertainties bred by the downfall of the Virginia Company of London and King Charles I's proclaiming the colony a royal dominion led by Governor Sir John Harvey. The revisal responded to settler concerns about religion, food, defense, land, labor, tobacco, and governance—local concerns that remained at the heart of legislative agendas deep into future years. Moreover, the method of its making established a precedent for the later overhauls into the eighteenth century.

By the 1640s, Virginia's features as an unequal society based on tobacco, bound laborers, and commerce around the rim of the Atlantic were set and were now increasingly matters of written law. Frequent additions to the Revisal of 1632 had defined those traits in often contradictory or redundant ways that heightened the difficulties of administering the acts in force. The need for another renovation was in order. Governor Sir William Berkeley seized the moment and maneuvered the more wide-ranging Revisal of 1642 through a newly bicameral General Assembly, which he invented. The revised statutes left few areas of the colony's polity untouched. They also symbolized the Assembly's centrality as Virginia's primary lawgiver and its members' growing abilities as lawmakers.

The execution of King Charles I and the overthrow of the monarchy ushered in an interlude of republican rule that produced the next two revisals. Hurriedly cobbled together, the Revisal of 1652 established a constitutional order that centered authority in the House of Burgesses and ditched most of the acts adopted after 1643. Prepared in 1658, the second revisal improved on the first, but it set off a splenetic row between Governor Samuel Mathews Jr. and the House of Burgesses, which the members won with an impressive demonstration of legislative craftsmanship and adroit parliamentary choreography.

The return to royal government was the impetus for the Revisal of 1662. Deputy Governor Francis Moryson and Clerk of the House of Burgesses Henry Randolph drew it up at the behest of the restored Governor Berkeley, who also had it printed in London. Unquestionably, it was the most far-reaching of the seventeenth-century revised codes. It was a bold iteration of the relative autonomy the General Assembly had enjoyed from the 1620s, and it became *the* snapshot of the General Assembly at the peak of its ascendency as a little Parliament.

There would not be another overhaul until 1705. Royal intervention in the affairs of the General Assembly contributed to the forty-year interval between the two. So did the inability of the governors, councillors, and burgesses to agree on how to reform the statutes. Persistent prodding eventually resulted in an approach that modified past methods of redoing the *corpus juris*. That breakthrough cleared the way to the sixth revisal. The record of the Revisal of 1705 is more abundant than the others, which makes it the most detailed snapshot of all.

Lieutenant Governor Sir William Gooch inspired the Revisal of 1748. Unlike the other six, it was primarily a modernized version of the statutory status quo instead of a blueprint for sweeping structural reforms. Its review by royal officials provoked a rancorous quarrel between the General Assembly in Williamsburg and a revivified, authoritarian Board of Trade in London that threatened the scope of the Assembly's legislative powers. The threat receded, but the Virginians began to see the home government's management of colonial affairs in a new and revolutionary light.

※ ※

In spite of an immense accumulation of literature about early Virginia law, nothing re-created the sweep of its statutory development. This book does. Its analysis of the seven revisals offers a systematic, if limited, narrative of the General Assembly at work fulfilling the purpose of legislatures—legislating. It uncovers unparalleled insights for gauging how codes of statute law were created. Some of the snapshots offer more detail than others, but when seen in succession they portray the ways governors and assemblymen used them to forge the Old Dominion.

❦ AUTHOR'S NOTE ❦

Dates are Old Style, meaning they are rendered according to the ancient Julian calendar, which was ten days behind the Gregorian calendar that is in use today. The English began the year on 25 March, and it was therefore customary for them to write both years, that is, 1 January 1600/01, in the interval between 1 January and 24 March 1601. That usage is retained here, although 1 January is taken as the start of any given year. Quotations are regularized only to the extent that modern orthography is imposed on proper names; archaic abbreviations or symbols are spelled out; sentences begin with capitals and end in periods, question marks, or exclamation points; and use of *i, j, u,* and *w* conforms to modern practice. Everything else remains as found.

STATUTE LAW IN COLONIAL VIRGINIA

❈ 1 ❈

Beginnings and the Acts of 1623/24

Representatives gathered in the church at Jamestown on a sultry July day in 1619. Summoned by Governor Sir George Yeardley, they sat as a "general Assemblie." Following instructions from the Virginia Company of London, they enacted laws that for the first time extended a measure of self-governance throughout the English settlements. Following that initial meeting, the General Assembly worked more or less as Company executives envisioned but its future and its authority fell into question after the Company bankrupted and Virginia became a royal dominion in 1625. The loss of the Company charter undercut the Assembly constitutionally whereas King Charles I's failure to recognize it cast it in legal limbo as well and effectively left the colonists on their own. Seeking a measure of stability amid war with the Indians, Governor Sir Francis Wyatt and leading colonists in the General Assembly of February 1623/24 took it upon themselves to adopt a body of statutes to exert order across the English settlements. In so doing, they claimed an unbridled legislative authority and commenced the Assembly's journey from a corporate adjunct to a little Parliament. The acts, which were meant as temporary measures, were foundational as they and the additions to them became the basis of the Revisal of 1632.

❈ ❈

Developing Jamestown turned out to be a more difficult undertaking than the investors in the Virginia Company could ever have imagined in 1607.

It limped along unprofitably until it verged on collapse. All the while backers and colonists squabbled over a way forward. Company treasurer Sir Thomas Smythe (ca. 1558–1625); his principal ally Robert Rich, second earl of Warwick (1587–1658); and Sir Edwin Sandys (1561–1629) each headed factions with decidedly different visions of ways to make Virginia prosper. Even the Crown evinced an interest in Virginia's survival because the burgeoning tobacco trade held the promise of replenishing the royal coffers. Sandys eventually outmaneuvered Smythe and Warwick and became treasurer. He scrapped the existing martial model of settlement in favor of one that would develop a diversified economy and transplant as much of an English commonwealth as conditions in Virginia would allow. To that end, in 1618, he set forth a scheme in a series of management documents.[1]

Those papers reformed land tenures and promoted the production of staples. There were provisions for improvements to local administration, one of which substituted elements of English common law for the much-hated *Lawes Divine, Morall and Martiall,* a stern regime of military regulations that constituted Virginia's earliest statute law.[2] To create a more palatable resident government, a new governor also received orders to convene a general assembly comprised of him, Company-appointed councillors of state, and representatives elected by the freemen of the colony. That body would sit annually. It was empowered to enact local laws, grounded in the Company's corporate rights, that addressed local needs or implemented directives from London, any of which the governor might veto or Company officers might reject. That so-called "Great Charter" also authorized the Assembly to act as a court of justice from time to time.[3]

Sometime around 25 June 1619, Governor Sir George Yeardley issued writs to the "freemen and Tenants," ordering them "by pluralitie of voices to make election of two sufficient men" from each settlement to meet with him and the Council of State as a *"generall Assemblie."* (These representatives would be called "burgesses" from that day until 1776 when their successors took the title of "delegate," which is still in use.) Qualifications to vote or to sit in the Assembly were looser than those that applied in elections to the House of Commons. A candidate or an elector had only to be English, free, male, and above twenty-one years of age, and did not have to own or rent real estate.[4]

The General Assembly convened on 30 July 1619, at the Jamestown church, which was the only building in the colony big enough to accommodate large gatherings. Twenty burgesses, who represented eleven constituencies; six councillors of state; and the governor, comprised the body. We know little of the burgesses individually; most never sat in a subsequent Assembly, but more can be said about the councillors. Three of them, Francis West, Nathaniel Powell, and Samuel Maycock, had lived in Virginia for much of its first decade, and they were notable chiefly for their knowledge of matters military and their successes as colonizers. John Rolfe, the fourth councillor, had pointed the way to the colony's eventual economic survival through tobacco culture. Whatever memory of him lingers now, however, has less to do with a weed than with his marriage to a young Indian woman the English knew as Pocahontas. The Reverend William Wickham is remarkable only because he was the first one of only three clerics who sat as a councillor of state before the American Revolution.[5] Secretary of the Colony John Pory was the sixth councillor, and more can be told about him than anyone else.

Pory (bap. 1572–ca. 1636) came from people who sat much higher up the social ladder than all save Francis West. Educated at the University of Cambridge, he was one of those Jacobean wanderers the historian Alison Games styled "cosmopolitans."[6] That is to say, he was a well-traveled Englishman who traversed the globe in search of adventure, glory for God, king, country, and personal fulfillment. After going down from Cambridge, he assisted the Reverend Richard Hakluyt the Younger, that most influential of late Tudor publicists of English colonizing in the Americas, who aroused Pory's own curiosity about exploring new worlds. By the early 1600s, Pory's reputation for honesty, erudition, and diligence produced exceptional political connections and a seat in the House of Commons during the Parliament of 1604–1611. The latter mark distinguished him as one of only three seventeenth-century members of the General Assembly ever to sit in the Commons or the House of Lords. A pronounced weakness for drink neither dulled his wits unduly nor prevented Sir Edwin Sandys's enemies from engineering Pory's appointment as secretary of the colony in order to keep an eye on Governor Yeardley. Pory would be instrumental in launching the General Assembly before he returned to England in 1623, where he lived out his days as an intelligencer for his patrons.[7]

For his part, Governor Sir George Yeardley (bap. 1588–1627), was a son of a middling London merchant tailor. Like countless other British lads of his class, he shunned his father's calling and in his case traded a needle and thread for a sword. Time spent with the English troops that the Crown had stationed in the Netherlands as guarantors of Dutch independence from Spain imparted lessons in soldiering. He throve on the military life, especially after another soldier of fortune, Sir Thomas Gates (d. 1622), took him under his wing. The two of them set off for Virginia in 1609—Gates as lieutenant governor and Yeardley as captain of Gates's guard. Gates's ship, the *Sea Venture,* foundered on the Bermuda coast; both men survived and eventually reached Jamestown in 1610. An increasing number of duties followed until Yeardley returned to England in 1617. A year later he married Temperance Flowerdew, who was John Pory's niece. By then he had already caught the eye of Sir Edwin Sandys, who named him governor, and in November 1618, James I tapped him for knighthood "to grace him the more" in his new office. Touches from the king's rapier and a good marriage hardly elevated Yeardley in the eyes of those Virginians who regarded him as a "meane fellow by way of provision." Nevertheless, he managed his assignment well enough, though he was never entirely comfortable with his position. He gave it up in 1621 but briefly returned to office under King Charles I before he died.[8]

Together Yeardley and Pory led the Assembly to a successful first ever meeting. Afterward, Pory prepared a "reporte of the manner of proceeding in the General Assembly," which he composed and sent copies off to London soon after the session. If he had done no more than this, his reputation would be secure because the "reporte" is the sole record of what happened during the meeting, even though it leaves a reader wishing for more. It omits as much as it includes; it does not reproduce floor debates verbatim or speeches in full; and it does not reveal who put motions or how the members voted on them. Notwithstanding such omissions, the "reporte" is the fullest record for any session of the General Assembly before the 1680s.[9]

Everyone gathered in "the Quire of the churche." According to Pory, Yeardley designated him "Speaker" before naming John Twine as clerk of the Assembly and Thomas Pierse its sergeant-at-arms. The Reverend Richard Buck, the resident priest, prayed for heavenly blessings and divine guidance. Members swore an oath of allegiance to the Crown and another that avowed their acceptance of the king as the supreme head of the Church of England. (The latter oath was meant to catch out crypto-Catholics and to prevent them from holding any office.) Everyone stood by until Twine called the roll for their admission one by one as members.

To anyone acquainted with the workings of a seventeenth-century Parliament, all of this has a familiar look to it, but a closer inspection discloses some significant differences in proceedings at London and at Jamestown. Governor Yeardley, the councillors of state, and the burgesses sat as one house, not two. The Reverend Mr. Buck merely prayed, whereas his counterpart at the opening of Parliament preached a sermon, and there was no equivalent to the royal speech from the throne. Although John Pory styled himself "Speaker," nothing in his account indicates that he acted like a Speaker in the House of Commons. Instead of being elected by the burgesses, Yeardley had appointed him. The burgesses did not drag a protesting Pory to his chair. Nor did he give the customary disabling speech. Yeardley, not Pory, presided over the body. Pory was no advocate for the burgesses, which was a principal duty of the Commons' Speaker early in the seventeenth century. Actually, Pory sat with his council colleagues and devoted the bulk of his time doing secretarial and clerical tasks and setting the Assembly's agenda.

Calling Pory "Speaker" has long fostered the misbegotten idea that the General Assembly took life as a bicameral legislature, in which each chamber enjoyed distinctly separated powers. As a result, generations of Virginians and scholars have conflated the General Assembly with the House of Burgesses, which is a little like saying the House of Representatives and the Congress of the United States are one and the same body, when they are not. Instead, the first General Assembly consisted of three elements: governor, councillors of state, and burgesses, all of whom constituted an entity that remained unicameral until 1643.

Pory brought his legislative experience to bear on the dispatch of the Assembly's business in several lasting ways. For one, when a challenge to the qualifications of two prospective burgesses threatened a lengthy delay in proceedings, Pory suggested that his colleagues act as Parliament might and judge for themselves who could sit among them, which they did. By ruling that the disputed credentials were improper, the members laid down a precedent that later General Assemblies translated into an exclusive right that obtains to this day. For another, Pory fixed the legislative agenda. To that purpose, he explained the rationale for the General Assembly and detailed the duties the Company assigned to it. Next, he read aloud the Great Charter for the benefit of the whole company, and in so doing he took the place of a parliamentary reading clerk. Then he apportioned the legislative work into four parts: determining which sections of the Great Charter needed modification, which Company instructions were to be adopted as local law, what new regulations should be proposed, and what petitions to the Company in London were in order. Finally, Pory seems also to have been responsible for introducing two additional parliamentary habits, the use of committees to send bills to the floor in a timely manner and giving bills three readings before their enactment as statutes.

That Pory exerted so much influence stemmed from an obvious though often overlooked fact. He alone among the members knew much about procedures in deliberative bodies. Thus, he was in a unique position to shape how the Assembly did its business, and he tailored his knowledge of legislative proceedings to the needs of the moment as well as to an evolving legislature. His efforts eased the adoption of laws that enacted a range of activities that ran from relations with the Indians to labor contracts and tobacco prices, and in keeping with its purpose as a court of justice, the Assembly also heard a number of criminal matters. As a result of Pory's leadership, the General Assembly of 1619 not only did its work smoothly and expeditiously, but also bequeathed a legacy of rules of procedure for later Assemblies to build on.

Pory and his colleagues contended with an oppressively humid Tidewater Virginia summer as they worked in the stifling, cramped little church. Muggy weather carried off an already sickly Walter Shelley, burgess for Smythe's Hundred, and resulted in an adjournment on 4 August, because in Pory's words, "(by reason of extream heat both paste [past] and likely to ensue, and by that meanes, of the alteration of the healthes of diverse of the general Assembly) the Governour, who him self also was not well, resolved should be the laste of this firste Session."[10] As Pory and the others left the churchyard, they had cause to be pleased with what they had accomplished in a mere five days. They had shepherded an appreciable measure of self-government into existence, they had passed laws, and they had begun a process for legislating statutes in the years to come. Thereafter the General Assembly grew in popularity with settlers who increasingly saw in it an instrument of effective lawmaking and a political mechanism by which they could share largely in running the colony.

Although Yeardley, with Pory's substantial help, successfully executed the launch of the General Assembly, his was a troubled administration. Despite his knighthood, his lowly origins diminished respect for him and his office, as did a grumpy demeanor, but his chief problem lay in carrying out Sandys's plans for Virginia. There was the added complication of making do with ever larger numbers of new settlers who arrived sick or without needed skills. No matter their condition or abilities they had to be maintained, but the supplies to sustain them were more often insufficient than not. More colonists meant expanded settlements, which put more pressure on the Powhatans and hardened relations and eroded an iffy peace. Yeardley grumbled incessantly to Sandys about his troubles. His crabbiness annoyed Sandys and it became ammunition for the Smythe-Warwick faction to attack Sandys. His patience exhausted, Yeardley asked to be relieved, and in the summer of 1621, the general court of the Company voted to replace him with Sir Francis Wyatt.[11]

Wyatt (ca. 1588–1644) belonged to a patrician Kentish family, albeit one with a checkered past. The Wyatts bore the taint of treachery against the Crown. His grandfather, Sir Thomas Wyatt, rebelled against Queen Mary Tudor, which cost him his head and the family its reputation and estates. His father recovered enough of both for Francis to attend St. Mary Hall, Oxford, and Clifford's Inn, London, before he was knighted in 1618. Marriage to one of Sir Edwin Sandys's nieces and his active involvement with the Virginia Company accounted for his appointment as governor, despite his want of political experience and practical military training.[12]

Wyatt was barely into his governorship before he confronted a devastating war and the breakup of the Company. Sandys's overly ambitious schemes miscarried and those miscarriages stiffened the tensions that fractured into the Anglo-Powhatan War of 1622–1632. The Indians mounted a sudden assault on 22 March 1622 that wiped out a third of the colonists and set off a merciless intermittent war of attrition. News of the conflict heightened festering feuds between the Sandys and the Smythe Warwick factions. Shortages of capital starved operations to the edge of bankruptcy.

The Company's distresses compelled King James I to intervene. On his command, in November 1623 Attorney General Sir Thomas Coventry filed a writ of *quo warranto* in the Court of King's Bench to compel the Company to show cause why its charter should not be revoked. The outcome was never in doubt, although six months passed before the Court found for the king. In May 1624, the Company surrendered its charter and was no more. Virginia reverted to the Crown. James temporarily retained Wyatt and his councillors while he and his advisors considered how best to oversee the colony. He preferred a reconstituted company as the managerial device but he died before his wishes could bear fruit. The decision of what to do next fell to his son, Charles I, who in May 1625 issued a proclamation declaring Virginia a royal dominion under his personal protection. Vowing to maintain the colony "as any other part of Our Dominions," Charles said that its government would "immediately depend upon Our Selfe, and not be committed to any Company or Corporation, to whom it may be proper to trust matters of Trade and Commerce, but cannot bee fit or safe to communicate the ordering of State-affaires, be they of never so meane consequence." He promised to honor Company land grants and to support "at Our owne charge" all "publique Officers and Ministers . . . as shall be fit and necessary for the defense of that Plantation." Then he ended with several provisions regarding the tobacco trade, declaring "We are resolved to take the same into Our owne hands."[13]

By proclaiming Virginia his royal dominion, King Charles altered the purpose and shape of the General Assembly forevermore. The Company reforms of 1618 had provided a constitution for Virginia's governance, which had empowered the General Assembly; however, destruction of the Great Charter eliminated the legal basis for Assembly. After 1625, Charles's proclamation, commissions and instructions to the governors, and other royal policy papers became the constitutional grounds of authority in the colony. The silence of those documents regarding the continuation of the General Assembly and the reach of its powers, while not necessarily abolishing it, certainly cast doubt on its legitimacy. Charles inadvertently threw it into even deeper constitutional uncertainty by failing to recognize its existence in his proclamation. Moreover, Charles's subsequent inattention left the settlers to their own devices legislatively, which, in a twist, would give them an enormous latitude to grow the General Assembly from a corporate appendage into a little Parliament. The first sign of that change of purpose happened at the General Assembly of February 1623/24.

Dismantling the Virginia Company came at an especially fraught moment for the colony.[14] By 1624, the war with the Powhatans was entering its third year and showed no sign of a favorable outcome for the English anytime soon. Defenses were weak and there were shortages of armaments and foodstuffs. Opinions regarding Virginia's future were sharply divided. Certain colonists ardently favored rejuvenating the Company; others were vehemently opposed. An injudicious royal commission of inquiry into conditions in the colony, chaired by Captain (later Sir) John Harvey, widened that rift. Perhaps most troubling of all, the breakup threatened to leave Virginia in legal chaos. Governor Wyatt perceived that a bout of lawlessness, however fleeting, threatened to make the chaos all the more chaotic. To guard against such an eventuality, he summoned the General Assembly of February 1623/24.[15]

In addition to Wyatt, thirty-four individuals—twenty-eight burgesses and six councillors of state—were present in the Assembly that began on 16 February 1623/24. As a group, the councillors and the burgesses were a mixed lot in terms of their origins. Some were genteel, some were seafarers, some were military, some were merchants, and some were adventurers. Whatever their backgrounds, all saw in Virginia opportunities to slake ambitions they could not quench at home. The six councillors were Raphe Hamor (bap. 1589–1626), Dr. John Pott (d. ca. 1642), John Pountis (ca. 1565–1624), George Sandys (1578–1644), Francis West (1586–1634), and former Governor Yeardley. Hamor first went out to Virginia in 1609 and for a time succeeded William Strachey as secretary of the colony. Returning to England in 1614, he wrote *A True Discourse of the True Estate of Virginia* (London, 1615), which yet stands as one of the major narratives of the Jamestown project's early years. While a councillor, he was a key leader in defending the colonists against the Powhatans, having himself narrowly escaped death the day the war broke out.[16] Pott was the least experienced politically before he joined the Council, but his value lay in his knowledge of poisons, which he used to kill Indian leaders as a terror tactic in the war against them. He was acting governor until his archenemy Governor Sir John Harvey took office in 1630. Harvey had him tried and convicted for hog stealing, but the case was eventually dropped and he retained his seat.[17] Pountis was a London cloth worker turned merchant mariner who was treasurer of Southampton Hundred prior to his rise to the Council. After the Assembly adjourned, he was appointed its agent to London but died at sea on his way to the metropolis.[18] Sandys, Sir Edwin's brother, became treasurer of Virginia in 1621, which automatically gave him his seat on the Council of State. He held it for four years before he went back to England, where he advocated reviving the Virginia Company until his death.[19] West was the senior councillor and a brother of former Governor

Thomas West, twelfth baron De La Warr. Named to the very first Council of State in 1609, he kept his seat until he died. He was acting governor for two years following the death of Yeardley in 1627. That set the precedent for the senior councillor to act as chief executive whenever a governor died or was out of the colony.[20] As for Yeardley, he became a councillor after Wyatt replaced him as governor and followed Sir Francis to his old post in 1625.

All six shared something in common with Wyatt. They owed their offices to Sir Edwin Sandys. That debt committed them to implementing the treasurer's plans for Virginia and set them opposite the colony's supporters belonging to the Smythe-Warwick faction. Moreover, aside from Dr. Pott, these were men of broad political experience in Virginia who enjoyed the confidence of the generality of planters, and that was surely a boon to Wyatt as he guided the Assembly through its paces.

Prominent political figures at the time, most of the burgesses are now little more than names on a page.[21] Of those for whom something may be said, William Peirce (d. ca. 1643) and William Tucker (ca. 1579–1654) were among the earliest settlers; Nathaniel Basse (bap. 1589–1654) and Samuel Mathews (d. 1657) were among the more recent. A soldier, Peirce shipped to Virginia in 1609. Around the time of his election he took command of Fort James and fought in the Anglo-Powhatan War. He sat in another General Assembly before moving up to the Council of State where he stayed until the end of his days. Tucker, also a soldier, arrived in 1610 and settled in Kicoughtan. He was a burgess in the General Assembly of 1619 and a councillor between 1626 and 1628. A Londoner, Basse alighted in 1619 south of the James River in Warrosquyoake, which became Isle of Wight County. Altogether, he represented Warrosquyoake in four General Assemblies and did a short stint as a councillor. Mathews went out to Virginia in 1622 as a member of the Harvey Commission. He established himself as a consequential landowner, merchant, Indian fighter, and politician. Possibly the most unusual burgess was Nicholas Martiau (1591–1654), who was a naturalized Frenchman. His election marked the start of a thirty-year career as a burgess, local magistrate, and militia officer. Richard Stephens, a London painter-stainer, was never again a burgess but he was on the Council for four years between 1632 and his death in 1636. He had a son, Samuel, whose widow, Frances Culpeper Stephens, became Sir William Berkeley's second wife. John Utie (d. ca. 1638) sat in two later General Assemblies before he became a York County magistrate and continued in office until he died.

Like the councillors, these men inclined politically toward Sandys. How those inclinations played out with those of the lesser known burgesses throughout the meeting are lost because the skimpy record of the proceedings contains nothing about the debates. What we do know is that combatting the Smythe-Warwick faction and legislating took a while before a two-pronged strategy was agreed upon. John Pountis became the Assembly's agent and was dispatched to London "to solicit the cause of the country to his majesty and the counsell." To that end, he was entrusted with a series of papers to present at Westminster. Two rebutted Sir Thomas Smythe's allies Nathaniel Butler and Alderman Robert Johnson who had fiercely condemned Sandys for what they claimed was his corruption and gross mismanagement of the Company. A petition to the king expressed the Assembly's "great Comfort" in the knowledge that James had assumed "your more neere and especiall care" for Virginia as it begged him not to allow "your poore Subjects to fall into the handes of *Sir Tho. Smith* or his Confidents, who have lately abused your Sacred eares with wrong Informations." It pleaded for "souldiers" and closed with the prayer that King James would give the Assembly "voyce" because no one in England "by reason of accidents and emergent occasions" could govern Virginia "so advantagiously as our presence and experience." An entreaty to the Privy Council for sanctioning the Assembly was even more insistent. "But above all," it concluded, "we humblie intreat your Lordshipps that we may retaine the libertie of our generall Assemblie, then which nothing can more conduce to our satisfaction or the publique utilitie." These papers never reached the Privy Council because Pountis's ship foundered, he drowned, and the papers sank with him to the depths of the Atlantic.[22]

When the time came to consider legislation, Wyatt cautioned the councillors and burgesses about the dismal consequences of dithering. Local laws were needed until the Crown decided on permanent arrangements for the future management of Virginia, and he urged swift action. He had his way because the councillors and burgesses shared his concerns and because they respected him as a "most just and sincere gentleman."[23] There was no Speaker to shepherd bills into law, and who wrote them is unknown. They may have been drawn up by Wyatt or a committee. Alternatively, they might have been distilled from proposals put forward by individual members as responses to their constituents. If the reading of bills three times was already an accepted practice, then it is probable that every member voiced an opinion and contributed in some manner to the bills that passed into law.

Wyatt initialed thirty-five statutes and council clerk Edward Sharples enrolled them into a fair copy that constituted an official text.[24] None carried a title but each received a number that gave it a unique identity. Sharples's manner of classification was a common method of scribal identification that later Assemblies adopted. Thereafter it was customary to refer to a particular statute by naming the General Assembly that enacted it and identifying it by its number.[25] It also became customary for the secretary of the colony to keep the enrolled laws in his custody and to supervise making authentic copies for distribution throughout Virginia.[26]

While the acts shared purposes akin to statutes of the realm, there are no indications that Wyatt and his colleagues automatically looked to Parliament for their models. Indeed, the form and substance of the acts suggest otherwise. Plain declarative statements, they were seldom more than a sentence or two in length. (As such, they contained only one of the elements that comprised parliamentary statutes: preambles that rehearsed Parliament's power, an enacting clause, a body that set forth things regulated by the act, and, where necessary, a penalty clause.) The vernacular substituted for Law French and Latin, the languages of parliamentary legislation, and that substitution established the precedent for English to become the vocabulary of Virginia law.

The shortest of them, for instance, merely said "That a dew watch be kept by night."[27] Nonetheless, it and the other acts filled the interstices between English law and Virginia legalities that addressed aspects of colonial life that neither statutes of the realm nor common law nor local customs contemplated or those in which the Crown had shown little interest after it took over Virginia. Briefly put, these were acts that spelled out rules for exerting order and a degree of safety across the English settlements. They also responded to settler concerns about religion, food, defense, land, governance, and the economy, which would remain political issues that drove legislating in future years.[28]

The laws that the Assembly designed to buoy a fledgling colonial church is palpable evidence of these intentions. Those statutes were the first to be enacted, and they were the first to be enrolled. That placement suggests a pressing concern for things of the spirit and an equally pressing earthly concern about sustaining the church as an instrument of social discipline, filling the void caused by the absence of an Anglican religious establishment. Company officials always took considerable care to supply the colony with priests. Those clerics were licensees of the bishop of London. Beyond issuing those licenses the bishop of London showed little diligence in extending the institutional church to Virginia and neither did his superior, the archbishop of Canterbury. Therefore, from its earliest days the Virginia church harbored in no diocese and strung none of the supports that traditionally rigged the Church of England. The church acts of 1623/24 were the first among many that for the want of an ecclesiastical alternative began to shift church oversight over to the hands of secular authorities.[29]

One of these laws required setting aside "a house or roome" of worship in every plantation and a ground "empaled in, sequestered only to the burial of the dead." Several others dealt with church discipline. Attendance at divine services was compulsory. Absences "without an allowable excuse" resulted in modest punishments. The penalty for missing a single Sunday was a fine of one pound of tobacco or fifty pounds if one were absent for a month.[30] Ministers were commanded to conform as "neere as may be to the canons in England." Priests who were absent from their parishes more than four months were liable to lose their livings, but they were shielded from disparaging remarks "whereby the minds of [their] parishioners may be alienated from [them], and [their] ministry prove the less effectual." They were also entitled maintenance in the form of levies in tobacco and corn[31] collected from their parishioners. Then there was the statute that mandated that 22 March "bee yearly solemnized as [a] holliday." That particular act incorporated the anniversary of the outbreak of the Anglo-Powhatan War of 1622–1632 into the Anglican cycle of holy days and special devotions.[32]

One of the secular acts created what might be deemed the first protected class of citizens in American law. It exempted certain colonists and their "posterity" from future military service and relieved them of "any publick charge" other than church tithes. To qualify, someone had to be an "old planter" who had settled before "the last coming of sir Thomas Gates" in 1611. Perhaps Francis West, William Peirce, or William Tucker sponsored the act given that all three were "old planters" who stood to gain by its passage.[33]

By a different law, planters were supposed to have their landholdings laid out by the colony's surveyor general.[34] That person went unnamed in the act but undoubtedly he was William Claiborne (1600–1679). The Virginia Company hired Claiborne as surveyor general right after he left the University of Cambridge. A short time later he sailed to Virginia aboard ship with Governor Wyatt and began a career in public life that lasted from the 1620s to the 1660s during which he was a councillor and secretary of the colony. He was an ally of Samuel Mathews. The two of them shared commercial interests that linked them to the Puritan mercantile community in London, and they dominated Virginia politics for years.[35]

Among the economic statutes, one continued existing price controls on an unspecified number of commodities. A second means of regulating prices was a prohibition against ship masters unloading or making private sales of their cargoes without the governor's leave or until they docked at Jamestown. Another was a war measure that put a dent in commerce with the Indians when it prevented the settlers from trading with the Indians for food. Still another sought to encourage agricultural diversity with its requirement that "every freeman shall fence in a quarter of an acre of ground before Whitsuntide next" on which to grow grapevines and mulberry trees. A fifth decreed "That there be no weights nor measures but such as shall be sealed by officers for that purpose," although the statute did not specify who those "officers" were or by whom they were "sealed."[36]

Several acts were intended to alleviate famine and to ensure adequate defenses against the Indians. Permitting planters to sell their surpluses of corn "as deere as [they] can" and creating granaries "for the publique uses of every parish by the major part of the freemen" was intended to ease food shortages. To fill the granaries, a levy of one bushel of corn was charged to every planter older than eighteen. So too was the appointment of three inspectors in every parish who were charged "to see that every man shall see that every man shall plant and tende sufficient of corne for his family." The law empowered the inspectors to present delinquents to the governor and council for "censure."[37]

Houses were to be fortified with palisades, and their owners and servants were not to go abroad or work their fields without the accompaniment of an armed guard. Local commanders were charged with stocking "sufficient of powder and ammunition" and to keep muskets in working order at all times. And under no circumstances were they or anyone else "to spend powder unnecessarily in drinking or entertainments, &c." Planters were taxed to support a new summer campaign against the Indians. Wounded militiamen would "be cured at the publique charge," whereas those who suffered permanent injuries would be "maintained by the country according to his person and quality."[38] Other statutes directly addressed the preservation of public order. Of these one gave legislative sanction to gubernatorial proclamations against swearing and drunkenness. Those edicts exacted fines from offenders because the act stipulated that "forfeitures shall be collected by [local commanders] to be for publique uses." A second demanded obedience to the "present government" despite the "rumur" of its alteration, which was probably a slap at colonists partial to the Smythe-Warwick interests. By a third statute, violators of this law, or those who were otherwise disobedient, were punished in a manner that accorded with their social station. Ordinary planters were publicly whipped or maimed whereas "persons of quality" were exempted from the indignity of corporal punishment, though they could be "ymprisoned" for petty violations or subjected to fines for more serious infractions. (What constituted general disobedience went undefined in this statute or elsewhere.)[39]

Members used the opportunity to give greater definition to ways of governance in the body and in the localities. They forbade the governor from taxing colonists any "other way than by the authority of the General Assembly," and they claimed a right to "ymploy" the taxes "as the said Assembly shall appoynt." He was also prevented from withdrawing "inhabitants from their private labors to any service of his own," although he and the "whole body of the counsell" might impress colonists under certain conditions. Burgesses were spared from arrest during and either side of a General Assembly session, which is a privilege that continues to this day.[40] Setting up monthly courts "in the corporations of Charles City and Elizabeth Citty for the decyding of suits and controversies not exceeding the value of one hundred pounds of tobacco and for the punishing of petty offences" eased the burden of the governor and councillors in their judicial capacity. But the law represented something else too. It was the Assembly's first statutory claim to regulate government beyond Jamestown, and in that regard the act opened the way toward the county court system of local rule.[41]

On 5 March, Wyatt signed the acts and adjourned the Assembly. It had been a productive meeting. In the space of just two weeks he had participated in enacting laws that on parchment held the likelihood of keeping Virginia intact for the time being, and to that end authenticated copies were sent throughout the settlements. The councillors, the burgesses, and

Wyatt learned something of the arts and politics of writing laws, and with that they began the transformation of the General Assembly into Virginia's primary lawgiver. Beyond tackling the imperatives of the moment, none of them could ever have imagined the greater significance of their handiwork. They had set the foundation for subsequent legislation and for the revisals that were to come.

2

Sir John Harvey and the Revisal of 1632

Sir John Harvey (ca. 1581–1646) was the very antithesis of Sir Francis Wyatt, whom he succeeded as governor in 1628. Enticed to blue water as a boy, he worked his way from the forecastle to the quarterdeck and became a ship captain. Successful voyages to the East Indies gained him a reputation as an expert, dependable merchant mariner and favorable notice from the Crown. Always cocking a weather eye toward profit, he bought stock in the Virginia Company and leased one of his ships, the *Southampton*, to the Company as a transport for new colonists to Virginia. The timing of his first voyage to the colony is uncertain, but he took up land in the New Town section of Jamestown where he raised a large house. Later in 1622, the Privy Council commissioned him chairman of a fact-finding committee it sent to Jamestown to inform King James about conditions in Virginia. Not unexpectedly, the colonists greeted Harvey and his fellow commissioners warily. He and the General Assembly of February 1623/24 clashed, which only added to the hostility and deep distrust he fostered, but he finished his assignment and sailed back to England. King Charles I eventually named him governor in 1628, and likely knighted him at the same time. Harvey's part in English naval operations against Cadiz and guarding British ports amid the Thirty Years' War, however, kept him from Virginia until 1630.[1]

Temperamentally, Harvey was prickly, short-tempered, and unbending. His ideas about governing were very much shaped by his maritime experiences. At sea the captain was a law unto himself. His chief responsibility was the well-being of his vessel and its cargo and ensuring that both arrived at their destination safely. That meant his ship was always to be kept tidy and in proper working order. He drilled his crew to perform their duties smartly; deviation from established routines was intolerable because it threatened safety. His orders were not topics for debate or compromises with his subordinates; they were to be obeyed without question. Disobedience was tantamount to mutiny and invited brutal punishment. Although Harvey's style of command suited rule at sea, it hardly suited governing from the Council chamber in Virginia.[2]

Harvey came to office in uncertain times. There was no end to the war with the Powhatans. Defenses were weak. Shortages of food and other goods were prevalent, which made prices dear. The transition from the demise of the Virginia Company to royal administration was still a work in progress. Apart from the governor and Council of State, Virginia had no permanent royal government. Land titles were in doubt. Despite King Charles's promise not to turn management of the colony over to a revitalized Virginia Company, a reconstituted company remained a disturbing possibility. Equally troubling was the king's consideration of a royal monopoly on the tobacco trade, which would undercut the likes of William Claiborne and Samuel Matthews, who had independent ties to London merchants. Inevitably, the news of Harvey's appointment, which reached Virginia well ahead of his arrival, inspired no joy among the settlers. They had reason to worry because to them the newly minted Sir John represented a king whose designs for their future were anything but certain. Those who recalled his contentious conduct when he chaired the Harvey Commission certainly had no expectation that he would be any different as their governor. He was not. Almost immediately he clashed with his councillors of state. Their brawls made for a tempestuous administration that lasted until his removal in 1639. However, those scuffles masked a record of considerable accomplishment, not least of which was Harvey's promotion of the first revisal of the statutes in force.[3]

The number of legislative acts had grown with increasing frequency after 1624. At Wyatt's behest, the General Assemblies of 1625 and 1626 had passed more laws as it seemed evermore obvious that the Crown would probably leave regulating Virginia's internal affairs to the colonists. There are no copies of the 1625 acts so it is impossible to know their number or what they entailed whereas a few of the statutes from 1626 are summarized in a minute from a Council of State meeting of 7 and 8 August 1626.

The summaries indicate that those laws were mainly amended versions of earlier statutes, one of which included a change in a church act that explicitly appropriated the canons of the Church of England "in substance and Circumstance."[4] In 1628, while Francis West stood in for Harvey, a second batch came into being. Those statutes are lost so there is no way of telling how many there were or which among them modified existing laws, which were new acts that extended the Assembly's legislative reach, or what was the manner of their preparation. Acting governor Dr. John Pott shepherded an additional nine bills into law before he dissolved the General Assembly of October 1629. The acts themselves are the only record of the session. They concerned renewed campaigns against the Indians, church law, immigration, and the possible fortification of the mouth of the James River at Old Point Comfort. Another was an appropriations bill that required the burgesses to collect the levies they raised, which is the first sign of how provincial taxes were collected before there were sheriffs.[5]

Governor Harvey intended to take control of affairs immediately, and not long after he landed at Jamestown he circulated writs for an election of burgesses. They met him and the Council of State in the General Assembly of March 1630. Harvey was authorized to construct a fort at Old Point Comfort and to hire Samuel Matthews as the prime contractor. He won passage of the first statutory control of tobacco with bills that encouraged staple crop production, controlled prices, and outlawed the slaughter of female cattle.[6]

Although the meeting went well for Harvey, he and the councillors quarreled about the extent of his authority. Their relationship turned even more vinegary after he filled vacancies on the Council without consultation, but everyone called a momentary truce to the sniping in a written agreement they signed in December 1631.[7] The lull led directly to the Revisal of 1632.

What stirred Harvey to propose revising the laws is unknown. For certain, he was aware of the bloated, jumbled, and otherwise defective nature of the laws, and he may have sought to make them easier to enforce. His concern may also have been a gambit to govern less acerbically with a favorable response to planter complaints about the confused condition of the current statutes. Whatever his calculations, Harvey called the General Assembly to Jamestown in February 1632. Of the councillors who attended, John West,[8] John Utie, and Richard Stephens were among Harvey's appointees. William Claiborne and Samuel Mathews were there too.

Having been members of three previous General Assemblies, the burgesses who were elected this time were not lacking in legislative experience, but there were only twenty of them, and they represented less than half the existing constituencies. As yet no regulation governed the number of electoral districts or their representatives. If they chose, voters in Jamestown, church parishes, settlements embraced by the monthly courts, and the remaining particular plantations could elect as many burgesses as they were willing to pay, which is why some districts had more than one burgess. Voters faced no penalty for not electing anyone. Other than inclement weather, there is no ready explanation for why the General Assembly of February 1631/32 was so unrepresentative of the colony as a whole.[9]

On the morning of 21 February 1631/32, everyone gathered in the Jamestown church for the opening rituals. Harvey and the councillors took their places in the chancel; the burgesses were seated in the nave. Everyone swore the oaths of office after the Reverend Francis Bolton prayed for divine guidance. A recess followed before they reconvened that afternoon when "The Commission from his majesty nowe in force was read before the whole bodie of the Assembly."[10] (The person who read the commission is unknown, but it probably was William Claiborne who was the secretary of the colony.) Speaking for himself and the Council the next morning, Sir John called for repealing the laws in force and replacing them with a new written *corpus juris*. The nature of his proposal significantly extended the Assembly's authority from merely adding to the statutes that had come into force since 1624 to undertaking a thorough overhaul whenever that seemed appropriate.

Scanty records are silent about how the revisal proceeded. Harvey's part is not known so it is impossible to detail his participation. The only certainty was his approval because he validated the revised acts with his signature. As yet there was still no Speaker so Claiborne and the clerk of the Council probably shared the tasks of moving drafts to bills to laws. Apparently, Claiborne, a mysterious someone, or a committee drew up a document that served as the basis for the bills that were debated. Whichever it was, the approach to the task was straightforward. All the laws enacted between 1619 and 1632 were reviewed and purged of those that were deemed no longer useful, blemished by confusion, or which bred misunderstanding. Some laws were retained without changes, others were edited to give them clearer purposes, and new ones were composed, but in the end the revisal bore a considerable likeness to the laws it replaced.

Sixty-eight statutes, one of which abolished existing laws, comprised the Revisal.[11] Organizationally they were patterned on the acts of 1624, which is to say those dealing with church polity came first and everything else followed. The arrangement of the secular statutes conformed to no discernible logical order, although it may be indicative of when a statute was adopted into the revisal.[12] One of the church laws reincorporated the constitution and canons of the Church of England "as neere as may bee," which meant that maintaining church doctrine and discipline continued to be a lay responsibility.[13] For the first time, moreover, a reenacted law that related to matrimony was amended to forbid priests from marrying couples who neglected to publish the banns or failed to obtain a "lycense graunted by the Governor."[14] There was a new law requiring all churchwardens to swear an oath of office "before those that are of the commission for the monthlie corts," and the text of that oath was written into the statute.[15] Others touched on church attendance, record keeping, baptisms, burials, clergy discipline, clergy compensation, and the maintenance of church buildings. Taken together, the new ecclesiastical acts extended lay management of the colonial church some distance further than heretofore.

Because of the late war against the Indians the specter of hunger lingered, which led to various acts that controlled commodity prices and required planters to raise at least two acres of corn annually.[16] Somewhat in the same vein were defense-related statutes that proscribed trade with the Indians and barred settlers from working their fields or walking to church without armed guards.[17] To reduce overproduction and raise prices, seven new statutes dealt with tobacco, stipulating planting time, crop size, marketing, and quality control. So far as can be determined, they constituted the first ever detailed regulation of the tobacco economy.[18]

Three acts appropriated, respectively, the Jacobean statute of artificers,[19] "the lawes of England against drunkards,"[20] and the "statutes . . . of England against forestallers, and engrossers."[21] All are notable because they are the first documented examples of direct borrowings from parliamentary legislation. They probably came from the Council's copy of William Rastell's *A Collection of Statutes Now in Force* although the existing record is too meagre to account precisely for the source or why the revisers singled these statutes out. Several contingencies would have come into play. Skilled immigrants were in high demand but often they were all too eager to farm tobacco rather than to work their trades. Public intoxication was a problem that was about as old as the colony itself, and adopting the English law represented the latest legislative effort to control it. Forestallers and engrossers were nefarious individuals who cornered commodities in order to drive up prices, and the English law provided the means to prevent their unscrupulous practices.

Equally prominent were two acts that related to Virginia's institutions of governance. One codified a conciliar habit of sitting four times a year as the Quarter Court, which recognized a gradual devolution of administrative and judicial authority to the various local monthly courts that had been established by statute in 1624. The other act extensively revised the existing monthly court law. It created five new courts; it included the text of the gubernatorial commission that set forth the duties of the commissioners at length; and it prescribed a commissioner's oath of office.[22] Nine acts restated verbatim laws that were first passed in 1624. Among these were ones that limited the governor's control over finances and his ability to impress men for his service, defined the Assembly's prerogatives, granted tax-exempt status to "ALL the old planters," and reestablished 22 March 1622 as a day of remembrance.[23] The ninth statute mandated "That these acts and ordinances be published [transmitted] throughout this colony, and the commissioners, for the mounthlie corts doe at the beginning of theire corts always read or cause to be read all these acts and that true coppies thereof be kept in the corts afforded to be read by all that shall desire the same."[24]

Harvey initialed the bills and sent the burgesses home on 6 March. Considering what happened next there is cause to suspect that this revisal was not well received. Sometime toward the end of August, Harvey issued writs for another General Assembly to meet him and the Council on 4 September 1632. Although fewer councillors attended, the West brothers, Claiborne, and Mathews were there. The polling defeated some burgesses who were present in February, but those who won reelection were in a large contingent that swelled the total representation to thirty-eight, and every electoral district across the colony sent one or more burgesses to Jamestown.[25] This outcome suggests that the voters who had gone unrepresented raised a fuss of sufficient magnitude that it inspired Harvey to aim for something better. That something better was the handiwork of the General Assembly of September 1632.[26]

A general preamble justified repealing the February laws in robust parliamentary language. "Divers acts" were deemed so defective that "the Governor and Counsell togeather with the Burgisses in the present Grand Assembly have taken the sayd acts into their consideration, and according as what was then provided where neede required have made a cleerer explanation of some of them, as likewise some additions and alterations, wee doe therefore hereby ordeyne and establish that these acts and orders in these presents following soe explaned and altered be in this colony and to be accounted and adjudged in force."[27] This preamble was an important improvement for it not only justified the overhaul, but also would become the model for future revisions.

A comparison of the two versions hints that the same persons were the authors of both because of the close metamorphic relationship between them.[28] Both contained the same arrangement, the same subjects, the same purposes, and they employed virtually identical language in a distinctly Virginia voice. But there were seven fewer acts in the September version because some of the February laws were consolidated with others or were dropped.[29] The September acts were frequently longer and more precise, and certain ones addressed previously unregulated matters. A revamped monthly court act was more streamlined than the one it replaced.[30] The earlier, somewhat disjointed tobacco statutes became a single, more polished comprehensive law. It was also among the first Virginia statutes to contain its own preamble, an enacting clause, and a penalty clause, which brought its form closer to an act of Parliament.[31] The English statutes about artificers, drunkards, and forestallers were specifically rewritten to reflect Virginia realities.[32] Besides modifications to earlier strictures on the Indian trade, a new law proclaimed the natives *"our irreconcileable enemyes"* and went on to declare that "yf any Indians doe molest or offend any plantations in theire cattle, hogs, or any thinge else, or that they bee found lurking about any plantation" the local "commander" was authorized to lead an armed force against them.[33] Finally, the September version went on to declare "all other acts and orders of any Assembly heretofore holden to be voyd and of none effect."[34]

What was now the Revisal of 1632 was silent about indentured servitude despite a growing number of servants and difficulties related to their employment. Nor did it recognize the presence of African slaves, whose population was small but growing too. It was equally quiet about land law, apart from requiring surveys and fences. Nothing was said about validation of wills, the disposition of inheritances, or the care of orphans and their property. Nothing explains those omissions except to say that these were matters that had yet to be regarded as worthy of statutory definition. And there was no definition of anything like a coherent Anglo-Indian policy akin to that devised in the future by Sir William Berkeley after the Anglo-Indian War of 1644–1646.[35]

Adding to the number of monthly courts was a forward step but their organization was still fuzzy. They lacked clerks, sheriffs, constables, coroners, and other lesser officials, and there were no provisions for courthouses or jails. Then too the Revisal contained little in the way of criminal law or civil procedure. It merely assigned the prosecution of petty offenders to the monthly courts but there were no statutes that covered the conduct of such trials. There were no felony statutes, although in this instance there is a plain explanation for a seeming omission. Offenses such as murder, treason, burglary, larceny, counterfeiting, rape, arson, robbery, and horse stealing were prosecuted according to the dictates of the English law of crimes, which in Virginia came into force wholesale and without formal reference during the Company years. Because felony charges put a defendant at risk of life or member, indicted malefactors were tried by the governor and councillors who alone held power over death or dismemberment. No rules of civil procedure were written beyond the right of suitors to appeal monthly court judgments to the Quarter Court.[36]

After the Revisal went into effect later General Assemblies did what legislatures routinely do: they amended it in response to pressure from their constituents or later unforeseen contingencies. Copies of much of this newer legislation went missing long ago but the surviving acts illustrate its drift into the 1640s. Some repealed and replaced the tobacco statutes the better to regulate the tobacco economy; some acts compelled tradesmen to practice their trades; and some tightened restrictions on trading with the Indians; others improved the collection of tithes and allowed remote parish churches to appoint deacons whenever they were unable to recruit priests; others authorized the settlement of Middle Plantation (later Williamsburg) and changed the monthly courts into county courts. The craftsmanship exhibited in these additions shows an incremental progression in the assemblymen's abilities as statute writers, which may suggest their greater reliance on parliamentary models for guidance.

As a snapshot, the Revisal of 1632 displays an enhanced General Assembly reaching toward becoming Virginia's little Parliament. What were deemed great imperatives frequently coincided with the members' ambitions. Even though the Assembly still sat on boggy constitutional soil, its members took as their right and bounden duty not only to craft statutes on an as-needed basis, but also asserted their right to revise all the laws in force whenever the need might arise. Further, the members revealed their desire to provide statutory constancy as best they could, which caused them to regard more closely the language of their laws. They also exhibited an eagerness to conduct themselves legislatively as they learned lessons in the possibilities and arts of statute making. As they laid down a precedent for the future, they established the device for statutory revision that other governors, councillors, and burgesses would use for the rest of the seventeenth century and beyond. Be that as it may, the reality was that as the 1630s yielded to the 1640s the *corpus juris* had grown bloated and in need of reform. That reformation took place in March 1642/43.[37]

❧ 3 ❧

Sir William Berkeley and the Revisal of 1643

The Revisal of 1643 was directly linked to the appointment of Sir William Berkeley as governor general and the division of the General Assembly into a bicameral legislature. Happenstance made Berkeley (1605–1677) governor. Born into the Somerset family of Berkeleys, he walked a familiar path to preferment for a younger son of the Stuart gentry. Educated at Oxford and the Middle Temple in London, he toured Europe before he obtained a situation as a privy chamber man in 1632 at the court of King Charles I. The responsibilities of this post were not onerous and it brought with it an asset of considerable value: it afforded him ready access to the king and to Charles's councillors, some of whom were also his kin. Action in the Bishops' Wars against the Scots in 1639 and 1640 gained him a knighthood but heightened his unease with the policies of a monarch he increasingly looked upon as feckless and very much out of touch with the mood of his people. Frustrated by his failure to advance higher at court, and deeply troubled by the widening breach between sovereign and subject, Berkeley decided to go abroad in the spring of 1641. A well-placed family friend recommended him for an ambassadorship at Constantinople that he sought but suddenly rejected in favor of displacing Sir Francis Wyatt as governor of Virginia. Friends and relatives arranged an amicable buyout of Wyatt, and on 10 August 1641 King Charles commissioned Sir William governor and captain general of Virginia. Berkeley reached Jamestown sometime in February 1642 and formally took office on 8 March.[1]

The Virginia he encountered little resembled places and sights he left behind but the Virginia of 1642 also had a look and feel that differed markedly from its appearance years earlier. Its main features—of an unequal society based on tobacco, bound labor, and commerce around the rim of the Atlantic—were now set. A decade of peace coincided with an upsurge of settlers whose dispersal widened the colonized spaces and put extraordinary pressure on the Powhatans.² The substitution of county courts for monthly courts fixed a permanent architecture for local government and determined a basic division of political power and legal responsibilities between province and county. That change of structure had one other durable effect. It enabled a few fractious, vaulting colonists who took places on county benches to cement themselves as a ruling class as they yoked position to land, laborers, social networks, and strategic marriages. Although still unicameral, the General Assembly more resembled a little Parliament than ever before, especially after King Charles I finally legitimized it when he reappointed Sir Francis Wyatt governor in 1639 and instructed him to summon it annually.³

Berkeley faced a daunting task that presented an exquisite test of skill for a newcomer, especially a newcomer little experienced in the rule of others. He had to govern in the interests of both king and colonist—interests that were not necessarily coincident. Success meant keeping Virginia loyal to the Crown, carrying out King Charles's instructions, retaining the good will of the Puritans in Parliament, and steering between competing factions of leading Virginians. On the one hand, pragmatism bolstered Virginians' loyalty to the monarchy. King Charles guaranteed their land titles and their political setup while his indecision stymied those London merchants and colonists who desired a resurrected Virginia Company, which they regarded as the best means of managing the colony profitably for themselves. Then civil war broke out in Britain in August 1642 and put colonial allegiances to the test. It compelled the settlers to take sides, it threatened religious strife, and it imperiled commercial relationships that were vital to everyone's well-being.

On the other hand, there were potential political difficulties with the Council of State. Although no longer governor, the always popular Sir Francis Wyatt still kept a chair at the Council table and his presence threatened to undermine the inexperienced Berkeley. An even graver threat were the factions that divided the Council. The most potent of these was one led by Samuel Mathews and William Claiborne. Barely seven years had passed since that group had violently overthrown Governor Harvey over disputes about his ability to act independently of them and his interference with their trading schemes. Most of them still sat at the Council, and they were fully prepared to contest Berkeley if he bucked them. On the other side, Secretary of the Colony Richard Kemp (ca. 1600–1649)[4] was a nominal Harveyite and something of a magnet for disgruntled councillors who were hostile to the Mathews-Claiborne faction. Then there were a few who spoke for middling and smaller planters who owed no fidelity to Kemp or to Mathews and Claiborne.[5]

Nothing in Berkeley's papers reveals the force of his grip on the issues and personalities he was about to confront. For certain he cannot have been entirely ignorant of them. From his youth, he knew things about Virginia vicariously through his parents who had invested in the Virginia Company and relatives who had gone out to the colony from time to time. His years at court brought him close to King Charles's privy councillors who sometimes wrestled with what to do with Virginia, and he was clearly aware of George Sandys's latest effort at reconstituting the Virginia Company. More recently he dealt with William Claiborne, who negotiated Sir Francis Wyatt's side of the bargain that made him governor. Shortly after that he encountered Secretary Kemp. No friend to Claiborne, whom he displaced as secretary while Harvey was in office, Kemp was a potential ally.[6]

The General Assembly was sitting when Berkeley landed at Jamestown and out of deference to him Wyatt prorogued it until 18 April 1642. Berkeley wanted to establish himself as the Assembly's leader as quickly as he could; making good that wish presented him with his first crucial political test: what to do with the prorogued General Assembly. He could recall it or he could dissolve it. If he dissolved it he would void pending legislation, which would not endear him to the members whose work would go to waste. But there was no local precedent for a recall because the Assembly had never before found itself in a similar situation and had yet to regard Parliament entirely as its model. Berkeley's instructions imposed no restrictions on when or how he might convene the Assembly. The controlling clause merely obliged him to "Summon the Burgesses of all and Singular of the Plantations" annually or "oftner if urgent occasion shall require." Nothing in that clause equated "summoning" and "electing" or contemplated the dissolution of a standing General Assembly upon his assumption of office. Constitutionally, that meant he could do as he thought best. He recalled it.[7]

Berkeley and the assemblymen greeted one another on 1 April 1642. He announced that the rumors about a possible revival of the Virginia Company were not just gossip because he had seen George Sandys's petition to that purpose laid before the House of Commons as he was leaving England.[8] His news goaded the Assembly to a swift response that shoved aside other legislative business and widened splits between councillors and burgesses. Berkeley saw an advantage that he quickly seized. He joined forces with those burgesses and councillors who stubbornly refused to countenance a renewed company and won adoption of a written protest against revival, the phrasing of which evinces unambiguous signs of his hand. Then to give the harshly worded "The Declaration against the Company" even greater weight, he got the Assembly to adopt it statutorily. The act contained an unusual proviso that proclaimed it took effect immediately in Virginia and within "five days after the Arrival of this our said Declaration Protestation and Act within the realm of England." Without saying so directly the General Assembly appeared to place its laws on an equal footing with English statutes. This was the earliest instance of a hint at co-equality with Parliament.[9]

The debate over the Declaration aroused such passions that further legislative business came to an abrupt standstill. A respite seemed in order, and after concluding that a break would not invalidate pending legislation Berkeley adjourned the Assembly "to the Thursday in Whitson week being the Second day of June next coming."[10] The recess produced the desired effect, and as soon as the unfinished bills were enacted Berkeley signed them and dissolved the Assembly.

In the months that followed events strengthened Berkeley's hand. Wyatt sailed back to England, never to return, and with him out of the way Berkeley no longer worried about his second-guessing him. Wyatt's leaving vacated one of the three council seats, which Berkeley filled with replacements who allied with him. He actively cultivated William Claiborne, which put some distance between Claiborne and Samuel Mathews. In another gesture toward winning the councillors, he openly shared his royal instructions with them, as he would do for as long as he governed. That was an extraordinary indulgence because it breached the secrecy of privy communications between the king and his vicegerent. The effect was a softening of resistance to Berkeley.[11]

As summer yielded to fall, Berkeley chose to call a General Assembly of his own. He consulted the councillors about an optimum meeting date. Everyone agreed on 2 March 1642/43, and he circulated the election writs to the county sheriffs who conducted the poll about six weeks ahead of the session. The polling resulted in a fresh crop of burgesses. Some were newcomers, several were veterans of earlier Assemblies, a few were even Berkeley's tenants or neighbors, but nearly all were in his pocket. Wasting no time in turning this advantage to good effect, he encouraged the General Assembly to accept two reforms he set before it. First, he called upon the burgesses to sit separately from the Council and himself. They accepted with alacrity, and so was born the House of Burgesses. Second, he charged the newly bicameral General Assembly to rewrite the acts in force, and that task became the sole business of the session.[12]

Both reforms consolidated Berkeley's hold on power. He could use a bicameral Assembly to play the two bodies against one another and foil potential opponents. A house of their own enhanced his popularity with the burgesses. Their approval strengthened when Berkeley prompted them to elect their presiding officer, and when they chose Thomas Stegge (d. 1652),[13] they brought the office of Speaker of the House of Burgesses into being. These changes raised the burgesses' collective stature legislatively and led to other parliamentary characteristics that had been lacking ever since 1619.

The new code invested Berkeley with greater leeway to chart Virginia's future and to steer clear of Britain's troubles. It continued the devolution of authority to local elites that had been ongoing since the 1620s. The acts themselves eliminated "the defects and inconveniences"[14] in those they replaced, which kept faith with the purpose of the Revisal of 1632. Like that codification, their arrangement duplicated that of the Acts of 1623/24: church laws came first; secular statutes next but in no discernible order.

Destruction of the legislative records and the drafters' working papers obscures the dynamics of how the recodification proceeded. Despite that obstacle, the identity of key figures, clues from Berkeley's papers, and the new statutes themselves are indicative of some of what went on. Aside from Berkeley, Speaker of the House Thomas Stegge and Secretary Kemp were active in the deliberations. So were members in both houses who had contributed to the Revisal of 1632. Their institutional memory now proved useful to their newer colleagues as well as to Berkeley. Council clerk

John Corker (ca. 1600–1670) and House clerk John Meade (ca. 1612–after 1645) probably shared the drafting chores.[15] They were practiced scribes, and, when necessary they might turn to the law books in the small Council library or borrow some from members.[16] King Charles I's instructions to Berkeley provided directions for certain acts and reinforced Berkeley's own ideas for others.

A general preamble, which Berkeley might have drafted, minced no words in setting forth the rationale for this revision. "Many and sundry acts and laws" enacted by previous Assemblies "have been found very prejudicial to the Collony," and they should be reduced into "a more exact method and order" to eliminate "all mistakes & pretenses which may arise from misinterpretation or ignorance of the laws in force." The preamble did not say so but these nuisances had come to pass through the years because the number of statutes trebled after 1632. (Copies of most of them disappeared long ago.) Up-to-date texts were often unavailable because clerks of court were notoriously sloppy copyists and sometimes they even neglected to enter new laws onto their records. Acts were ill-conceived or ambiguously crafted, others were outdated, and there had been no prior efforts to throw out the clutter. Therefore, the most expedient remedy was to recur to the precedent of 1632: repeal the entire *corpus juris* and begin with a clean slate.[17]

In due course, the Assembly jettisoned a laundry list of one hundred old laws and adopted a slimmed-down code of about seventy-three acts.[18] Among the former was the law for reading aloud of all the statutes at the opening of county court meetings. Gone too were those laws linked to the defunct office of marshal and virtually all defense statutes, outdated revenue measures, and fee schedules. Every tobacco law was swept away too. Such a drastic change seems curious on its face because past General Assemblies had routinely regulated the weed, and as recently as 1640 one even went so far as to restrict production as a means of driving up prices. This so-called stint act restricted the size of an individual planter's crop to 120,000 pounds, which was supposed to reduce the colony's annual output to approximately 1,200,000 pounds of the leaf. An additional clause, enforced by locally appointed inspectors, compelled planters to burn accumulations of old tobacco and any new crops that exceeded their allotments.[19] It appears that law had the desired result because prices were on the rise, and the prospect of better returns likely dampened enthusiasm for renewing the stint, though that does not account for the elimination of the other tobacco legislation or the lack of replacements.[20]

Laws that pertained to the county courts and the appointment of their commissioners disappeared too but there is a ready explanation for why they were not kept.[21] King Charles ordered Berkeley to "appoint in places convenient Inferior Courts of Justice and Commanders for the same," which Berkeley interpreted as constitutionally sanctioning the existing county courts. Because he did not regard the king's instruction as a limitation on the authority of the General Assembly, he encouraged it to institute a series of statutes that expanded the county courts' jurisdiction and clarified the duties of their officers.[22] One reauthorized monthly sessions and empowered the commissioners to adjudicate civil causes valued at 1,600 pounds of tobacco or less. (Individual commissioners could dispose of suits involving less than 20 shillings.)[23] Another extended trial by jury in civil litigation to "any of the courts of this colony," at the request of either party.[24] County courts were prohibited from contravening acts of assembly or gubernatorial proclamations, and they were forbidden to issue blank warrants or to directing the same writ to more than to more than one sheriff.[25] Two other statutes gave clearer definition to the office of sheriff. One limited his term to a year and required him to "yield vp at everie March quarter court yearly to the Governour and Councell a just accompt of all publique commands committed to [his] charge."[26] The second made sheriffs responsible for jailing accused felons prior to their trials at the Quarter Court, and it required the "commissioners of the severall countyes [to] take care that sufficient prisons be built" or else face fines for their delinquency.[27] Finally, an earlier law was reproduced to protect public officials from being "molested or troubled" in the performance of their duties and to allow them to recover "such charges and damages as should be justly determined . . . in the severall courts of this colony" in those instances where they were disrespected.[28]

There were improvements to the Quarter Court's conduct of its business. For the first time a statute put the court's rules of civil procedure in writing. It did away with the "want of due formes not before sett downe . . . which occasioned much trouble to the Government and great charge of inhabitants of the colony." Although it placed no restriction on the volume of cases the court tried in its capacities as either a trial or an appellate court, that act apportioned the number of suits that the judges heard at each quarterly session according to a schedule it prescribed. Suits were docketed sequentially in the order in which they were filed with the council clerk. Plaintiffs initiated their causes by writ or petition; defendants answered in writing too. Both litigants posted appearance bonds and presented their evidence personally or through their attorneys. Suitors who were dissatisfied with a court decision had a final avenue of relief. The act allowed "Appeales to lie from the quarter courts to the Assemblies with the former cautions," although those "former cautions" went unstated.[29]

An act that regulated attorneys wrought another improvement and broke new ground as well. Passed in response to popular complaints against "the great fees exacted by them," it was designed to mitigate those excesses by licensing attorneys. Henceforth, would-be practitioners applied to the Quarter Court for a license, and after receiving it, they could litigate in the court and no more than one county court. The fees they could charge were limited to 20 pounds of tobacco per action in a county court or 50 pounds in the Quarter Court, and if someone attempted to charge more he was liable to stiff fines of respectively 500 and 2,000 pounds. But the statute specifically exempted attorneys who prosecuted pleas of the Crown or those who produced "letters of procuration."[30] Quite apart from being the first of its kind in Virginia, the act had an enduring significance because it established a precedent for the General Assembly's regulation of the practice of law that continues to this day.[31]

Of equal importance were signs of the burgesses' growing awareness of their importance as the voter's representatives. They reenacted a prior law freeing themselves from arrest "from the time of . . . election vntil ten days after the dissolution of the Assembly" and declared the supremacy of statutes over court orders or gubernatorial proclamations.[32] Another law taxed "the inhabitants of the severall counties and precincts [for] the defraying of the Burgesses charges expended in their imployment," which was the first to embed the costs of representation in the statutes.[33]

Five statutes committed an emerging law of indentured labor to paper. Those acts probably responded to planter demands. They either codified currently unwritten practices or they were new legislation meant to address things their authors saw as problems created by their fellow planters' unruly servile population, which was on the rise. In either case, they represented an extension of the General Assembly's jurisdiction into the area of labor relations. One kept a 1639 act that is the very first piece of servant legislation on record. Directed at planters who traded "with other mens' servants and apprentices which tended to the great injury of masters," it imposed a penalty of "one month's imprisonment without bayle or mainprize" and a fine of up to four times the value of the traded goods.[34] Another settled the question of how long a servant who arrived in Virginia without an indenture was expected to serve. Men and women above the age of twenty could be bound for four years, adolescents between twelve and twenty for five years, and children younger than twelve could be held for seven years.[35]

Secret servant marriages were banned. Any manservant who married without the master's or mistress's permission faced an additional year's service whereas a maidservant received double that time. (If a free man was involved he merely paid fines to the maidservant's owner and the local parish.) The same statute also tried to curb fornication by imposing similar fines and additional service for those who flouted it.[36] Given its grueling nature, indentured servitude encouraged an unstoppable gush of runaways that the last two statutes were especially written to staunch. The first targeted planters who hired or harbored fugitive laborers; those who did faced a fine and such extra penalties as the governor and Council chose to inflict. The second chastised runaways in several pitiless ways. It visited felony prosecution on any runaway who bartered muskets and ammunition to the Indians. First-time runaways faced an addition to their indentures that equaled twice the length of their absences. Repeat offenders got worse. They received a harsh punishment that was appropriated from the English statute of incorrigible rogues: branding on the cheek with the letter R and a whipping.[37] A proviso allowed accused runaways to avoid the imposition of these penalties if they could convince a commissioner of the peace that they absconded because of abuse by their masters.[38]

When he acceded to the reenactment of a law from the Revisal of 1632 that prohibited the governor and the Council from laying "any taxes or impositions vpon this collonie their lands or commodities otherwise then by the authority of the Grand Assembly to be levied & imployed as by the Assembly shall be appointed," Berkeley consented to a significant attenuation of his power.[39] His concession won him chits that he cashed throughout the session. He spent one to win approval of a law that sustained a vital channel of commerce without offending London merchants. It kept Virginia open to Dutch traders so long as the Hollanders obtained "good and sufficient letters of credit directed to the Governor from some merchants or merchants inhabiting within the Citty of London of knowne repute and ability."⁴⁰ Some were used to pass acts that governed mortgages, debt suits, and certain types of land cases, among others.⁴¹ He cashed the rest on the revision of Virginia's ecclesiastical laws.

Arriving in Virginia with scant foreknowledge of the colonists' religious habits, he chanced upon an institutional church the like of which he had never seen in England. Several dozen parishes scattered across the colony comprised the organized body of the church. Some congregations had no priests; some lacked housing and other forms of maintenance for their clergy; and some had church buildings that were in decrepit physical condition. He discovered that, lacking any episcopal oversight from England, ecclesiastical supervision had of necessity dispersed into the hands of congregants, local magistrates, the General Assembly, and the governor. Berkeley learned that in matters of doctrine and discipline the majority of believing Virginians inclined toward a version of Anglicanism that accepted moderation and avoided the rigid, unyielding orthodoxy that King Charles I sought to impose across his kingdoms. Berkeley's own predilections were closer to the colonists' preferences than to Charles's, but as governor he was obliged to implement the king's views, which were set forth in two of his instructions. He put both into play, though not quite as Charles expected.

The first instruction ordered him to "Administer the Oaths of Allegiance and Supremacy to all such as come thither, with the intention to Plant themselves in the Country," and immigrants who refused "were to be returned and shiped from thence home." (That was King Charles's way of curtailing Puritan immigrants whose numbers in the colony were on the rise.) Berkeley finessed that commandment in a fashion that the burgesses and councillors found most appealing. He included it in the act that forced the oath of allegiance upon Catholic recusants and barred them from public office.⁴² Then, in a direct nod to the instruction, he proposed a statute that imposed conformity on "all ministers which shall reside in the collony" and ordered the expulsion "with all conveniencie" of any nonconformists.⁴³ Although the inclusion of this statute aroused little dissent in the General Assembly, it did not sit well with the affected Puritan congregations along the south side of the lower James River, whose complaints would cause difficulties for the governor in the years ahead.⁴⁴

The second instruction told him to "be carefull that Almighty may be duly and daily served according to the forme of Religion Established in the Church of England both by yourself and the people under your charge."⁴⁵

A Sunday closing law and the reconfirmation of the boundaries of some recently erected parishes addressed that directive but the set piece was Act I of the Revisal. Drawn up in seventeen sections, this statute refined legislation that had been on the rolls in one version or another ever since 1624, and it included new features that Berkeley advanced. Of the latter, one called for the creation of a vestry in every parish. An unspecified number of parishioners, who served no fixed terms, constituted each vestry. Vestrymen were bound by oath to elect wardens, raise parish levies, maintain the fabric of their church, and to present parishioners who committed moral offenses for prosecution in the county courts. They were responsible for recruiting priests and recommending clerical appointments to the governor. In turn, the governor inducted, that is, installed, appointees, and he could suspend them for cause, but only the General Assembly could dismiss them permanently from their livings.[46]

With a bit of creative tinkering Berkeley converted a body whose primary duty in an English parish was overseeing relief of the poor into a unit that administered parish affairs. It grew into the tier of self-government closest to the people and the one that most frequently touched the routines of their lives. That adaptation not only made Virginia vestries self-perpetuating, but also turned the place of vestryman into a gateway to higher political office. Berkeley's claim of the right to induct ministers for himself and his successors circumvented the need of bishops to appoint ministers to their cures, and in doing that he resolved an issue that had long taxed the imagination of previous lawmakers.

Reflected in the making of the Revisal of 1643 is how its realization variously marked Berkeley, the General Assembly, and the legal order. For Berkeley, it was an opportunity to hone his skills as a legislator and a way for him to forge common cause with the big men. Not only that, it signaled his willingness to interpret his royal instructions in ways that enhanced rather than upset the colony's polity as he found it. For the General Assembly, the Revisal of 1643 was a singular accomplishment for a just-made bicameral body. Becoming bipartite cemented the Assembly's position as the colony's primary lawgiver and sent it along its journey toward becoming a little Parliament. The process of revision opened a generations-long, sometimes bumpy quest to understand the meaning of bicameralism in a colonial setting as governors, councillors, burgesses, and even the Crown felt their way toward delineating which powers stayed wholly with the executive, which responsibilities lodged in the Council, which dwelt mainly in the House, and which were shared prerogatives. For the legal order, the Revisal of 1643 met the priorities that brought it into being.

Their work done, Berkeley, the councillors, and the burgesses left Jamestown probably congratulating themselves on having produced a clean, up-to-date codification of the laws in force, though they knew from past experience it would be modified as future conditions warranted. However, no one could have foreseen the two extraordinary episodes that powered most of the new statutes onto the rolls before midcentury—the Anglo-Indian War of 1644–1646 and the overthrow of the monarchy. Their preoccupations with the civil war in Britain and the relative peace they maintained with the Powhatan chiefdom had led Berkeley and the colonists down the path of carelessness. For the great weroance Opechancanough their negligence was an unmatched opportunity to mount a surprise attack on the English and possibly expel them from his homeland. Success depended upon his ability to best Berkeley on the battlefield. Opechancanough struck on 18 April 1644. The attacks killed more than 500 colonists and an untold number of Powhatans during the first days of a vicious war that wrought terrible destruction on Indian and colonist alike.

Berkeley's reaction was as quick as it was purposeful. He called the General Assembly and together they mapped out a battle plan to defeat the Powhatans. Militias were called up, William Claiborne was appointed general-in-chief, and his forces were ordered to burn Indian villages and cornfields as they sought to destroy enemy warriors. Everyone agreed that Berkeley should speedily "repair for England and Implore his Majesty's gracious assistance for our Releife," and he was given letters of credit to replenish the colony's stock of war matériel. His two-year trip proved unsuccessful. Not quite empty-handed, he returned to Virginia to find that war had not favored the English. Claiborne had proven to be an indifferent general more interested in contesting Marylanders for the ownership of Kent Island than in besting the enemy.[47] Berkeley put him aside and took the field himself. At the same time, he relied on the General Assembly for the authority to raise more troops and for appropriations to buy whatever stores of war he could purchase abroad. He also turned to it for the legislation to succor wounded and displaced colonists and to encourage the resettlement of areas that were burnt out or otherwise abandoned. He decisively defeated Opechancanough and captured him. The ancient weroance became a prisoner at Jamestown where he was murdered. His successor Necotowance sued for peace. At the General Assembly of October 1646, Berkeley secured the enactment of the treaty with Necotowance that ended the conflict.

By its terms Necotowance acknowledged that he and his people were now English tributaries, in recognition of which they had to give the governor twenty beaver skins annually. The Powhatans exchanged most of their ancestral home lands for a reservation north of the York River. Their contact with the English was prohibited without special license from the governor, and licensees who passed through English settlements were required to don identifying coats and badges. Henceforth, colonial law, not tribal custom, became the basis for settling all civil or criminal disputes between themselves and the English. An amplifying act called for erecting forts strategically situated along the frontier that would form a defensive boundary and an early warning system against tribes to the north and west of the colony's borders. Here, then, was a scheme of the moment that rested on an unambiguous reckoning. Without the subjugation of all Indians who lived near the English there could be no durable peace. Colonist and Indian should be kept apart, and it would be within the governor's power to regulate all interaction between the two peoples. With the General Assembly's ratification of the treaty, it became the first Anglo-Indian agreement ever to receive the imprimatur of a statutory enactment. More importantly, it formed the core of a comprehensive Indian policy, which the General Assembly would enlarge statutorily for the next three decades.[48]

Even as the colonists fought Opechancanough, the English Civil War posed its own dangers. It pinched vital commercial lifelines that sustained Virginia. It cracked open fissures along religious and political fault lines that separated colonists who adhered to the royalist or parliamentary causes. And the more King Charles's hold on his crown weakened, the greater the chance that Berkeley would be displaced. He was indeed ousted after Parliament overthrew the monarchy and proclaimed an English republic. That revolution also accounted for a new constitutional order in Virginia.[49]

4

A New Constitutional Order

The Revisals of 1652 and 1658

King Charles I lost his head in January 1649. Half a year later the republican Council of State in London officially informed Governor Berkeley of the late sovereign's execution and commanded his obedience to Parliament. Instead of bowing to the new order, Berkeley condemned it and proclaimed the dead king's son the rightful ruler of Virginia. He urged royalists to emigrate and use Virginia as a base from which to attack the parliamentarians. To hold the colonists loyal to King Charles II he called the General Assembly to Jamestown in October 1649 and secured legislation defining as treasonable any public utterances that championed regicide, doubted the divine right of kings, or questioned the succession of Charles II. The parliamentarians in England reacted cautiously, but Virginia was too important and Berkeley was too visible a monarchist for them not to bring both to heel. Wanting as little trouble as possible, their first reaction was low key but calculated. They promulgated two orders-in-council that interdicted English commerce with Virginia, and a navigation act that barred foreign vessels from trading in Chesapeake waters. Berkeley angrily denounced those papers at a one-day meeting of the General Assembly in March 1651 and theatrically threatened to forfeit his life in defense of his king.[1]

His obdurate refusal to countenance those whom he snidely called "the men of *Westminster*" showed that words alone would not cow him. Force was in order, but the parliamentarians were in no position to deal with him militarily until they had crushed Charles Stuart's campaign to recover his throne. Oliver Cromwell ended that threat when he utterly smashed

Charles's army at the Battle of Worcester. In the months following Cromwell's victory the men of Westminster gathered warships, transports, soldiers, and supplies for an expedition they dispatched to reduce Virginia. Among its leaders were the Virginians Thomas Stegge, William Claiborne, and Richard Bennett (1609–1675),[2] who happened to be in London lobbying Parliament to exclude Dutch shippers from Chesapeake waters. After the flotilla set sail for America and captured Barbados, it survived a fierce storm at sea that drowned Stegge before it anchored in the James River off the site of the present-day city of Newport News in January 1651/52. Messengers from Bennett and Claiborne rowed up to Jamestown and demanded Berkeley's surrender, but he paid them no heed. Instead, he called up a thousand militiamen and situated them strategically around the capital, making it appear as though he would match strength against strength. Neither side thirsted for blood, however, so they agreed to negotiate a peaceful settlement. Berkeley called the General Assembly to town to join him in haggling with Bennett and Claiborne over terms. Two treaties of capitulation, initialed on 12 March 1651/52, formalized the transfer of Virginia and the Assembly to Parliament's control, whereupon Berkeley dissolved the Assembly and went into retirement at Green Spring.[3]

The shorter of the two treaties applied primarily to Berkeley. In return for his surrender, he was spared from swearing "any oath, [or] engagement to the Commonwealth of England." His "Lands, howses, and whatsoever else belongeth" remained his, though he could sell them and remove unhindered either to the Netherlands or England. He would receive outstanding salaries and other debts due from the General Assembly. Providing he bore the cost, he could dispatch an emissary "to give an accompt to his Majestie of the Surrender of his Countrie." The second treaty involved the General Assembly. Because their submission was a "Voluntary Act not forced nor constrained (by a Conquest) upon the Country," the Assembly and the colonists would "have and Enjoy such freedom and Priviledges as belong to the free-born people of England." Everyone had twelve months to decide whether to pledge allegiance to Parliament or leave, and they could keep their weapons. The House of Burgesses was sovereign, just so long as it enacted nothing "contrary to the Government of the Commonwealth of England and the Laws there Established." It alone could levy taxes and raise or garrison troops. Parliament guaranteed the colony's "Ancient bounds and Limits," existing land titles, and continuation of the headright system.

Finally, there was an explicit promise of a charter that would codify these provisions.[4]

Surrendering to "the Obedience and Government of the Commonwealth of England" upset Virginia's prevailing constitution. To put things right Claiborne, Bennett, and the incumbent councillors assumed executive control. They commanded sitting justices of the peace to stay in place and "do & act in all things in as full & ample manner as [they] have heretofore done . . . Untill further order." This assured continuity in the localities until a General Assembly could meet and make the necessary changes. On 15 April 1652, writs for an election of burgesses went out to the county sheriffs.[5] The polling returned a mixed bag of newcomers and former members. Some spoke for voters who sided with Parliament, but not aggressively so, while others represented freeholders who were monarchists or neutrals. How many burgesses coalesced into each of these groups is speculative, but given the depth of sentiment for the Crown throughout Virginia, most of the members were probably royalist sympathizers. Whatever their persuasion, all accepted the situation for what it was and strove to make the best of it.[6] The new General Assembly convened on the 26th of April and dissolved ten days later. Because only the burgesses held the powers of appointment and legislation, their first order of business was organizing the House. For Speaker, they chose Edward Major (1615–ca. 1655),[7] a protégé of Richard Bennett, and they kept John Corker as their clerk. Next, they decided on the form of the General Assembly. Unlike the reconstituted Parliament in the Commonwealth, it remained bicameral, and for the time being all the incumbent councillors were reelected to their seats. Richard Bennett was elected governor and William Claiborne was chosen for his old place as secretary of the colony.

Then the burgesses tackled recasting the laws in force. That entailed decisions about which laws to scrap, which to keep, and which new ones to enact in order to establish Parliament's writ and to stamp out every vestige of royal authority. Who was responsible for those decisions and their incorporation as the Revisal of 1652 is uncertain. Perhaps it was a committee of burgesses named by Speaker Major. Possibly it was Clerk Corker, who was long experienced as a drafter of statutes and who was also custodian of "the book of the Acts uppon Record at James Cittye."[8] More to the point, when William Waller Hening compiled the *Statutes at Large*, he was unaware of this revisal's existence, and it was unknown to later scholars too. It lay hidden until the 1970s, when the only copy in existence turned up among a volume of seventeenth-century records housed at the clerk of court's office in Surry, Virginia. A unique find, its rediscovery disclosed a manuscript of singular value for its revelations of how the burgesses adjusted Virginia law to a new constitutional reality.[9]

Ditched were 160 of some 220 statutes enacted between the Revisal of 1643 and 1651. Approximately a third had been passed for short-term purposes that were outdated and therefore easily abolished. Roughly another third that dealt with the courts was eliminated too. The final third was a miscellany that among others related to the Anglican establishment, agriculture, commerce, and even Berkeley's speeches to the General Assembly of March 1650/51.

Sixty saved acts joined about two dozen new ones to constitute the Revisal. It was arranged in a familiar design. A preamble preceded the church laws, which preceded everything else, although there was an outstanding difference between it and its predecessors. The first fifteen acts, which were new, were classified by titles and identifying numbers that ran from 1 to 15. Next came the retained laws. Whether they were incorporated unchanged or amended, each of them still carried its original title and number.[10] Seven new acts, numbered 17 through 22, completed the collection. This quirky classification system has no explanation other than the haste with which the revisal was cobbled together.[11]

The preamble is remarkable more for what it left unspoken than for what it said. A short paragraph, it contained no reference to Virginia's surrender or the overthrow of the monarchy. It merely promoted this latest codification of the statutes in force in language reminiscent of its forerunner from 1643. Existing "Acts, and Lawes of this Collony through Multiplicityes, Alterations and Repeales, are become Difficult, and not so Easy to be knowne, as is Requisite for things of that nature" and thus should be replaced. That the burgesses struck a familiar tone argues their intention of refraining from rumpling the constitutional fabric any more than was necessary to bring Virginia into Parliament's orbit. That Claiborne and Bennett voiced no objection on Parliament's behalf suggests their acquiescence as well.[12]

Among the new acts, a pair dismantled the Anglican church in the colony and drew the establishment into concert with Puritan conceptions of religious polity. A second pair enforced Puritan views of public behavior by declaring that the English laws against adultery, drunkenness, Sabbath breaking, cursing, and other lewd conduct "shall be putt in Execution in this Countrey." Those acts were buttressed by a retained statute that prohibited arrests on Sundays and muster days.[13] A stopgap measure provided for land patents to be "drawn upp in a forme relatinge to the present government," and "untill a Seale may be procured," the signatures of the secretary and the governor sufficed to validate them "as any Pattents formerlye granted under the Collonye Seal, and the like for all things that hath usually passed under the Seale."[14] Other temporary acts addressed conveying public letters, issuing writs and warrants, preventing the spread of rumors, and paying the expenses of Councillor Samuel Mathews Sr. as Virginia's agent in London.[15] Another act amended the Indian policy that the Assembly had devised in October 1649 to enable magistrates along the frontier "to settle peace with the Indians in their Countyes." Pressure for the change came from the freeholders in Northumberland and Northampton Counties, which is one of the few visible indications of the burgesses' responsiveness to voter complaints.[16]

No law dismissed incumbent officeholders or disenfranchised royalist sympathizers, and there was no confiscation of anyone's possessions. Instead, the Assembly codified the decree of "indempnitie and oblivion to all the inhabitants of this colony" that Bennett, Claiborne, and Edmond Curtis guaranteed at the surrender.[17] County commissioners, sheriffs, constables, clerks, and surveyors received new commissions, oaths of office, and several significant enhancements of their powers. The position of "surveyor for highways" formally came into being. Appointed annually, his duties involved keeping roads and bridges in good repair according to the "course used in England to that End."[18] (Responsibility for maintaining thoroughfares was first assigned to the monthly courts in the Revisal of 1632 but that act did not assign it to a specific individual.)[19] Individual commissioners of the peace were authorized to decide cases involving up to 350 pounds of tobacco, whereas two, one of whom was a senior judge, could settle suits between 350 and 1,000 pounds. In both instances, litigants were allowed to appeal to the full county court.[20] Saying the "Tryall of Criminall Causes att James Cittie is very Chargeable and burthensome to the People," for the first time a different act permitted justices to prosecute felonies. The law may have been a temporary measure because in the past local courts had lacked jurisdiction, and the act's headnote bears the notation "Expired."[21]

An important increment in the county courts' power was an act that authorized the commissioners to determine "Marityne Causes," which also empowered sheriffs to make shipboard arrests. Henceforth the commissioners were qualified to adjudicate routine maritime matters like wage disputes and the condemnation of prizes, which took some of the burden off the Quarter Court. The statute "Concerninge towns and Corporations" encouraged urban development. Raising towns in addition to Jamestown had long been an aim of the home government and Virginians, although it had never been expressed statutorily in the past. To any planters who wished to found a town, the new law offered generous inducements via the county courts, the Council, and the governor. They included a right of incorporation and a power to elect mayors, aldermen, sheriffs, and burgesses, as well as "such priviledges and freedoms as any the Incorporated townes of England doe, or may Enjoy by the Customes and Lawes of England." Both acts assumed an added weight in light of Parliament's budding scheme for eliminating the Dutch as commercial rivals and fitting Virginia into a closed Atlantic mercantile community centered on London. As such, they represented the Assembly's first steps toward the implementation of that policy.[22]

The new code is remarkable for things it did not include. Although an old law that spared burgesses from arrest while on public business was retained, there were no stipulations defining the constituencies they represented, their compensation, or the manner of their elections, all of which had been dealt with by earlier Assemblies. Inexplicably, meeting dates and procedural rules for the Quarter Court and the county courts were missing, which was contrary to what had been done in 1643 and built on in later years. No act set out a schedule of fees that the secretary, clerks of court, and sheriffs received for drawing up various court papers. Abandoned too was the Anglo-Powhatan Treaty of 1646 despite its being foundational to the Indian policy that was reenacted and to some extent enlarged. Most curious of all was the want of clearly defined relationships between the House, the Council, and the governor.

Were these oversights brought on by the rush to finish, or was something else in play? A little of both, it might be argued. There were substantial constitutional differences in the relationships between the elements of the General Assembly under the monarchy and under Parliament. Under the Crown the power to rule Virginia devolved from the king to his vicegerent, who acted in his stead according to the commission and instructions he gave the governor. Councillors of state and the secretary of the colony shared administrative, executive, judicial, and military responsibilities with the governor and were also Crown appointees. They and the governor served at the king's pleasure. Burgesses, elected by the voters, were the lower house of the bicameral General Assembly, which met at the call of the governor. They served no fixed terms. More often than not, the governor set the legislative agenda and he had veto power both as chief executive and council president, meaning that no bill ever became law without his consent. Even so, with the acquiescence of Governor Berkeley, the House had swiftly developed into an independent, self-conscious body that by 1652 was quite mindful of its liberties and equally capable of defending them. It elected its Speaker and clerk without gubernatorial interference, it controlled its internal procedures, and it initiated legislation that addressed voter complaints.

Under Parliament the authority to govern Virginia devolved from Parliament to the General Assembly, or more precisely to the House of Burgesses. No one in London mapped out the metes and bounds of that power. Indeed, having captured Virginia, the parliamentarians left the colony mostly alone. The closest thing to a chart of the new political landscape was an ambiguously worded passage from the treaty of surrender that the General Assembly "as formerly shall converse and transact the Affairs of Virginia."[23] Whereas royal governors, councillors, and secretaries held office by virtue of royal commissions and kept their places during good behavior, under the parliamentary regime all three were elected by the burgesses by statute to specific terms of years. The House gave them neither commissions nor instructions but that was of no importance because in effect they were adjuncts of the House who had to swear "the oath Burgesses take."[24] Even so, the burgesses conceded degrees of executive and judicial authority akin to those exercised during royal rule. The imprecisely defined relationship between the Assembly's constituent elements caused conflicts that the burgesses later manipulated to their advantage when they decided to scrap the new code.

For now, though, stitched together as quickly as it was, the Revisal of 1652 achieved its purpose of redefining Virginia's constitution. Very likely, some of the burgesses recognized its limitations and deemed it a temporary solution against a later day when another House would come up with a more comprehensive, well-designed replacement. Quirks and all, the

Revisal stood for six years. Future Assemblies routinely added to it but were slow to supersede it.[25] Their slow motion was directly tied to a political climate that repeatedly fostered animosities between the burgesses and the governors. Governors Bennett, Edward Digges (1621–1676),[26] and Samuel Mathews Jr. (ca. 1629–1660)[27] were creatures of the House. They answered to the burgesses in ways Berkeley never did, which became an open invitation for conflict. Their lack of political instinct or skill at finessing troublesome issues only heightened the likelihood of conflict. The upshot was that neither Bennett, Digges, nor Mathews enjoyed tranquil tenures. Bennett remained in office until 1655. The unpopularity of Parliament's commercial policy, which led to the First Anglo-Dutch War, diminished him in the eyes of House members. Consequently, he showed little interest in promoting statutory reform, which deepened the frostiness of his relations with the burgesses, a majority of whom tended to be royalists. Relations turned much icier when he interfered in the election of Walter Chiles, a Berkeleyite, as Speaker in 1653 and the burgesses forced him to back down.[28] Two years later they denied his reelection and chose Digges as his successor. An able, personable man better known for his gifts as an agriculturalist than for his political adroitness, Digges owed his election to a coalition of anti-Bennett and royalist burgesses. He proved more lukewarm than hostile to revising the statutes but avoided any involvement with the issue and within a year of taking office, he left for London on colony business. Samuel Mathews Jr., who filled Digges's unexpired term, and then sat in his own right, turned out to be the most controversial of all.

Son of Councillor Samuel Mathews, and still in his twenties, young Mathews was an odd choice to succeed Digges. He brought little in the way of reputation or deep political experience. His shortcomings suggest that Secretary Claiborne, the councillors who proposed him, and the burgesses who elected him purposely wanted a person of low standing instead of a veteran politician on the assumption that they could mold him into their biddable creature. If that was the thinking, then it turned out to be a grave miscalculation. Pliable Mathews was not. Headstrong, he impetuously breached the limits of his authority. His transgression plunged him into a fight with the burgesses, who humiliated him and forced their version of a new code down his throat.

In December 1656, Speaker Francis Moryson appointed Francis Willis, Abraham Wood, George Reade, and John Wilcox as a committee "for

Review of the Acts" in preparation for the next revisal. Well-seasoned legislators, Willis and his colleagues searched for copies of every law they could locate, even those that had been cast aside in former codifications or repealed by earlier General Assemblies. They handed their findings over to a second committee, also chaired by Willis. That committee vetted the findings before they drew up a draft text (now lost) that was supposed to be debated when the Assembly met in the spring of 1657. For reasons unknown, Mathews refused to convene the Assembly for more than a year, and when he did, the burgesses of the General Assembly of March 1657/58 went to Jamestown in a rancid mood and spoiling for a fight.

No sooner had the House come to order than the scrapping started. It broke out because Mathews and the councillors objected to three components in the draft: curbs on attorneys' fees, elimination of several conciliar monetary emoluments, and retention of House delegations at their current numbers. When the burgesses stood firm, Mathews saw only intransigence in their unwillingness to give way to his demands, and without looking before he leapt, he angrily tried to dissolve the House. The burgesses countered instantly, declaring unanimously that the governor's dissolution order was "not presidentiall neither legall according to the lawes, now in force." Speaker John Smith (alias Francis Dade)[29] commanded the members to stay in town, on pain of censure, to "act in all things and to all intents and purposes as a whole and entire house." The business of the House would now proceed secretly, and the Speaker was forbidden to "signe nothing without the consent of the major part of the house." Snared in no-man's land, Mathews looked for a way to disentangle himself. He suggested rescinding his order in return for referring the controversy to Oliver Cromwell and allowing the Lord Protector to decide whether Mathews had the power to dissolve the House.

The burgesses wanted none of that. They forced a settlement to their liking that they maneuvered into law that was quite parliamentary in its design and execution. Speaker Smith picked seasoned veterans John Carter, Wareham Horsemanden, John Sidney, Thomas Swann, Richard Webster, Jerome Ham, and William Mitchell and charged them to prepare a "manifestation and vindication of the Assembly's power which after presentation to the House to be sent to the Governor and Council." That done, they drew up "all such propositions as any way tend to or concerne the settling the present affaires of the country and government." After examining the precedents, the Carter committee determined that the "present power of government" rested solely with the burgesses, who were not "dissolvable by any power now extant in Virginia but by the House of Burgesses." As a sop to the governor and his supporters in the upper body, it recommended the reelection of Mathews and the councillors "for two yeares ensueinge." Members embraced the committee report but amended it with measures that strengthened it even further. The House sergeant-at-arms could execute precepts issued by the Speaker and no one else.

Mathews and the Council had no choice but to give way. Secretary Claiborne was humbled when he was forced to surrender custody of the public records to Speaker Smith. He, Mathews, and the other councillors were compelled to kneel at the bar of the House to admit their inferiority to the burgesses and to swear new oaths of office. Clerk Henry Randolph entered the outcome in the House journal on 31 March 1658. "THIS day," he wrote laconically, "all the former acts having been perused by the committee for viewing and regulateing them were by the said committee presented to the house, where being read and seriously discussed they were approved of in the House and a committee appointed to present them to the Governour and Councill, and to advise with them and his council about explanation or alteration of any seeming difficulties or inconveniencyes, Yet with this limitation not to assent to anything of consequence without the approbation of the House."[30] Mathews and the Council might suggest changes in the Revisal but the burgesses had the last word.

When William Waller Hening prepared the Revisal of 1658 for inclusion in the *Statutes at Large* he turned to a document he called the "Randolph Manuscript" for his source text. He noted that the manuscript had once been in the possession of Sir John Randolph (1693–1737), a one-time Speaker of the House of Burgesses and attorney general. Following Randolph's death, the manuscript passed to his son Peyton, and after Peyton Randolph died Thomas Jefferson bought it. Jefferson lent it to Hening, and now it is among the Jefferson Papers at the Library of Congress.[31] Unbeknownst to Sir John Randolph, Jefferson, or Hening, a different rendition found its way to England and into a collection of manuscripts assembled by the antiquary Sir Hans Sloane (1660–1753) now at the British Library.[32] Comparing them invites questions about how they came to exist and the connection, if any, between them.

The Randolph Manuscript is not an independent item. It comes from a handwritten book of statutes and orders that the General Assembly adopted between 1642 and 1662. Transcribed in the 1690s, that book was copied from an earlier volume, and it was done at the direction of House clerk Peter Beverley before it got into the hands of Sir John Randolph, who borrowed it from the House library. Randolph never returned it, which saved it from the Richmond fire of 1865.[33] Most importantly, the Sloane Manuscript is an older stand-alone document that originated around the year 1659. Its copyist was someone called Thomas Brewster, who may have been a deputy clerk for the House, a scribe from the secretary's office, or an employee of a prominent York County merchant-planter named Jonathan Newell. Similar repealed acts, similar revived acts, similar new acts, and identical numbering systems are the most obvious common traits shared by both versions. There are some differences. Brewster's copy contains thirteen more acts than are in the Randolph transcript. (Those thirteen were adopted by the General Assembly of March 1658/59.) Brewster also included an index, which the Randolph Manuscript does not have. Peter Beverley's scribe also edited about half of the acts' titles, thereby clarifying their meaning quite considerably.

The Randolph transcript was taken from a now-lost book of enrolled acts and it is attested to by Peter Beverley. What then is the Sloane Manuscript and what is the connection between the two? If Brewster was Jonathan Newell's clerk, then he prepared it for his master's private use. That is a believable conclusion because Newell's name was thrice written on a detached blank leaf by somebody other than Brewster, although the handwriting cannot be linked to the merchant. The more plausible explanation is that Brewster was in the employ of the House. He took down the copy, signed it, and passed it on with all the other copies that were made and distributed throughout the colony after the General Assembly recessed in March 1659.

Both versions reveal much about the content of the Revisal that was familiar. The preamble from 1652 was brought back. So were eighty-one former acts that went unchanged or were altered slightly. Eighteen were rewritten, and thirty-three were new. Each act was numbered consecutively from 1 to 131, and each was identified by its title. Generally, the arrangement of the acts resembled the one adopted in 1652, except there was a minimal effort at grouping them by subject matter.[34]

Some of the reinstituted laws antedated the 1640s, but the majority came into force between 1643 and 1656. Among the former was one that freed burgesses from arrest while on Assembly business, which had first gone on the rolls in 1624. Another controlled the prices of drugs and medical services; one exempted any planter who had settled in the 1610s from taxes; and a fourth declared 22 March and 18 April holy days in remembrance of the outbreak of war with the Indians in 1622 and 1644.[35] Among the latter were acts that touched on the Quarter Court and the county courts: jurisdictions, calendars, procedures, appeals, and membership. Statutes that bore on Indian affairs, including the Anglo-Powhatan Treaty of 1646, were resurrected, as were those that concerned the broader arena of colonial life, which the burgesses had come to regulate in earlier times. There was also a temporary law from 1652 that should have been repealed but was reenacted. Originally intended as a short-lived means of validating land patents and other public records, the act was meant to stand only as long as it took Parliament to authorize a new seal for the colony. Parliament never did, and its failure is a small insight into how inattentive it was to Virginia while it controlled the colony.[36]

A number of new acts curtailed the governor's powers. Two of them dealt directly with the issues that started the fight between the burgesses and Mathews. An election law detailed when the sheriffs should conduct the polls and when they should send the results to the secretary. It left the sizes of delegations unaltered but stipulated that burgesses be "persons of knowne integrity . . . and of the age of one and twenty years" and that all freemen had the vote.[37] The second act banned lawyers it styled "Mercenarie Attorneys," who charged exorbitant fees, from practicing in any of the courts.[38] A corresponding statute lessened the need for such barristers by outlawing mistakes in suit papers as grounds for dismissing cases and constraining magistrates to "give judgement according [to] the right of the cause."[39] (What to do with the councillors' emoluments was put aside for another day.) Other acts allowed the county courts to name their clerks and required the burgesses to confirm the governor's nominees to the courts, while a third permitted the courts to divide their counties into parishes where none existed.[40]

For the first time an act codified a definition of titheables, meaning taxable, persons to include all Africans, all Indians, and all English, sixteen or older, who were held in any type of bondage. Its stated purpose was the prevention of tax fraud but it had the added effect of broadening the tax base.[41] A contrasting law set forth what might be styled an immigration policy because it provided a legal identity for resident foreigners. It promised "aliens and strangers," such as Hollanders and other Europeans, who lived in the colony for four years, maintained a "firme residence," and swore an oath of "ffidelitie" to the "government of this countrey" could become free denizens of Virginia. A variation on how denizens were made in England, the act conferred permanent resident status and many of the same rights as English Virginians enjoyed. Instead of receiving letters patent from the Lord Protector, the proof of their status arose from a commission passed by the General Assembly and signed by the governor.[42]

Mares and sheep could not be exported; neither could their hides nor wool or iron. These restrictions represented extensions of a series of retained acts that were meant to promote greater economic diversity. Sericulture was encouraged anew and so represented a small step toward reducing the annual tobacco crop. Perhaps the most radical feature in the Revisal was an act that shifted the "burthensom and vnequall waie of laying of taxes by the pole [i.e., ratepayer]" to the exporters of tobacco for one year as a further inducement to diversification. The tax amounted to 2 shillings per hogshead to be collected at the time of lading shipboard. Collectors appointed by the House would be stationed at the usual shipping points and would receive 10 percent of the taxes they collected. The funds were in the exclusive control of the burgesses. In part, fostering these kinds of economic development came about because of the failure of the town act of 1652. Passed to satisfy Parliament, that statute never had a chance of success. The most avid town builder of the time was Sir William Berkeley, who had spruced up Jamestown in 1649 and planned to do more before he was turned out of office. None of his successors shared his enthusiasm for urban development, and so it languished.

The Revisal of 1658 bore witness to the purposeful way in which the burgesses had gone about their task. It was an ordered and comprehensible revision of the *corpus juris,* which embodied consequential improvements over its predecessor. Nevertheless, it turned into an unusually partisan document. Ensnared in the struggle between the House of Burgesses and Governor Mathews, it was the catalyst that heightened the burgesses' consciousness of their power and their willingness to combat challenges to their place at the center of the provincial government.

A threat to that position arose during the General Assembly of 1658/59. On 8 March, Governor Mathews summoned the burgesses to the Council chamber and read them a letter from Henry Lawrence, the president of the Council of State in London. Directed only to Mathews and his councillors, Lawrence's letter told of the death of Oliver Cromwell. It bid them to proclaim Cromwell's son Richard the new Lord Protector, and it commanded them to apply themselves "with all seriousness, faithfulness and circumspection to the peaceable and orderly management of the affaires of that collony." Hearing Mathews out, the burgesses excused him and the councillors to discuss a response. Everyone agreed to proclaiming Richard Cromwell but they disputed "their Lordships' intentions for the government of this country" arguing "That wee owne the power and the whole contents thereof." As the hour was late, the talking wound down, and they adjourned for the day. Next morning, they told Mathews and the Council to join them in sending an address to London informing the Lord Protector that the "supream power" of governing Virginia inhered in their house by virtue of the "present lawes resident in the Grand Assembly." Therefore, they asked "That what was their priviledge now might be his or their posterities thereafter."[43] Their bold claim of privilege provoked no rebuke from Henry Lawrence. By the time news of it reached London, he was no longer president of the Council of State and republican England was falling to pieces.

Returning to legislative business, the House approved five acts that responded to a range of issues that the Revisal of 1658 had not addressed or they spoke to recent complaints from the planters. Civil appeals from the Quarter Court to the General Assembly were limited to judgments of more than 2,500 pounds of tobacco, which shrank the volume of appeals. Appeals from the Eastern Shore county of Northampton to the Quarter Court were prohibited in suits below 3,200 pounds of tobacco, or £32, which was likely intended to soothe complaints from the Quarter Court about its ever-growing caseload. The third set down rules for compensating burgesses who represented church parishes, the fourth repealed an act about grand juries, and the fifth forbade sheriffs and clerks from pleading cases in their courts.[44]

Then the burgesses finally codified their relationship to the governor and the councillors. They enacted a statute that controlled gubernatorial elections and conciliar appointments and another that prescribed an exact method for convening the Assembly to elect governors. The former elected

Mathews to a two-year term, starting in 1659, after which the House would choose "a Gouvernor as the they shall think fitt" who must be a councillor. It continued the incumbent councillors in place. Thereafter, the governor could nominate new councillors whom the burgesses would accept or reject. Councillors would hold their places for life, although the House could remove any of them for "high misdemeanors." Another act dictated the rules for electing governors to come after Mathews. In an election year the Assembly was to convene on 10 March, having been called to Jamestown two months prior, and the governor was compelled to schedule the poll. If he failed to issue the election writs, then the secretary of the colony was required to circulate the call no later than 10 February.[45]

Their work finished, the House recessed until Mathews called them back to Jamestown in March 1660. However, that call never came to pass.

Governor Mathews died suddenly in January 1659/60. His death not only left Virginia without a governor, but also revealed a structural defect in the colony's constitution that prevented the immediate elevation of a successor. There was no lieutenant governor, and neither the Speaker of the House of Burgesses nor the secretary of the colony was lawfully entitled to replace Mathews. No one in 1652 or 1658 had foreseen a need for a mechanism to supplant a governor who either fell into incapacity or dropped dead. It had sufficed in both revisals merely to confer the power of election on the burgesses. That provision only worked if the burgesses were sitting or an incumbent called them to Jamestown. But in January 1660 the General Assembly was in recess, and without Mathews there was no one to convene the burgesses to conduct an election. Because tales out of England rumored the unravelling of the parliamentary regime and the restoration of King Charles II, it was vital to pick a new governor quickly. But how? Some councillors of state came up with a solution. They would nominate a placeholder who would recall the Assembly promptly, and then the burgesses could either confirm him or choose someone else. Within days of Mathews's demise they tapped Sir William Berkeley, and in mid-February he summoned the General Assembly to gather in the capital on 13 March 1659/60.

That day the burgesses took up the matter of picking a permanent chief executive. Over the objections of some, Berkeley emerged as the preferred choice, assuming he and the House could negotiate acceptable terms. Speaker Theoderick Bland deputed a committee to dicker with him.

Berkeley seemed surprised at the offer and quite reluctant to accept it, but Bland's committee persisted and after a week's hard bargaining, he and they came to an agreement. Berkeley would stay only until the political situation in London clarified and the wishes of whoever was in power there were made known in Virginia. He insisted that the sitting councillors concur in his election; he accepted the "supreame power" of the House of Burgesses as the sovereign authority in the colony; he swore to govern according to the "aunctient lawes of this country," summoning the General Assembly once every two years, or "oftner if he [saw] cause"; and he promised not to dissolve the Assembly without the consent of the House. On their part, the burgesses allowed him to name his own councillors of state and secretary of the colony. They pledged an immediate payment of all his pending financial claims against the provincial government. These conditions did not entirely please Berkeley, but his choice came down to accepting them or forgoing election. On 19 March, he stood before the House and announced his acceptance. Two days later he delivered a similar announcement to the Council. Back in the governor's chair, he and the Assembly turned to pending legislative business before recessing until 20 March 1660/61.[46]

Reports of Berkeley's return to office made their slow transit across the Atlantic to Whitehall and reports of the situation in London went no speedier in the opposite direction. Nearly six months elapsed before Berkeley received confirmation of who held the government in England. The news arrived one day in mid-September 1660 when a ship tied up at Jamestown dock.[47] Scrambling down the gangway her captain quickly sought out Berkeley and handed him a packet of mail that Secretary of State Sir Edward Nicholas had entrusted to him. Breaking the seals Berkeley unwrapped three documents: an official announcement of the return of King Charles II to his throne, a warrant from Charles that "Graunt[ed] unto Our trusty and welbeloved Sir William Berkeley Kt. of the Place of Governor of Virginia," and a revived commission of office that Charles had given to Berkeley in 1650. As soon as he digested the contents of those papers Berkeley dictated two proclamations to one of his scribes who penned fair copies for circulation throughout Virginia. One heralded Charles's restoration and commanded obedience to that "most potente, mightye & undoubted King." The other ordered the colony's civil and military officers to remain in place until further notice and to issue all "writs & warrants . . . in his Majesyes name."[48] Those edicts pointed toward the Revisal of 1662.

❦ 5 ❧

Safeguarding Virginia's Autonomy

*Sir William Berkeley, Francis Moryson,
Henry Randolph, and the Revisal of 1662*

No one understood better than Governor Berkeley that the resumption of royal authority involved more than his merely proclaiming the return of the monarchy. Restoring Crown rule meant rewriting Virginia's existing constitution, and that was something he could not do by himself, even if he wanted to, which he did not. Reframing the constitution required a General Assembly to dismantle what its predecessors had constructed in 1652 and 1658. Those realities led him to a series of political decisions that culminated in the fifth revision of the *corpus juris*.

Berkeley faced the matter of what to do with the General Assembly that had elected him governor in March 1660. His promise not to recall it until 21 March 1660/61 presented him with a predicament. Should he summon that Assembly or should he dissolve it? Ignoring his pledge would be perfectly lawful because the parliamentary regime was dead and he could honestly maintain that his promise no longer mattered. That was a risky choice, however. It would ruffle feathers at a fraught moment and it would invite resistance from politicians whose acquiescence he counted on to smooth the return to royal governance. Going back on his word was personally obnoxious because to him a pledge made was a pledge kept. Holding to the letter of his promise, on the other hand, posed an unacceptably long delay in finishing the transition due to the length of time that it took for an election to run its course. Was there a way around those stumbling blocks? There was, and he read it in a law that the General Assembly had enacted when it reelected him. The statute stipulated that should the governor happen to "find occasion by importance of affaires" to recall the Assembly sooner than 21 March 1661, then he "should promptly issue forth his sumons to the present Burgesses." And within days of his proclaiming Charles II king Berkeley sent forth a writ of summons for the Assembly to meet him on 11 October 1660.[1]

Although fire destroyed the journals of the October session when Richmond burned in 1865, a copy of the acts still exists, and it is the only window into what went on. Berkeley began by greeting members with a convivial opening speech. He told everyone of the state of affairs as best he knew them. Then he outlined his agenda and urged prompt action on it. Burgesses and councillors alike warmed to his remarks and generally welcomed the prospect of returning Virginia to its former loyalty. But not all. Several dissenters loudly objected to being recalled to Jamestown, claiming that Berkeley had summoned them "with out a new election" which threatened the legitimacy of this General Assembly. Berkeley finessed their objection. He agreed to insert a justification into the preamble of the session's statutes. The operative language in the preamble flatly asserted that "upon the Immergent occasions of the Countrey which could not well admit of soo much delay As must upon necessity have attended a new election, the authoritie of this present Grand assembly, is by presidents [precedents] in England warrantable and legall." Berkeley's "presidents" had been laid down by the Convention Parliament when it legislated the restoration of King Charles to his throne. And, as that Parliament had done, the General Assembly declared its acts "good and valid . . . to all intents and purposes and that who ever shall presume to question the power thereof shalbe adjudged a seditious person, and bee liable to such Censure as the lawe in such case do infflict."[2] That solution seems to have satisfied the dissenters because no further complaints are evident.

Once the objection was resolved, the members began recasting Virginia's constitution. They called upon Berkeley to intercede with the king for a general pardon of the colonists for their having defected from their loyalty to the Crown. They named Berkeley, Speaker Theoderick Bland, and their colleagues Nathaniel Bacon,[3] Miles Cary, Robert Ellyson, Henry Soane, and Robert Wynne an extraordinary committee, which they charged to petition King Charles for validation of "several favours," including confirmation of the General Assembly as the colony's legislature, land titles, and free trade. Then they repealed all the statutes adopted during the Interregnum that were in any way repugnant to monarchy; everything else in the Revisal of 1658 remained good law and fully enforceable. Finally, they affirmed the only "authority" in Virginia was that of "the Kinges most excellent majestie."[4]

These steps reestablished the king's writ but they were quite modest when compared to how the General Assembly of April 1652 had approached constitutional change after Berkeley surrendered Virginia to Parliament. That Assembly had massively recast the laws in force as the principal means of adjusting to new rulers and new constitutional government. Was an overhaul in order in October 1660 as it had been a decade earlier? Berkeley did not advocate such an undertaking. He put it off to another day.

Neither his surviving papers nor the remaining General Assembly records hint at why Berkeley temporized, though several possibilities come to mind. Berkeley had been out of office for a decade, which was an absence that weakened his relationships with the colony's leaders. He needed time to rebuild a following especially among newer politicians who had come to prominence during his enforced retirement. He was well aware that back in March 1660 some burgesses and councillors had opposed electing him. They were among the grumblers who objected to reconvening the Assembly. Quite possibly those realities made him skittish about challenging potential opponents while he was still in a tenuous political spot. Perhaps he listened to members who advised that a thorough reform was unnecessary. Others may have told him that enacting a revisal would compel everyone to stay longer at Jamestown, and they wanted to go home. Whatever his thinking, he eventually concluded that law reform should be left to another day; he dropped the matter and dissolved the Assembly.

Events during the winter of 1660–1661 moved Berkeley to revive the issue after he started hearing news that both disquieted and pleased him. He picked up intimations coming out of London of King Charles's inclination toward binding England and the colonies into an Atlantic economic entity that would exclude the Dutch from the American trade. Then he got rumors about a scheme to revive the Virginia Company of London. If true, this combination of prospects boded ill for the colony's autonomy, its institutions, and his own conception of Virginia's right relationship with the Crown.[5] The promising intelligence was a tip that the king had named a committee of knowledgeable individuals to advise him about the state of affairs in his American plantations. Early in 1661 Berkeley learned the veracity of that tip when he received a royal commission appointing him to the newly formed Committee for Foreign Plantations. The appointment instantly persuaded him that an agent must go to London to guard Virginia's interests. And who better than he? He had connections at court like no other Virginian. Besides, his gubernatorial commission permitted him to return to England in emergencies, which this was. Then, too, his seat on the Committee for Foreign Plantations implied his attendance at Whitehall at some point in the none-too-distant future. All he needed was the approbation of the General Assembly and its funding of his agency.

Acting on this mix of news, Berkeley issued writs for a new General Assembly to meet him on 23 March 1661/62.[6] The polling for the burgesses returned a few holdovers from the October session but the majority were newcomers who were inclined to follow Berkeley's lead, which indicates that he pulled enough strings to deliver a favorable House majority. Changes at the Council table also assured a more pliant upper chamber. Once again, no text of his opening address exists, but the tenor of that speech may be supposed with fair assurance. Berkeley would have recounted what he knew about the Crown's emerging colonial policy and would have explained its undesirable implications for Virginia. He would have remarked about a threatened revival of the Virginia Company, he would have noted the dangers a resurrected company could create for the planters, and he would have told of his appointment to the Committee for Foreign Plantations. Then he would have stated a case for sending an agent to London to lobby for Virginia's interests. He was the obvious choice, he would have said, because of his close personal and family links to potent courtiers who had the ear of King Charles II. Without hesitation, the members agreed and charged him to go to Whitehall and "oppose the invaders of our freedoms and truly to represent our condition to his sacred majesty." They also appropriated 200,000 pounds of tobacco to support his agency.[7]

Berkeley urged the Assembly that this was the right moment to take up another revisal because updating the statutes would strengthen his hand by satisfying a mandate from his instructions as a foreign plantations' commissioner. Again the members complied with his wishes by ordering "Collonel Francis Morrison [i.e., Moryson] and Henry Randolph clerke of the assembly [to] review all the acts, peruse the records, give dates to the severall acts, from the first time of their being in force and present a draught of them with such alterations & amendments as they shall find necessary to the next assembly [i.e., in March 1661/62] and that there be paid to them for their paines fifteen thousand pounds of tobacco out of the next levy." Prior to sailing to London Berkeley conferred with both men about what the revisal should entail. He told them that as soon as the revisal passed into law they were to send him a fair copy, which he would have printed for distribution to the Crown and for use in Virginia.[8]

Moryson and Randolph were sound choices for this assignment. Respected, highly placed lawmakers, both men enjoyed the confidence not only of Berkeley but of leading councillors, burgesses, local magistrates, and the generality of the planters as well. Moryson (ca. 1628–ca. 1680) shared a relationship of some intimacy with the governor that dated back to the days before the English Civil Wars. His sister Lettice's marriage with Lucius Cary, 2d viscount Falkland, related him to a Berkeley patron, and it was through his sister that he first met Berkeley. One of his brothers, Richard Moryson, commanded the fort at Old Point Comfort (in modern-day Hampton, Virginia) until he died in 1648. Francis Moryson, an ex-colonel in King Charles I's army, escaped to Virginia in 1649 and lived for a time with Richard's widow before setting up a farm near the governor's Green Spring plantation. Berkeley encouraged him to involve himself in the colony's public life and he gave him a boost by putting him on the James City County court. After the parliamentary takeover Moryson's open loyalty to the Stuarts proved no impediment to the advancement of his political career. In 1656, he took his seat in the House of Burgesses, after which his colleagues chose him for their Speaker. Before he quit the House, Speaker Moryson had overseen the selection of the men who drew up the preliminary draft for the Revisal of 1658. The burgesses elected him to the Council of State in March 1660. Berkeley kept Moryson as a councillor and gave him two lucrative posts: commander of the fort at Old Point Comfort and deputy treasurer of the colony. He promoted him higher still when he named him deputy governor for the duration of his mission to London.[9]

Henry Randolph (1623–1673) was typical of the middling sorts of Englishmen who beached up in the colony and prospered by dint of ability and connection. A merchant from Little Houghton, Northamptonshire, he landed in Virginia in 1643. Setting himself up in Henrico County, he grew friendly with Moryson and got to know Berkeley. His gift with a pen, his skill at record keeping, and his smattering of legal knowledge drew the notice of the Henrico County justices who named him their clerk in 1656.

That same year he succeeded Charles Norwood to the clerkship of the House of Burgesses, a post he retained until his death. Barely into that job he received a crash course in statutory reform when he assisted the two select committees who prepared the eventual 1658 revisal. That experience, his deepening appreciation of the records of the House, its procedures, and closer proximity to leading House members effectively turned him into an indispensable legislative author who drew up the bills that eventually passed into law.[10]

How Moryson and Randolph apportioned the work among themselves can only be guessed. In all likelihood, Randolph did most of the preliminary labor because his knowledge of the legislative archives in his custody greatly exceeded Moryson's and his clerical duties in Henrico County were lighter than the deputy governor's executive responsibilities. After reviewing all of the "severall acts," the journals of both houses, and other pertinent records, he composed a preliminary draft. Moryson went over it, adding parts, refining others, and subtracting some sections altogether until the draft was mostly to his liking. Then the two of them sorted out their differences, and after that Randolph drew up the report that they laid before the General Assembly when it reconvened.

When the General Assembly gathered on 2 March 1661/62 it confronted what proved to be a copious agenda, fuller perhaps than Moryson, Randolph, or anyone else could have anticipated. Besides the usual spate of routine legislative business and action on the draft revisal there were extraordinary matters to be met. The most immediate of these was choosing someone to replace Speaker Henry Soane who had recently died.[11] Robert Wynne (bap. 1622–1675)[12] won the election. A Cantaurian, Wynne was reared in a well-placed family. Named after a lord mayor of Canterbury, he also had relatives who represented the cathedral city in the House of Commons. What Wynne did before he left England is unknown, though he may have read law. That possibility is implied by the survival of one of his books, a first edition of Sir Edmund Plowden's *Commentaries*.[13] A probable royalist, Wynne likely emigrated to Virginia around mid-century because he was a member of the Charles City County Court as of 1656. Two years later, he was elected to the House of Burgesses for the first time. After sitting out a session he returned to the House and participated in Berkeley's recall. He retained his seat in the election of March 1661, which positioned him for the Speakership.

The next great worry was finding a prompt way of tamping down the latest skirmishes with the Indians who were not signatories to the Anglo-Indian Treaty of 1646 and whose lands were being gobbled up by expanding English settlements. If left unchecked those clashes threatened serious violence along the frontier.[14] Another apprehension was a challenge to the established religious order posed by the rapid spread of Quakerism.[15] At what point the draft revisal came up for consideration is uncertain, although an extant order of the House offers a clue to how the adoption proceeded. A scrap from a House journal notes that "Upon the committees report, *it is ordered by this present grand Assembly* that those excellent proposalls presented by the right honourable governor to the assembly be drawne into acts except the first article concerning an interstitium[16] being very difficult to effect."[17] Moryson submitted the draft to Speaker Wynne who summarized it for the burgesses and decided where to docket it on the legislative calendar.

When the draft actually came up for consideration, Wynne commanded Randolph orally to recap the subject of each of its proposed acts. Then Wynne resorted to one of two procedures. Either he referred the draft to the standing Committee for the Review of the Acts for its disposition, which was then the usual way of moving most bills to enactment, or he entertained a motion to resolve the burgesses into a committee of the whole House for its recommendations. Whichever procedure he imposed resulted in a report that went to the floor for debate and perfection into bills that was forwarded to the Council of State. The councillors had their say and sent their amendments to each bill back down to the House for additional consideration.[18] An ad hoc conference committee of burgesses, councillors, and Randolph met to reconcile outstanding differences, and that was probably when the "first article concerning an interstitium" was eliminated. As soon as the conference committee report was agreed and vouchsafed in both houses, it went to Moryson who signed it into law.

The new revisal consisted of 142 statutes. It mirrored its predecessors in certain features. Apart from the inclusion of the preamble, the general configuration stayed consistent with the one first instituted in 1624; that is, church laws came first followed by everything else. Borrowing innovations initially employed in 1658, Randolph and Moryson clustered the acts roughly by types of regulation that contained as few as one or two laws or ran into dozens, and they gave every law its descriptive title as well as its number. They retained quantities of existing acts, some unchanged in content, some repurposed, but all rewritten in a style of statutory language that they imposed throughout the entire revisal. Crisper and less convoluted, that language brought the acts nearer to the point and purpose of parliamentary statutes than ever before. Perhaps that improvement speaks to Randolph's growth as a legislative draftsman as well as his reliance on one of the full-text editions of acts of Parliament, such as William Rastell's *Collection of Statutes in Force* (London, 1615), which were readily available in the Council of State library.

A full-throated preamble explained the reasons for the revisal. It began by declaring that "the late unhappy distractions caused by frequent changes in the government of this country" left the law in such a confused state that "the people knew not well what to obey nor the judge what to punish." For that reason, the General Assembly reviewed "the whole body of the laws" to rid them of "all unnecessary acts & chiefly such as might keep in memory our inforced deviation from his majesties obedience" with the intention of bringing the laws in force "into one volume." Hence, all existing statutes were "repealed, and expunged." In their place were new laws "(as neere as the capacity and constitution of this country would admitt) to adhere to those excellent and often refined laws of England, to which we profess and acknowledge all *due obedience and reverence*." Also "sett downe" were "certaine rules to be observed in the government of the church, until God shall please to turne his majesties pious thoughts towards us, and provide a better supply of ministers among us."[19] Berkeley insisted on the inclusion of such passages before he went to London. His underlying rationale for inserting them was political. Aimed at the Crown, they were in keeping with two of his instructions as a member of the Council for Foreign Plantations. The one alerted royal officials that Virginia law sometimes diverged from English law, while the other foretold how the Assembly sidestepped the shortage of priests until the king rectified the shortage.[20] Of greater importance, perhaps, was his desire to steer clear of as much of the Crown's or Parliament's intrusion in the colony's internal affairs as was possible.

Acts I–XVII reset the church on its Anglican bearings. Primarily concerned with governance, they were modeled on the Revisal of 1643 and its various amendments down to 1652, but not slavishly so.[21] For instance, Randolph and Moryson chose to break apart the church government act from 1643 and redistribute its pieces as separate laws. Act II repurposed parts that defined vestries, fixed their membership at twelve per vestry, and required them to swear the English oath of allegiance and supremacy. Another piece made explicit provisions for the governor to induct clergymen into their cures and to expel ministers who refused to obtain gubernatorial licenses. Priests leading divine services were forbidden to deviate from the liturgy as it was written in the Book of Common Prayer, and they were enjoined to preach weekly. Church attendance was compulsory. Sundays were not "to bee prophaned." Any parish that had no priest was at liberty to choose a layman of "grave and sober . . . good life and conversation" to lead prayers and deliver canned sermons. That was a new Berkeley-inspired innovation designed to meet a perennial shortage of ordained ministers. To combat the Quakers, Act IX incorporated an Elizabethan recusancy statute that outlawed conventicles and provided stiff fines for any nonconformist who refused to attend the Anglican church.[22] Two new laws declared annual days of remembrance: 30 January to mark the execution of King Charles I and 20 May to commemorate the restoration of his son.[23] Drawn from former acts, an additional six statutes prescribed various administrative responsibilities of both vestrymen and the clergy.[24]

Act XVIII revised and codified an earlier law that was intended to found a "colledge" to promote "learning, education of youth, supply of ministry, and promotion of piety."[25] The inspiration for this law came from the Reverend Phillip Mallory (d. 1661), a York County parson. Mallory accompanied Governor Berkeley to England intending to lobby both the Crown and prominent churchmen to support the college financially. Sadly, Dame Fortune did not smile on him. He died soon after he got to England, and the realization of a Virginia college would languish for another three decades.[26]

Although this section of the Revisal restored the church to its former place, none of its statutes remedied the perennial shortage of clergy that had existed ever since the fall of the Virginia Company of London in 1624. There were only about a dozen resident priests in 1662, who could hardly have tended to the spiritual needs of sixty parishes scattered across the colony. The reasons for that scarcity were manifold, but they need not be summarized here, except to say the most obvious one. Few men of the cloth regarded Virginia as an inviting place for a ministry.[27]

Another section dealt with the General and county courts. The changes to the General Court did not affect its membership or the boundaries of its original and appellate jurisdiction. One was no more complicated than a name change. From its earliest days, the court had borne the name "Quarter Court" because it sat four times a year. That name became "unsutable" after one of its sittings was abolished in the 1650s but the title remained. Calling it the "General Court" was a more "sutable" appellation because it was reflective of the place "where all persons and causes have generally audience and receive determination." A vastly more substantive change standardized and amplified the rules of civil procedure. Here the goal lay in furnishing judges and suitors with fairly precise instructions regarding the dates of sittings, the number of cases to be tried on given days, the form of timely appeals, the issuance of writs and subpoenas, the presentation of evidence, and the prevention of frivolous lawsuits.[28]

When it came to criminal procedure an act vested the General Court with the exclusive power to try accused felons, thereby purposefully renewing the prohibition the Assembly imposed upon county courts in 1656. That law enshrined the English principle that petit jurors must be "chosen out of the neighbourhood where the fact was committed" but bent it with a Virginia twist. The tenet was difficult to apply in the colony because unless the crime happened in the capital or one of its close-by counties twelve jurors could not readily be drawn from the vicinage of an accused and transported to Jamestown. To clear that barrier the act modified an English writ known as *tales de circumstantibus* (i.e., "such of the bystanders").[29] The writ enabled an English judge to complete a jury by ordering a sheriff to collect as many jurors as necessary from the spectators hanging about the court. The Virginia variation required a county sheriff to gather six men from the "neighbourhood" who accompanied him with the accused to Jamestown. On trial day, the court ordered him to produce those men and six more that he pressed from onlookers who stood about the Council chamber or in the yard. That twist overcame a procedural impediment unknown in England and kept Virginia law faithful to a venerable rule of law.[30]

As for the county courts, another cluster of acts delineated their place in Virginia's governance with greater specificity than ever before. For the first time, county courts were limited to "eight of the most able, honest and judicious persons of the county," which reduced their size to an exact number. Hereafter explicitly designated "justices of the peace," local magistrates received a general power when in court to enforce English and colonial law and when not in session to "act, and doe all such things as by the laws of England are to be done by justices of the peace there." New and rewritten laws completed the devolution of routine ecclesiastical matters into the justices' hands. Chief among these was an act that empowered them to probate wills and to grant administrations on intestate estates, which relieved the governor of a burdensome, time-consuming task and spared colonists a trip to Jamestown. By implication, it also meant that disputes about the validity of wills or the settlement of estates originated in the county courts and that eased the General Court's caseload.[31]

Rules akin to those in the General Court set out county trial procedures. The role of grand juries was clarified. First introduced by the General Assembly of November 1645 and retained in 1658, their use had never been set forth with any degree of particularity. That imperfection vanished with the requirement that sheriffs convene grand juries twice yearly for the express purpose of looking into breaches of law and presenting miscreants for trial. The right to a petit jury was reformed too. Ever since 1643, it had been the practice to hold jury trials only when suitors requested them. Randolph and Moryson considered that habit contrary to English law so they eliminated it. In its place, they substituted a rule for a sheriff to empanel a jury each morning his court sat to try whatever cases the justices put before them and to deny jurors "meat and drink vntill they have agreed on their verdict."[32] In other words, juries remained sequestered without relief until they decided the case.

Who was a sheriff and what one did had come quite a distance since Sir John Harvey appointed the first of them. Those early sheriffs were not even considered members of the monthly courts and their duties lacked much by way of written definition, but the understanding of the office changed with time. Around mid-century, though still not a member of the court, a sheriff had come to be regarded as a county's chief administrator as well as its policeman. In those capacities, he summoned prospective jurors, served writs and warrants, executed judgments, inflicted corporal punishment, arrested and jailed criminal suspects, collected taxes, acted as bailiff and crier for his court, and conducted elections. By the 1660s many of these functions already had statutory definitions, and in those instances Moryson and Randolph had only to clarify whatever clarification was indicated. They added several acts of their own design that put sheriffs on county commissions of the peace, made them post performance bonds, imposed limits on their tenure, and exacted stiff fines for failure to do their duty. These changes not only enhanced the powers of the office, but also made it more attractive to hold.[33]

Although clerks were integral to the working of the courts they had always escaped the General Assembly's attention, except when it came to regulation of their fees. Moryson and Randolph paid them scant heed too. The apparent reason for that inattention was tied up in the nature of colonial clerkship. Virginia clerks never sat on the bench because they never were justices. Their paramount duty was recording the business of court and colonist. Their office seems to have evolved from an early amalgamation of the record-keeping functions of an English justice of the peace called the *custos rotulorum* (keeper of the records) and his underling, the clerk of the peace, who was basically a scrivener.[34]

The county court acts firmly concentrated local control in fewer hands and permanently cemented the political division between county and province into written law. While that outcome was something that gratified the great men, it encroached upon executive rights by limiting the size of county benches. Berkeley tolerated the intrusion. It gave him protective cover to reshape the magistracy by displacing justices who denounced the return to royal rule, and it was consistent with his deference to county grandees.

A small cluster of laws dealt with the burgesses, who came in for tighter supervision of their office. They faced fines of 350 pounds of tobacco for every day they were absent without the Speaker's leave or an excuse acceptable to the whole House. Because their "immoderate expences" caused "diverse heart burnings" among their constituents, their compensation was limited to 150 pounds of tobacco per diem and reimbursement for their traveling to and from Jamestown. A more important measure reduced the number of burgesses to two per county. As an exception, voters in James City County got to elect three, one of whom sat for Jamestown, and voters in any other county could elect an additional burgess if its justices laid out a town that attracted at least a hundred titheable persons as residents. These changes were inducements to promote towns, but they also proceeded from palpably political motives that were meant to keep certain types out of the House and to tighten the justices' hold on the office. Reducing the number eliminated church parishes as electoral units, which effectively prevented dissenting parishes south of the James River from electing their coreligionists. The limitation also meant that from 1662 onward no one would sit in the House unless he also sat on a county court.[35]

Laws about land, servants, Indian affairs, economic diversification, and tax policy stand out among the remaining clusters. With one exception, the land laws grouped rewritten versions of former acts. Toward the end of the meeting Moryson and Secretary Thomas Ludwell (1629–1678) secured the exception when they proposed a written method for disposing of real estate that reverted to the Crown whenever a decedent died heirless.[36] The servant law cluster was similarly put together. Important modifications, at least for indentured servants, abolished branding runaways, outlawed cruel usage, and clarified bondage by bringing it into conformity with the English law of indentures for apprentices. Perhaps because their numbers were still small, no statute distinguished African slaves from English servants at any length. Randolph and Moryson did no more than write a 1661 statute about English servants absconding with "negroes who are incapable of making satisfaction by addition of time" into the revised act about runaways.[37]

A single act merged decades of law about Indian policy that Berkeley formulated after the Anglo-Powhatan War of 1644–1646 and later Assemblies had expanded. However, nothing in it altered the underlying strategic concepts of that policy of keeping the tributary nations separate from the English and guarding the frontiers from those Indians who were not signatories to the Treaty of 1646. Modest restraints on tobacco cultivation and tentative inducements to producing alternatives anticipated Berkeley's grand scheme for diversifying the colony's economy. And a two-act cluster raised the possibility of supporting the provincial government with a tax on tobacco exports.[38]

The concluding act ordered that a certified transcript of the new code be "sent to the honorable Sir William Berkeley into England and that he be requested to procure his majesties royal confirmation; . . . [and] after they be confirmed the said honorable Sir William Berkeley be pleased to deliver them to the assignee of Henry Randolph . . . to be printed."[39] Randolph's "assignee" was Anna Cotes (fl. 1661–1667), a London bookseller whose shop was located at the Tiger's Head in Fleet Street near Saint Dunstan's Church. She hired nearby printer Ellen Seile (fl. 1661–1667) who produced the book.[40] Seile finished the job shortly after 3 September 1662. That was time enough for Berkeley to send copies to King Charles and his privy councillors for their confirmation and to pack a trunkload when he sailed for America later in the month.[41]

Seile designed *The Lawes of Virginia Now in Force* for utility instead of beauty, which was typical of mid-seventeenth-century English legal publishers. A plain-looking book, it has the usual license, title page, and dedicatory epistle printed on six front leaves. Those elements are followed by eighty-two numbered leaves of text and a four-leaf unpaginated index. The index is arranged in the order in which the acts are printed instead of by subject, which was a common way of indexing at the time.[42]

Moryson opened the book with a flowery dedication to the governor. He thanked Berkeley for having *"impos'd on me and the Clerk of the Assembly, the charge to peruse our Laws, and to reduce them into as good a Form, as our weak abilities could perform."* But Moryson craved pardon for not having done better because *"the Troubles of the Indians, and Quakers, and other emergent Occasions of the Publique, depriv'd me of much of that time I had devoted to that most serious Imployment."* Despite the obstacles, he and the Assembly succeeded in retaining laws that *"your self had done in the time of your Government"* while cleansing them of *"what vitious Excrescencies had grown in them, by the corrupt humor of the times"* and erased *"the memory of our enforc'd Defection from his Sacred Majesty."* Calculated to strengthen Berkeley in the eyes of King Charles and the Privy Council, the dedication ended on this note of praise: *"though the remoteness of this place, hath yielded the glory of . . . your Honourable Actions; yet I, and all that here with me . . . must, and ever will acknowledge that you, next to his Majesties goodness, we owe both the Laws we Govern by, and the Countrey it now Govern'd by those Laws."*[43]

Berkeley may have written the dedication over Moryson's name. Whether or not he did, it was of a piece with his intended use of book itself. He had gone to London seeking to protect Virginia's autonomy by convincing King Charles to embrace his schemes for urban renewal at Jamestown and for economic diversification.[44] To both ends, he aggressively showered royal officials with petitions and other documents to make his case. On the one hand, he targeted one of those items, *A Discourse and View of Virginia*,[45] at the Council for Foreign Plantations to demonstrate a Virginia capable of producing desirable staple commodities. On the other, he aimed at the king and the Privy Council with *The Lawes of Virginia Now in Force* to reveal a stable legal order that required little interference from the Crown. No response to his presentation has ever come to light.

The distribution of *The Lawes of Virginia Now in Force* throughout the colony is impossible to calculate with any degree of precision. How many copies of the book Berkeley brought with him cannot be reckoned. Neither can their owners be identified or counted since the loss of Randolph's papers cancels any discovery of who bought them. It is reasonable to suppose that justices, burgesses, and councillors numbered among his customers, but here again no proof sustains that assumption. Even William Waller Hening was unaware of the book since he failed to cite it in anywhere in the *Statutes at Large*. The few copies that escaped destruction ended up in research libraries where they rest as generally forgotten artifacts from a distant legal past.[46]

Without question, the Revisal of 1662 represented the most wide-ranging of the seventeenth-century codifications. It defended the relative autonomy that Virginians enjoyed up to the 1660s. It reflected the creative skills of their makers, especially those of Francis Moryson and Henry Randolph. It not only refined old statutes and added new laws but also extended the law's reach and gave clearer definition to Virginia's internal polity. And, with Governor Berkeley's blessing, it allowed grasping colonists to tighten their grip on power more than ever before. As a snapshot the Revisal was the reflection of the General Assembly at the peak of its preeminence as the little Parliament it now was.[47]

❦ 6 ❦

The Long Road to the Revisal of 1705

Moments before proroguing the General Assembly, Lieutenant Governor Edward Nott remarked how "Very Glad" he was "to see so great a Body of Laws agreed upon And passed this Session, . . . and did not doubt but their proceedings would be very agreeable to her Majesty and for the hon^r and Service of the Country."[1] Although Nott did not refer to them as such, this "great Body of Laws" comprised the Revisal of 1705. Decades in the making, it was an element in a redefined nexus between Crown and colony that diminished the General Assembly and circumscribed Virginia's autonomy. What does the Revisal of 1705 say about the condition of statutory law, the colony, and the Virginians' relations with the Crown that did not exist forty years earlier? The place for answers starts at the restoration of Charles Stuart. As a snapshot those answers yield the most comprehensive picture of the seven revisals because the volume of available evidence on the 1705 Revisal exceeds that which exists for all the others combined.

❦

A penurious King Charles II returned to London in 1660 with his equally strapped courtiers desperate for money to restore the monarchy as a working government. An empty treasury set them off in search of ample permanent revenues, a search that inspired the Crown to bind Virginia and the other colonies commercially and politically into an imperial community centered on London. In time, boards, committees, and departments, assisted by knowledgeable bureaucrats, took on ever greater administrative responsibilities for managing the colonies, and they would seek to hedge Virginia's autonomy. Governor Sir William Berkeley went to London in 1662 intending to exempt Virginia from provisions in the emerging navigation system that excluded the Dutch from the Chesapeake and ended the colonists' freedom to trade wherever they might. He failed, although King Charles sanctioned his schemes for diversifying the Virginia economy and empowered him to run the Old Dominion pretty much as he saw fit. For fifteen years Berkeley governed with little interference from London. Yet they were not his best years. Diversification failed, Dutch naval raiders attacked during the Second and Third Anglo-Dutch Wars, restive servants and slaves kept their masters on edge, complaints of misgovernment mounted, and Berkeley physically declined.[2] His inept responses to renewed conflicts with the Indians caused his kinsman Nathaniel Bacon (1647–1676) to revolt in 1676. Bacon's Rebellion, which began as a contentious quarrel between two hard-headed men, threw Virginia into civil war, destroyed Berkeley politically, and ended royal apathy.[3]

In London, the immediate concern lay in restoring order. Berkeley's superiors marshaled redcoats, ships, and a commission of investigation to uncover the causes of the upheaval. But there was more in the moment than merely crushing Nathaniel Bacon and dismissing an elderly, disgraced governor. Here was a sudden opportunity to redefine the Crown-Virginia linkage. Quieting the malcontents could be the way to drawing Virginia closer into the empire, which would only be achieved through robust applications of the royal prerogative. King Charles and his minions were quick to intervene in the colony in ways the Crown had not since the 1620s. Royal interference did not go unchallenged. Indeed, Whitehall's reach for ascendancy provoked sharp protests, especially from the burgesses who bewailed the assaults on their "ancient" privileges. Grudgingly, they yielded to a force they could not overbear and acceded to a recalibration of their relationship with the Crown. The overthrow of King James II and war with France slowed the incursions, but the likelihood of future infringements remained a distinct possibility. So did the fear that an aggressive Crown and assertive governors general would someday result in an acutely dangerous strengthening of the royal prerogative at Virginia's expense.

Throughout the 1680s and the 1690s, royal officials purposefully undercut the General Assembly such that it lost much of its unbridled authority.

Annual sessions were a thing of the past. Gone too was the its long presumed "right" to sit as the colony's highest court of last resort. Its control of the purse was diminished. Internally the House of Burgesses ceded a measure of control over its choice of Speakers and clerks, and it was forced to accept new forms of statutory language. Its nearly absolute right of legislating disappeared. For a while it was forbidden to sit, except in dire emergencies, without explicit orders from the king and then only to adopt bills drafted by the governor and Council of State with approval from London. When there were no General Assemblies, the governor and the Council ruled by proclamation, which was a perennial rub that chafed but about which the burgesses could do little except howl. Politics took on a different coloration. Local issues had dominated ever since 1619 but with the Crown's reach for greater control, those concerns receded as the game of politics increasingly moved toward broader imperial issues and the elite's efforts to defend its position.

Revising the statutes grew into one of those issues. Virginia politicians and English officials warmed to legal reforms but for different reasons. To the home government compelling a revisal to its liking became important to a vigorous reassertion of the royal prerogative and another way of weakening the General Assembly. After 1676, King Charles required session laws be sent to London following every meeting of the Assembly. His underlings also pressed for some sort of compilation of the existing acts for their determination of which ones intruded on the king's authority and which laws were necessary to make Virginia conform to the Crown's colonial policies. To that end they relied on the governor and councillors to draw up periodic compilations and then to compel the burgesses' concurrence. At first the Virginians regarded reform as a way to improve their law as they had done repeatedly since the 1630s, but soon they saw reform not only as a means to obstruct the Crown's aggressiveness but also as a device in their struggle to guard against royal overreach.

For a while Virginia's great men were of divided counsel about how to minimize the intrusion. Some of the older ones became adamant foes of the governors in the hope of exhausting them into leaving the colony as it had been before Bacon. Philip Ludwell (ca. 1637–ca. 1723) and Robert Beverley were the most obstinate of these. Both Ludwell and his brother Thomas were Berkeley's stoutest adherents. As younger men they were clients of Berkeley's brother John, 2d baron Berkeley of Stratton, who secured

Thomas's place as secretary of the colony in 1660. The two brothers sailed to Virginia together and befriended Sir William, who elevated Philip to the Council of State and other provincial positions. Philip developed a closeness to Berkeley's wife that turned into marriage with the widowed Dame Frances. After Thomas died in 1678 Philip became one of the hard-liners' most visible spokesmen, and for more than fifteen years he was constantly at cross-purposes with royal officials. The proprietors of Carolina appointed him to govern their colony, and he held the post for four years before he returned to Virginia in 1694. The James City County voters then sent him to the General Assembly of 1695–96 where Ludwell became Speaker. He sat out the 1696–97 session, he returned for the short meeting in 1698, and he was elected for the last time in 1699. Then he left Virginia and lived out his days in England.[4]

Around the year 1663 Robert Beverley (1635–1687), a Yorkshire mariner from Hull, hauled up in Lancaster County where he prospered as a land surveyor, attorney, and import-export merchant planter. He and Berkeley were drawn to one another. When the General Assembly carved Middlesex County out of Rappahannock County in 1669, the governor put him on the initial Middlesex commission of the peace and named him the new county's surveyor and one of its militia officers. An unswerving Berkeleyite, Beverley proved harshly effective at suppressing Bacon's rebels. He was elected to the General Assembly of February 1677. The burgesses picked him for their clerk, which led to his first clash with Berkeley's successors. That collision happened in April 1677 when he refused turn over legislative journals in his custody to acting governor Colonel Herbert Jeffreys. His refusal caused the Privy Council to dismiss him and to mark him as a troublemaker who bore constant watching. Their assessment appeared justified in 1682 when he was arrested and tried for high treason in the General Court. He stood accused of leading planters in Middlesex County who destroyed their own and their neighbors' tobacco crops, which they expected would create shortages that would raise prices. The treason charge failed for want of evidence, but he was convicted of "high misdemeanors" to which he confessed and was pardoned. Reelected clerk in the General Assembly of 1685–86, he incurred the wrath of then Governor Francis Howard, 5th baron Howard of Effingham, who accused him of turning the burgesses against him and fiddling conciliar amendments to a much-desired town bill. Such was the depth of their disagreements that the governor sought King James II's permission to remove Beverley from the clerkship and his other offices. James complied but Beverley died in 1687 before Effingham could carry out the order. By then the number of politicians of his stripe was thinned by dismissal, retirement, or death.[5]

Opposite Ludwell and his like were old-timers such as Francis Moryson and Nicholas Spencer and younger politicians like Isaac Allerton, John Armistead, William Fitzhugh, Henry Hartwell, and Mathew Kemp who were on the edges of the Berkeley clique. They bore no abiding affection for the old governor or his vision for Virginia. Often, they underwent conversions akin to that of Francis Moryson. Long an intimate of Berkeley's, Moryson walked the road to Damascus while he was in London acting as Virginia's agent. He witnessed firsthand the unfolding royal policies toward the colonies and slowly internalized the underlying rationale about where Virginia properly fit into an imperial order. Little by little he inched away from Berkeley while at the same time seeking the king's patronage. Bacon's Rebellion horrified him and solidified his conviction of the necessity for a redefinition of the Crown-Virginia nexus. Had he lived longer, he could have shown royal officials where to strike hardest at the General Assembly and its statutes because he understood both better than anyone else in London.[6] Others of his stripe accepted the changing times readily. To them an Atlantic world order that pivoted on London offered the benefits of security, social contentment, and economic gain that Berkeley's way had not. By their lights officeholders who accepted this new reality stood to benefit. They would remain safe in their places just as they would reap the rewards of additional royal preferences. Self-interest eased any reluctance to trade the General Assembly's autonomy for personal advantage.[7]

Then there was an amorphous middle bloc. Foremost among them was the rebel's cousin Nathaniel Bacon Sr. (bap. 1620–1692). Over a forty-year career that took him from the county court to the House of Burgesses to the Council of State, he outlasted parliamentary rule, Berkeley, and post-1677 governors. William Byrd (ca. 1650–1704) and Augustine Warner (ca. 1643–1681) were prominent among the councillors, burgesses, and local magistrates who belonged to this loose coalition that also included immigrant lawyers and native-born Virginians. They always stopped short of open confrontations with the governors but hindered them whenever doing so posed no threat to their places. Actually, the younger ones regarded making Virginia law more like English law a good thing, and they actively participated in the efforts at law reform throughout the 1690s.[8]

None in the latter blocs ever constituted a "king's party" primarily because none of Berkeley's successors enjoyed much luck in creating one in the House of Burgesses. Truth be known they did not try because they had few tools to engineer one. They might hold the House of Burgesses through prorogations or they might dissolve a stubborn one but those tactics were blunt instruments of little effect.

In the view of King Charles and his advisers Sir William Berkeley's way of governing had substantially weakened the governor's office and by extension the royal prerogative. Bolstering the post was a top priority, and to that end policymakers in London looked to recruiting a different sort of governor. Apart from Francis Howard, 5th baron Howard of Effingham, Berkeley's successors—Colonel Herbert Jeffreys; Thomas Culpeper, 2d baron Culpeper of Thoresway; Francis Nicholson; Sir Edmund Andros; and Major Edward Nott—were tested army officers. Time spent in command of garrison towns instructed them in ways to manage oft-times unruly and hostile civilians. All six shared an imperial outlook. Dependent upon their royal masters for preferment, their loyalty to the Crown was beyond question although their successes in reforming Virginia law precisely to the Londoner's wishes came up short.[9]

Jeffreys (d. 1678) entered military service in 1642 when King Charles I gave him a lieutenancy in a regiment of foot. A taste for combat and a talent for command led to his promotion to a regimental captain but fighting for a losing cause blighted his chances for higher rank. He went into exile and attached himself to the staff of James Stuart, duke of York, whose devoted servant he remained until his death. After the Restoration he was posted to Dunkirk, Portsmouth, York, and France before the duke chose him to lead the redcoats sent over to smash Bacon's rebels and to replace Berkeley temporarily. He showed no regard for the General Assembly or for Virginia politicians, whom he regarded as so much rabble. The Virginians matched contempt for contempt and insult with insult but trod carefully lest Jeffreys set loose his troops and impose martial law upon them. They harassed him as much as they dared and made his eighteen-month tenure as lieutenant governor so miserable that they literally hounded him to death. He ordered Robert Beverley to prepare an abstract of all the acts the Assembly passed between December 1662 and February 1676/77, which he sent to Secretary of State Henry Coventry just before he died.[10]

Culpeper (1635–1689) lived his early years at the family seat in Hollingbourne, Kent. In his teens he joined his father and other indigent expatriates who were King Charles II's court-in-exile, and in his twenties, he married a Dutch heiress whose wealthy family gifted him with a handsome dowry. After the Restoration, he returned to England shortly before his father died and bequeathed him an insolvent barony of Thoresway, an interest in the Northern Neck proprietary land grant, and King Charles's undying gratefulness to the Culpepers. Endowed with such assets, the personable young nobleman set about enriching himself. Charles II graced him with several clerical places in the rolls' office, each of which was worth some £1,500 annually, and gave him charge of the Isle of Wight and Carisbrook Castle. The latter posting greatly enriched Culpeper, though it did nothing to sweeten his tastes for governance or any inclination to sugarcoat them. The king's favor did not flag. He was given a commission as a high-ranking infantry officer and a seat on the Council for Foreign Plantations. Then he secured a reversion to the Virginia governorship on the death of Sir William Berkeley.[11]

Contemporaries judged Governor Culpeper "one of the most cunning and covetous Men in *England*."[12] Nothing about his tenure disproved their verdict. He cared little for governing Virginia. What captivated him about the place was the possibility of profiting from his claim to the Northern Neck proprietary. The prospects seemed unusually promising because the other proprietors were dead or had bargained away their rights, leaving him and Henry Bennett, 1st earl of Arlington, the sole claimants to a huge tract of Virginia real estate. Governor Berkeley initiated a series of complicated court actions and a round of enormously expensive, lengthy negotiations to rid the colony of the proprietary. Dickering turned knottier in 1673, after King Charles assigned all unpatented land in the colony and all Virginia quitrents to Arlington and Culpeper for a period of thirty-one years. Berkeley raised more taxes to fend them off, which contributed to Bacon's Rebellion and stopped further dealings for some time. Lord Arlington sold out to Culpeper, who appointed land agents who issued patents in his name and collected rents for him.[13]

Culpeper was sworn governor just weeks after Berkeley's burial at Twickenham in July 1677, but he dawdled in London for almost two years before Charles II finally sent him packing. He took up residence at Green Spring House with his cousin Dame Frances Berkeley. Their dalliance turned her later husband, Philip Ludwell, into an ever more stubborn foe of royal governors. As instructed Culpeper summoned the General Assembly of June 1680. He cajoled it into granting the Crown a permanent revenue and forced it "to observe in the passing of Laws That the stile of Enacting the same [be] By the Governor, Council And Assembly bee henceforth used & none other."[14] Then he blithely adjourned the Assembly and sailed to England without giving fair warning of his intentions or asking anyone's leave to abandon his post.[15]

While Culpeper enjoyed the delights of London the colonists rioted in a desperate attempt to drive up the price of tobacco. Order was restored well before his lordship returned to Green Spring House in December 1682 and conducted his own investigation into the riots. The episode was fraught with implications that corroborated his failures as governor. Worse was to come. He stole some £9,500 out of the provincial treasury, a theft Councillor Bacon exposed when, unbidden, Culpeper returned to England. An exasperated king summarily dismissed him and replaced him in August 1683 with Effingham.

Effingham (1643–1695), the eldest son of Sir Charles Howard of Great Bookham, Surrey, had a thoroughly conventional gentry childhood before he was packed off to Oxford. Not having a penchant for learning he came down without a degree though he formed connections that worked to his advantage in later life. He married Philadelphia Pelham (1654–1685) who belonged to a prominent Sussex family and the couple had eight children, only three of whom survived. At the death of his father in 1673 he became a deputy lord lieutenant and a justice of the peace for Surrey. He might have lived in obscurity for all his days but for the death in 1681 of his cousin Charles Howard, 3d earl of Nottingham and 4th baron Howard of Effingham, leaving him heir to the barony. Little income or estates attached to the barony, though the title raised the visibility of the new Baron Effingham at court. Two of his kinsmen, Henry Howard, 6th duke of Norfolk, and Henry Mordaunt, earl of Peterborough, introduced him to the duke of York and William Blathwayt, and by their contrivance King Charles II chose him to supplant Culpeper.

The appointment thrilled Effingham who saw in it the opportunity of a lifetime. He not only got to serve his king, but he was entitled to a salary of £2,000 and other monetary perquisites. Those financial emoluments were especially appealing because he needed money to support appearances and a large household. He, one young daughter, and an aunt embarked for Jamestown late in November 1683; the rest of his family stayed behind until Lady Philadelphia recovered from having birthed her eighth child. His ship dropped anchor in the York River in February 1684, and he was greeted warmly by the Council of State and other bigwigs who hoped their new governor was not another Culpeper or Jeffreys. Effingham was neither a Jeffreys nor a Culpeper, but nor was he willing to deviate in the slightest from his determination to carry out the king's wishes to the letter. Determination was the mark of his administration. Nothing—not his fights with Philip Ludwell and Robert Beverley, not his tussles with the General Assembly, not his own sickly constitution, not even the tragic death of Lady Philadelphia, whom he deeply loved—deterred him.

Like Culpeper he was under direct orders to revise the statutes. Despite four attempts he was no more successful than Culpeper.[16] He avoided any mention of the king's command in his inaugural address at the General Assembly of April 1684. Apparently, though, there were informal discussions about the possibility of reforming the laws because the burgesses pressed him to appoint a committee of their members to draft a revisal, which was the Virginia custom. He bluntly spurned them, invoking King Charles who he said was pleased "to Command me with the assistance of your Councell to take care that all the Lawes now in force be revised." Point made, he promised to present a draft to the next General Assembly for its "Consideration & Approbation." His promise came to nothing because it got lost in quarrels with the House over his refusal to countenance appeals to the Assembly. It was buried again in the disastrous first meeting of the General Assembly of 1685–86 when a town bill provoked a monumental row over its agreed text. The meeting came to dead stop, and a furious Effingham lost his temper. To punish the burgesses, he withheld his signature from all pending bills and prorogued them to October 1686, which nullified the legislation.[17]

During the second session, the burgesses lobbied him again. Now Effingham informed them that "sometime since I appointed a select number of worthy & discreet Gentlemen of his Majesties Councell" as a revisal committee who were at work "and a fair progress therein made." Philip Ludwell, John Page, and Secretary Spencer were the committee. Their selection was sound because all of them were experienced lawmakers, and Spencer's staff of clerks could provide logistical support. Naming Ludwell was an attempt to win him, but the overture failed, and the doughty Ludwell lost his place in February 1687.[18]

Ludwell, Page, and Spencer confronted a task of considerable magnitude. Before they could even begin to prepare a working draft, they needed to determine what constituted a reliable body of the existing acts, which was a formidable chore. Copies of Moryson's *Lawes of Virginia* were scarce and long out of print. Another printed version, John Purvis's *A Complete Collection of all the Lawes of Virginia* (London, 1684), was untrustworthy due to an abundance of errors that infected it; moreover, the General Assembly had suppressed it. Acts in manuscript passed after 1662 were scattered and often incompletely recorded. Ludwell's dismissal entailed an even greater burden on Page and Spencer but they soldiered on. By fall 1687 their report was ready for the Council's consideration. Gout got the better of both of them. Indisposed, they were unable to present their proposed bills when the Council met that October, and further action was delayed until their health improved.[19]

The postponement extended into May 1688 when a sickly Effingham laid the Council's draft before yet another querulous House of Burgesses. He urged its acceptance, but the burgesses stubbornly refused to cooperate. Their obstinacy was among the reasons a frustrated Effingham huffily dissolved them on 12 May. He never recalled them. The following February he returned to England seeking a cure for his deteriorating health as well as answering complaints against his government and persuading King William and Queen Mary to retain him. Just before he sailed off, the Council pleaded with him to take a copy of their revisal to London for royal sanction.[20]

The fate of that document is uncertain. Effingham may have lost it somewhere between Jamestown and Whitehall. It may never have existed. It is not in the governor's papers or the Council's archives, nor is a copy among the colonial papers housed in the British National Archives, the British Library, or any other repository that keeps seventeenth-century Virginia records. None of the letters Effingham wrote to William Blathwayt and the earl of Sunderland in May and June 1688 say anything about the revisal or his failure to get the burgesses to embrace it. No one knew of his leave-taking until the day he announced it at the Council, which would account for why the councillors asked him to bring a copy with him. If he was in a hurry to be gone as the Council minute unequivocally indicates, then he was quite unwilling to be delayed while copies were made.[21]

Arriving in London Effingham already knew that King James was deposed and that the House of Burgesses through its agent Philip Ludwell was lobbying for his dismissal, so one of his first concerns was keeping his place. He fended off the burgesses' attempt at dislodging him and was overjoyed with the Privy Council for upholding him and confounding Ludwell. King William and Queen Mary recommissioned him governor in February 1690. However much these happy turns buoyed him, it was quite evident that he was physically unfit for sea travel and the rigors of governing Virginia. Reluctantly, he agreed to the appointment of a lieutenant, Francis Nicholson, who stayed until he resigned in 1692. Three years later he died in obscurity.[22]

Francis Nicholson (1655–1728) was an army officer who over a lifetime filled assorted administrative slots across the empire. Most recently he had served as lieutenant governor under Sir Edmund Andros in the Dominion of New England, but that posting was no impediment to the Virginia assignment given that William and Mary favored James II's colonial policies and looked to the same officers to enforce them. So, his patrons had little difficulty inserting him as Effingham's second. Happy to have Effingham gone from their midst, the councillors and burgesses enthusiastically greeted Lieutenant Governor Nicholson, and an aura of calm pervaded the Council of State and the House of Burgesses as it had not since Berkeley's best days. Nicholson contributed to the mood by choosing not to challenge the General Assembly with objectionable legislative proposals. He knew that his was a precarious position. No redcoats were around to back him up as they had Jeffreys. He could not depend on the Crown in quite the same way as had Effingham, plus Effingham might choose to return, which would displace him. Astute army officer that he was, he weighed the risks and ignored the potentially troublesome portions of his instructions. He chose not to revisit law reform, and it never came up during either session of the General Assembly of 1691–92.[23]

Nicholson tried but failed to succeed Effingham. William Blathwayt, who had promoted Effingham, saw in Sir Edmund Andros (1637–1714) the preferred successor to Effingham, and he more than any other royal bureaucrat maneuvered Sir Edmund into place. Andros had the distinction of governing all of the royal colonies in North America. Native to the Isle of Guernsey, he answered his call to arms as a youth and passed up the ranks to become one of the Crown's ablest soldier-administrators. More particularly, he attached himself to the household of James, duke of York, whose faithful servant he forever was. James dispatched him to govern the ducal province of New York in 1674, and when he was king James sent him to rule the Dominion of New England. During the Glorious Revolution, the Massachusetts colonists deposed their hated governor general and clapped him in a dungeon on Castle Island in Boston Harbor. Nine months of incarceration slipped away before Bay Colony authorities shipped him off to stand trial in London on charges stemming from his execution of James II's orders. The prosecution failed for want of evidence and because Andros's judges were also his allies.[24]

Redeemed and reinstated, now as governor of Virginia, Andros reached Jamestown in the fall of 1692, but he let six months pass before calling the General Assembly of March 1692/93 partly to give himself time to recover from the voyage and partly to familiarize himself with his government. Within days of convening, the burgesses urged Andros and the Council to join with them so that the "whole body of the lawes of this Colony may be revised & methodically digested." Andros responded saying that "It is mine and the Councill Unanimous opinion that so good a work . . . should as soon as conveniently, be effected." He suggested a conference between four councillors and "such of your members as you shall appoint" to work out the details. Speaker Thomas Milner named nine burgesses including Samuel Swann, who spoke for them. The conference went nowhere. Swann and his colleagues argued for a joint committee that would meet after the session and prepare a draft for consideration at the next General Assembly. According to Swann, the councillors rejected that suggestion out of hand. They countered by insisting that the House should proceed on its own. Later conferences failed too, and revising the statutes was put off for another day.[25]

That day arose during the General Assembly of October 1693. In his opening address Andros expressed the hope "that I need not remind you of what import & how necessary the Revisall of our lawes is to all concerned in this Colony & hope you are now Satisfied it is not a worke of Such difficulty or labour as not to be effected even during an ordinary Session." Charging the House to create a revisal along with other legislation posed a nearly impossible task to the burgesses. Without a preliminary draft to work from someone had to draw up individual bills for every revised act before adding them to the stack of other bills that awaited House action and Council concurrence. That meant sifting through each of the existing statutes to determine which ones should stay, which ones should go, and which ones required amendment or consolidation. Speaker Milner assigned the onerous chore to the standing Committee on Propositions and Grievances.[26] Milner's choice was an obvious one, given that the committee normally vetted all nonmoney bills before it recommended the ones that should proceed to the floor for debate. Committee chairman William Fitzhugh (1651–1701) was a long-time advocate of law reform. Son of a Bedford woolen draper, Fitzhugh gained a considerable measure of formal legal education before he left England and settled down in Stafford County about the year 1670. His marriage to Sarah Tucker tied him to a kinship network that linked him to important families who seated along the upper Potomac River watershed. Those connections prospered him as a planter and an attorney. First elected to the House of Burgesses in 1677, he was in a crop of post-1677 members who had no prior political experience as justices of the peace. An unsuccessful run at Speaker in 1684 and support for Governor Effingham cost his election to the General Assembly of 1685–86. Effingham named him to a seat on the Stafford bench, though he did not seek reelection to the House until the fall of 1693.[27]

As a sitting justice and a busy trial advocate, Fitzhugh routinely confronted the confused condition of the colony's *corpus juris,* which caused delays and frustrations that annoyed magistrates and litigants alike. Exasperation made him a determined law reformer who appears to have devised a scheme for a revisal, which he carried with him to Jamestown and then laid before the General Assembly. That would account for the rapidity with which the committee produced draft bills for the House's consideration. The supposition is borne out by this bit of evidence. The day after becoming chairman of the Committee on Propositions and Grievances "Mr *ffitz-hugh*" brought a batch of 17 reform bills to the floor, and within a two-week span he moved an additional 116 in several batches. As the bills in each batch were introduced, they were read three times, engrossed, and sent to the Council—but the councillors were slow to take them up. Their sloth impeded the House's dispatch of other business, including legislation to establish the College of William & Mary. Seeking to break the impasse, Speaker Milner sent Andros a message reminding him that the House started the revisal at his command. The burgesses, continued Milner, undertook "the Revisall of the Lawes & have acordingly gon thorough with the Revisall & methodicall digestion of the whole body thereof & laid the same before the honorable Councill Some time since for their concurrence." Therefore, the expectation was "the Same can be finished by them." Andros answered in reply "That we had offered something in or among those bylls which had caused the Councill to be at some stop, that he knew not, when it might be done, & how it might be rec^d in *England* when it was done." Frustrated by his response, the burgesses saw the latest try at law reform vanish when the governor dissolved the Assembly and sent them home.[28]

Fitzhugh never returned to the House. That did not mean he abandoned his hope of seeing some sort of reform come to pass. He changed his approach. As he explained to Nicholas Haywood, his agent in London, he had crafted "a summary discourse of Virginia, & a full & methodical digest of our Laws" that he would forward as soon as he located "a convenient passport to get them to your hand, without the great charge of Postage."[29] After these papers came to hand, Haywood was supposed to engage a printer to print 1,000 copies, which Fitzhugh would have licensed for sale in Virginia and Maryland. Several years passed before Haywood found a willing printer. By then Fitzhugh was in declining health, and the digest was never printed.[30]

What became of the "summary discourse of Virginia" is unknown because no copy has ever come to light although two copies of the digest exist. One was prepared for Governor Andros and the other was for Philip Ludwell. Both are in scribal hands and were executed in summer of 1694. That timing is consistent with Fitzhugh's letter to Nicholas Haywood about his intent to secure a royal license to print the digest, and they satisfied that purpose.[31]

A digest, or an "abridgement," as Fitzhugh actually called his, was a common species of seventeenth-century legal literature. Widely used on both sides of the Atlantic in Fitzhugh's day, some abstracted the English statutes at large; others arrayed statutes alphabetically by topic rather than chronologically. Fitzhugh chose the latter variety and called it "An Alphabeticall Abridgment of the Laws of Virginia." It abstracted all the acts of Assembly adopted between 1662 and 1693 that Fitzhugh arranged under some five dozen subject headings that ran from "accounts" to "wolves." Each abstract summarized the name of the act, the year of its adoption, who was governor, who was on the throne, and how many acts were passed at each meeting of the General Assembly. If more than one statute related to a topic then they were filed in the order of passage. The abstracts also indicated a location for the full texts. Moryson's *Lawes of Virginia*, which Fitzhugh referred to as "the printed laws," was his source for the acts as they existed in 1662; everything else was in manuscript and identified by the General Assembly that produced it. He incorporated addenda that he meant to be reference guides. Quite possibly the most useful of these was his list of all the repealed, expired, or "disused" statutes. Abstracts of private acts, a table "Shewing the yeare of the King 1661 to Anno. 1694," one that showed who was governor from Berkeley to Andros, and another that itemized the meetings of the General Assembly between 1661 and 1693 completed the supplements. Had Fitzhugh succeeded in publishing the "Abridgment" it likely would have been widely popular, given its potential usefulness as an accurate, comprehensive guide to the statutes in force. Even though Fitzhugh failed, the "Abridgment" left a mark. Ludwell's copy was one of many documents that contributed to the Revisal of 1705.[32]

Andros did not summon another General Assembly until April 1695. The burgesses came to town keen on taking up law reform again. Andros was not. England was in the middle of King William's War, and his main concerns were protecting the colony and securing an appropriation to help the New York government fend off the Canadian French and their Indian allies. The burgesses balked at aiding the distant New Yorkers before they eventually allocated £500 sterling from a liquor tax for the war effort. When the Assembly reconvened in 1696 a smallpox epidemic effectively forced Andros to dissolve it before it legislated much of substance. The inaction caught the eye of the newly constituted Board of Trade. Created by the Navigation Act of 1696, the board, among its other responsibilities, reviewed all colonial legislation and recommended to the King-in-Council which acts of the General Assembly should be disallowed as contrary to the royal prerogative or the trade laws.[33] Consequently, it had an interest in law reform in the colony. The board rebuked Andros and the Council of State for their slow pace with a revisal and ordered them to send a copy of the existing statutes to London post haste.

The governor blamed the General Assembly for the lack of progress but in March 1698 he designated Councillors Ralph Wormeley, William Byrd,

Edward Hill, and Edmund Jenings a committee who were "to proceed on the Reviseall of the Laws as soon as possibly may be & to call Mr Attorney Generall [William Randolph] to their Assistance." Within a month the committee claimed their task was of such "great Moment" that they needed more time, which caused the Council to put off further consideration to a later date. Andros forwarded a clear text of the existing statutes to the Board of Trade. Andros received yet another letter from the board demanding to see the "Laws Now in force." It was read in council, and notice was given to the committee to make its report to the next meeting, which Andros mailed to London in July.[34]

Andros was on his way out. He had never adjusted to the Virginia climate, which aggravated his sickly constitution. Recurring illnesses reduced his effectiveness especially after his widening rifts with the Reverend James Blair. At first the two got along until Blair concluded that Andros was insufficiently attentive to the needs of the College of William & Mary and the colony's clergy, and he used his considerable clout in London to lobby for Francis Nicholson as Andros's replacement.[35]

Nicholson returned and took over in December 1698. Four months later he met the General Assembly. In his opening address to the House he informed the burgesses that the Board of Trade commanded that they and the councillors "take Care that all Lawes now in force be revised and considered . . . to the End his Majesties Approbation or Disallowance may be signified thereupon," and they should proceed. (Actually, Nicholson fibbed because the board had expressly ordered that he and the Council draft the revision without regard to the House.) It was agreed that the preliminary work should be assigned to a committee of burgesses and councillors but as before everyone was soon at odds over the composition of that committee, when it should meet, where it should meet, and for how long. Negotiations deadlocked until Nicholson and House leaders bargained their way through the logjam, finally agreeing on "An act appointing a committee for the revisall of the whole body of the laws of this his majesties colony and dominion of Virginia."

The act itemized in exquisite detail the who, the what, and the how of the revisal should go forward. Its preamble recognized that no revisal could be "conveniently effected dureing the session of an assembly," which was a concession to the burgesses. A clause created an independent commission that would continue even if the Assembly dissolved.

The nine commissioners were identified by name. Three came from the Council—Edward Hill (1637–1700), Matthew Page (1659–1703), and Benjamin Harrison (1645–1712)—six were burgesses—Miles Cary (d. 1709), John Taylor (d. 1707), Robert Beverley (ca. 1673–1722), Anthony Armistead (d. 1705?), Henry Duke (d. 1713), and William Buckner (d. 1716). Peter Beverley would perform clerical duties, and Benjamin Harrison (1673–1710) and Bartholomew Fowler (d. 1703) were designated committee assistants. The nine were invested with "full power and authority to revise, alter, add to, diminish, repeal, amend or revive all or any . . . Laws" and to report back to the next General Assembly "from time to time till all the said laws be fully and absolutely revised." They were authorized to call for any records that could be located, which was probably a work-around to the archives that had burned or been scattered in the statehouse fire of 1698. Other clauses set forth the work schedule and other procedural matters. Lastly, there was a provision to retain the existing laws in force until the completion of the entire revisal, or such of it as won the Assembly's approval.[36]

Why these men? The commissioners and their staff mingled interest and experience, and having been at the forefront of the negotiations for the act, all of these men were logical appointees to be active in preparing a draft revisal. Councillor Harrison had risen to prominence in Charles City County before he joined the Council in 1698. He was an original trustee of the College of William & Mary and the Reverend Mr. Blair's father-in-law. Hill, the eldest of the councillors, retained a wealth of institutional memory and legislative savvy, having been Speaker of the House before he gained his place at the Council in 1691. Matthew Page, newly appointed a councillor, was of a conciliar family connected to Gloucester and York Counties. He sat on the Board of Visitors of the college and was nominally allied to Blair. Cary followed his father and grandfather as a burgess for Warwick County, starting with the General Assembly of 1684. Armistead came from another robust family of Warwick politicians, and Beverley was a son of Effingham's old archenemy. Peter Beverley, Robert's older brother, was clerk of the House of Burgesses. A relative newcomer to Virginia, Duke was a James City County burgess ever since 1691, as was Buckner who had just begun his second term as a member for York County. Taylor, who represented Charles City and first went to the House in 1696, was a county militia officer and clerk of court.[37] Fowler had been a deputy council clerk before his recent appointment as attorney general, and the younger Harrison was the current clerk of council.

Blair influenced some of the choices too. His concern was for supporting the college and steering oversight of the church away from the laity to the bishop of London Henry Compton's commissary, that is, himself. Something else figured into the calculus. Everyone on the committee and staff lived in counties that lay within easy reach of Jamestown and the soon-to-be capital Williamsburg. Being close to their meeting places lessened the likelihood of low attendance because of inclement weather or difficult travel overland or across Chesapeake Bay. Proximity was important for another reason. A clause in the enabling legislation authorized the commission to oversee raising a new capitol building at Williamsburg.[38]

Convening for the first time in July 1699, the committee spent several days organizing for work. Peter Beverley was sworn in as their clerk, after which he prepared the members' request to Nicholson for the same "liberty and freedome of Speech and debate as is accustomed to be allowed the Members of the General Assembly in their proceedings." They perused "Certain Instructions of the Lords Justices of *England*" before telling Nicholson that they would take them into account as they went about their business and considered "Matters of the like Nature."[39] The previous October fire in the statehouse had consumed writing supplies and burned an unknown quantity of law books in the General Court library. At his colleagues' behest, Councillor Harrison undertook to offset those losses. To replenish the burnt writing supplies, he ordered "Two gallons of best Recording Ink, Two Thousand of best dutch Quills, A pound of pounce,"[40] and ten reams of fine writing paper, all of which he probably bought from a London dealer who routinely furnished such items to the secretary's office. Then he arranged to buy copies of law books that contained statutory models and compilations of writs and other documents that moved suits through the royal common law courts at Westminster. That purchase suggests an intent to fashion the revised statutes in a form and fashion similar to those in England, which could have been prompted by the "Lords Justices of England."[41]

The committee devoted much of a day to discussing its role in building the Capitol before it adjourned for three weeks. Reassembling in August, they started on the revisal. Their point of departure was listening to a reading of the existing statutes, which took more than a week to finish. Afterward they decided to arrange the laws by numbered titles under thirty-nine separate headings that were divided into three equal groups. Each group was assigned to an assistant and a clerk who were charged to summarize the acts in their group and to write their abridgments down on paper leaving ample space for annotations. Benjamin Harrison Jr. was tasked to abridge one group; Bartholomew Fowler and Peter Beverley would condense the other two. Their digests became the basis for discussion and decision making.[42] When the commission rose on 10 August it instructed Harrison, Fowler, and Beverley to report at its next meeting "and so from tyme to tyme as they proceed therein."

At the next meeting in October, Fowler told of his progress in abridging the church statutes. That prompted an invitation to the Reverend Commissary Mr. Blair for his comments on ecclesiastical affairs. He grabbed the chance to advance his agenda for recasting church government. Given who he was, his remarks were not to be discounted but deliberations were unexpectedly interrupted when Councillor Harrison and John Taylor abruptly left to tamp down Indian troubles along the Charles City County frontier. Back at work in November, the commission finished with Blair's comments and moved ahead with the other sections of Fowler's abridgment and several of those done by Harrison Jr. and Peter Beverley. They rose in mid-month, adjourning to April 1700, but not before ordering the assistants to draw up bills about the church, marriages, courts, officers, and money for the eventual presentation to the General Assembly.[43]

The committee had gotten off to a good start. It had designed a workable scheme for moving the revisal along, and it had made an appreciable dent in preparing the bills. As 1699 gave way to the new year Nicholson and the members held high expectations of greater headway in 1700. The work went steadily according to plan until it stopped during the summer, and from then on it slowed, stopped, started, and slowed again.[44] Each in its own way—a new monarch, war with France, changes in committee membership, building Williamsburg, inertia in the House, and fracases with Nicholson contributed to the lack of progress. The death of King William III and the accession of Queen Anne were responsible for three short sessions of the General Assembly, none of which considered the revisal. Queen Anne's War pushed concerns for defense to the fore. Hill, Page, and Armistead were dead by 1704. Although Nicholson passed a law that eased requirements for a committee quorum, absenteeism remained an impediment.

Duke went to the Council. Peter Beverley quit and became Speaker of the House. Robert Beverley sailed away to London to lobby against Nicholson whom he had come utterly to loathe. Overseeing the construction of the Capitol in Williamsburg was a time-consuming interference. Nicholson's spats with Blair and squabbles with other councillors so distracted him that he lost his place.[45]

So it was that the General Assembly received no report until 1703. When it finally came the report proposed the adoption of 39 bills as replacements for around 500 acts that were either set aside on the Crown's order, no longer used, or still in force. The burgesses debated three of those bills but none came to a vote before Nicholson prorogued the Assembly. Their texts were in the House journal that he subsequently forwarded to the Board of Trade together with a copy of the entire report. Afterward Nicholson reconvened the Assembly three times but in spite of his prodding the burgesses declined to take up the revisal because they no longer trusted him and wanted him gone. Frustrated, he adjourned them again around the same time that Queen Anne's notice of his dismissal crossed the Atlantic.[46]

His replacement, Major Edward Nott (1657–1706), is an elusive figure because of scanty details about his background. Apparently of Kentish stock, he began a military career in 1677 when he received an ensign's commission in the duke of York's regiment. Thereafter, he rose through the ranks to become a major and governor of Berwick-upon-Tweed. Duty took him to the West Indies where he participated in the Martinique expedition of 1693 before returning to England just ahead of his posting to Virginia. Endorsed by George Hamilton, 1st earl of Orkney, Nott was named governor by Queen Anne in April 1705.[47] Greeted warmly, Nott was a welcomed change from the tempestuous Nicholson, for he was kindly and easily liked. Even the ever-acerbic Commissary Blair commended his "very calm healing Temper," but that mildness did not impede toughness and adeptness, which were Nott's hole cards.[48]

Nott arrived in Williamsburg in August 1705 and formally took over from Nicholson. He immediately dissolved the General Assembly and issued writs for a new one to meet him in October. The composition of the new House differed from the last one. About half the seats went to burgesses who were new to the House or who replaced retirees and lately dead members. Miles Cary, the Beverley brothers, Nathaniel Harrison, William Randolph, and Benjamin Harrison returned and were chosen for key leadership positions. From the outset, this House begot a spirit of cooperation that the mild-tempered Nott quickly bent to his advantage.[49] In his opening speech Nott called upon the burgesses to enact "Those Suitable Laws which were Revised and Compiled by The Direction of the General Assembly." His reference was to the revisal commission report and to the amended version of it that the Board of Trade gave him when he left for America. Nicholson had sent that copy to the board. The board in turn took advice from Secretary of the Colony Edmund Jenings, a former reviser, who was in London seeking Nicholson's ouster. Jenings (1659–1727)[50] explained the design of the draft revisal and helped with several changes before the board entrusted it to the governor. Nott sent it to the House together with additional proposals the board wished the Assembly to consider.[51]

The day after Nott's address the House voted that it "do proceed upon The Revisall of the Laws This Session." All those bills received a customary vetting in both bodies. Two were defeated in the House, and Nott vetoed a third. Some were amended although most sailed through the two chambers unchanged almost as quickly as the Committee on Propositions and Grievances presented them. Then they were forwarded to Nott who signed them. As straightforward as this procedure is in the telling it was truly time-consuming in its execution. Every bill received its first reading and was referred to a committee of the whole. Depending upon the legislative calendar, days went by before the House resolved itself into that committee. Committee discussions might extend over several more days before its version of the bill went back to the floor. Sometimes the bill was now subjected to a long debate ahead of a second reading; at other times postponements delayed the third reading and adoption. After the Council got the engrossed bill it was treated in like fashion, and when disagreements cropped up conference committees took more time to reconcile differences. Then, too, because it had been years since the revisal committee submitted its report, House members brought forward additional bills for consideration, which were debated and disposed of in the same orderly manner. The work moved steadily along. Here and there disagreements sprang up. Nott calmly but firmly stifled them before any irreparable damage was done. Approaching winter brought with it a recess that stretched into the spring. At the beginning of April, the Assembly reconvened and worked through to the end of June 1706. Nott signed the acts, congratulated everyone, and they went home.[52]

And so, the revisal was done. Nott achieved what his predecessors could not.

The Revisal of 1705 invites comparisons with what it abolished.[53] In both the 1662 and 1705 revisals, the acts were arranged by the order of their introduction to the House; they were numbered accordingly; and their titles were indicative of their content.[54] The revisal from 1662 contained 142 acts whereas the new one had only 58. The latter were of greater length, and of them 36 came from the original revisal commission report.[55] In 1662, the General Assembly stuck to precedent and incorporated a general preamble that set forth the rationale for its revisal. In 1705, instead of a single, general preamble, each statute received its own preamble, enacting clause, and repealing clause that voided whatever it replaced. The language came nearer to contemporary British statutory prose than had that of Henry Randolph and Francis Moryson, which is a likely indication of the Board of Trade's influence.

Arguably the most eye-catching difference involved four significant bills that miscarried. Three were proposals from the revisal commission and the fourth came from the Committee on Propositions and Grievances. One of the three related to ecclesiastical governance. It fit within the scheme for diminishing the laity's authority in church matters that Commissary Blair laid out for the revisal commission in 1699, and it drew his vigorous backing. His embrace attracted inflexible opposition from his foes in the House and Council who disliked him intensely, and that put the bill in trouble even before its first reading to the House. Anti-Blair burgesses favored abolishing the existing self-perpetuating vestries, which they suggested were too susceptible to undue clerical influence, and they argued that electing new ones to fixed six-year terms would reduce the parsons' sway. Blairite councillors killed that amendment, claiming that it was too radical and disruptive. The Council tried to fix clergy stipends at 16,000 pounds of tobacco, plus emoluments for tobacco casks and maintenance, on the grounds that higher salaries would attract a better class of priests. House members rejected the inclusion of any fringe benefits, saying that 16,000 pounds of tobacco was more than adequate to support any clergyman's annual needs. Both bodies disagreed over the governor's powers to induct priests into parishes where vestries neglected to fill vacancies within a two-year period. The burgesses rejected the creation of a church court, to be staffed by Blair, three councillors, and three burgesses, who would prosecute clergy offenses. Contentious, unfruitful hearings in a committee of the whole led to shrill debates. Votes were postponed while the burgesses, councillors, and Nott struggled for a compromise. None was possible. The bill died. Its failure rested in Blair's hand who prodded too hard, and its death accounts for the absence of a revised statute in place of the 1662 church laws. Consequently, those statutes were not repealed, and they continued to be good law until the postrevolutionary disestablishment.[56]

Members of the revisal commission had advocated appropriating the English Habeas Corpus Act of 1679 to safeguard the liberties of Virginians. Their "bill for the better securing the liberty of the Subject" sped through the House only to hit a snag in the Council. Without any debate the councillors urged Nott to veto it even though they did not question that they and "every man who has settled himself in this Colony would be very desirous to Secure to themselves, and their posterity such considerable priviledges and libertys as this bill enacts." They objected owing to the directions of the Board of Trade "being so plain against the passing it," and the bill was lost.[57]

The third defeat was the revisal committee's bill for "establishing the County Courts & for regulating & Settling the proceedings therein, and directing the manner of granting probates of Wills and administrations upon Intestates Estates," which repealed the existing statutes. Introduced in November, it lay dormant until the House forwarded it to a committee of the whole in May. Repeatedly amended there and by the Council it finally landed on Nott's desk. Nott refused his endorsement, saying that he could not pass "that Bill without further advice." The sticking point for him was a clause empowering five councillors to advise and consent to the governor's nominees for justices of the peace, which appeared to go against his instructions. His refusal provoked no push-back from the councillors or the burgesses. They believed there would be just a temporary delay because he promised "to obtain her Majesties Leave for passing [it] at another Session if it be thought convenient."[58] Nott never got the chance. He died quite suddenly in August from a fever. The General Assembly of 1705–06 died with him, and the lower tier of the court structure was constitutionally nonexistent until Lieutenant Governor Alexander Spotswood passed a county court bill without the questionable clause in 1710. Probates were in limbo too.[59]

Near the end of the session, Speaker Benjamin Harrison instructed the Committee on Propositions and Grievances to bring in the fourth bill. It prescribed the appointment of county clerks and established the fees they received as well as dues for sheriffs, constables, and the secretary of the colony. Threatened by a loss of some fees, Secretary Jenings and others on the Council came out in opposition. Their intransigence led to conferences upon conferences that lasted almost to the end of the session before the bill was quietly scrapped. If the bill had succeeded it would have made the clerkship a statutory office for the first time in its history. The failure of the proviso for a renovated, equitable fee schedule meant the continuation of a long-time source of planter griping that escaped any remedy for years into the future.[60]

Nonetheless, there were enhancements that updated the written law. Such an act disposed of a question always triggered by "the great distance of this colony and dominion of Virginia from our mother kingdom of England," which was this: Whenever a monarch died, what became of General Assemblies and executive or judicial decisions from the Council of State? The act allowed for the continuance of General Assemblies and the validation of conciliar actions before such time as a new sovereign was proclaimed in the colony.[61]

A different statute redefined the Council as General Court. A novel provision in one of its clauses expressly mandated "That at some one certain place . . . there shall be held one principal court of judicature . . . by the name of the general court of Virginia." The governor and councillors, any five of whom made a quorum, were designated "judges or justices" to hear "all suits and controversies which shall be depending in the said court." Besides the usual oaths they swore to the Crown, they were required to take a judicial vow that was written in the statute. Its wording appears to have been a modified version of a model drawn from Richard Garnett's *Book of Oaths* that Councillor Hill had ordered in 1699 for the revisal committee's use. Whenever they convened as judges in chancery they were to take a special oath that was also in the law. Its inclusion was a novel addition. The act went on to elaborate the court's appellate and original jurisdiction in civil and criminal causes. Well-established procedures were clarified in more detail. Some clarifications clearly codified practices long in use but never before spelled out in writing, and at greater length as well. Overall, the statute was cast in a direct, more comprehensible style and terminology than in the previous act. In toto, the judges, officers of the court, attorneys, suitors, and witnesses had a clearer appreciation of the workings of the court and where they fit into to the maintenance of an orderly society.[62]

A cluster of acts tightened up some rules of civil procedure. Complaints about the colonists' litigious propensities were addressed by one law that limited the number and types of actions that could be brought, and it also forbade certain actions from being filed at all. A statute of limitations determined how long judgments and instruments essential to commercial transactions remained in effect. Better protections for the estates of intestates, widows, and orphans were added in an act about the distribution of estates. Attorneys whose clients lived outside Virginia were required to post performance bonds to cover court costs and adverse judgments while those advocates who represented locals were not.[63]

The shrievalty underwent modifications. One change fixed the manner of appointment in such a way as to increase the governor's nominating power. Another dictated that only a justice of the peace could hold the place. A third limited the term of office to one year, which broke with a decades-old practice. The same act laid out a far-reaching elucidation of the sheriff's police powers and the consequence of malfeasances or misfeasance.[64]

For the first time, the composition of grand juries was particularized in "An act concerning Juries." Rounded up by the sheriff, county grand jurors would sit at all court days in May and November and hand up indictments or presentments as they determined them. At the General Court the James City County sheriff empaneled grand jurors from the bystanders who hung around on court days. The rules for picking petit jurors were reworked from earlier acts, although the Virginia variation on the use of the writ of *tales de circumstantibus* was more lengthily itemized than the original version from 1662.[65]

The old statutes that governed the burgesses changed somewhat. There were more exact steps that set forth everything from the issuance of election writs to the method of polling, certifying the results, and challenging an outcome. As in the past, voters in each county were charged to elect two burgesses, while voters in Jamestown and the College of William & Mary each got a burgess of their own. Again, in keeping with past legislation, voters were admonished to choose from the "most fit and able men" in their district. In order to qualify voters had to be white males, of age, and possessors of an undefined amount of real estate. They were also compelled to vouchsafe their qualifications by swearing an oath that was part of the act, although it said nothing about whether one was entitled to cast a ballot in every county where he satisfied the property qualification. Any planter who could but would not vote was answerable for a fine of 200 pounds of tobacco that went to the informer. In the section about the privileges of burgesses the act tweaked the venerable protections from arrests or legal actions during meetings by estopping litigation filed beforehand but allowed any such suits to proceed whenever an Assembly was prorogued for more than twenty days. The compensation burgesses received for their attendance and travel expenses had been a source of ratepayer complaints since before Bacon's Rebellion, and this act attempted to dampen them once again. It permitted a member a per diem of 130 pounds of tobacco, down from 150, and varied his travel allowances according to the distance between his home county and Williamsburg.[66]

"An act declaring who shall not bear office in this country" originated in the revisal committee. It applied to all civil, military, and ecclesiastical offices. Blasphemers, perjurers, forgers, or persons suspected of a crime punishable by death or maiming were excluded; Indians, free Africans, and mulattos were too, but pardoned convicts were not. Colonists who had not lived in Virginia for "the full term of three years" were also banned. Violators faced fines of £500 in current money and an extra £20 for every month they illegally held on to the position. Remarkably, the law came partially from clauses the committee found in the vacated acts of the General Assembly of June 1676. That they did is the lone glimpse into the depth of their research through the old legal records.[67]

Although the bill to regulate ecclesiastical governance failed, two other pieces of church-related legislation made it into the revisal. One aimed at controlling moral behavior; the other reformed marriage law. Both were drafted by the revisal committee. The force behind the morals act was Thomas Tenison, archbishop of Canterbury, who sought to outlaw atheism, drunkenness, swearing, adultery, fornication, and other immoral behavior not only in Virginia but also in the rest of the English colonies across North America and the West Indies. Nominally Virginia fell within the territorial jurisdiction of Bishop Compton, who delegated the task of securing the law to Commissary Blair. Besides contenting English church leaders, the new law fused Virginia acts of a similar nature. The reformed marriage law mainly updated and merged all former acts into a single statute. It is apparent that both were conceived as part of a group of church laws. They and the failed bill for church governance were introduced within days of one another early in the session but the tortured debate over the latter held their approval in abeyance until the final weeks of the session and after the governance bill had been defeated.[68]

The land act significantly altered the headright system and land policy more generally.[69] A device for distributing unclaimed land, the headright had come into being as a consequence of the Crown's indecision. King James I claimed Virginia as an adjunct of the royal manor of East Greenwich and all its landholders as his tenants. That declaration was repeated in the three charters of the Virginia Company of London but neither those charters nor any amplifying instructions set forth a coherent land policy.[70] To the contrary, the Company was authorized to distribute land. It devised the headright whereby every free immigrant got a fifty-acre bounty for herself/himself and another fifty acres for anyone imported at her/his expense who paid the Company an annual quitrent.[71] Lacking direction from the Privy Council after 1625, the royal governors and their councillors continued issuing headrights, and by default the system endured even though it was easily corrupted to the advantage of large landholders with close connections to the governor and Council who snapped up huge tracts.[72]

Officials in London took little notice until the 1680s. William Blathwayt, the surveyor and auditor general of revenues owed to the king from the royal colonies, investigated what the Virginians did with the quitrents, fines, forfeitures, licenses, prizes, and escheats that by right accrued to the king, and him only, but that investigation stalled. Then in 1697, Commissary Blair, Henry Hartwell, and Edward Chilton leveled a searching critique of the headright system that highlighted its corruption and the ways in which King William was being defrauded of his revenues. Their criticism caught the attention of the Board of Trade, which ordered Nicholson to induce the General Assembly to adopt a new system of land grants. Nicholson got the revisal committee to propose it, and a bill was duly drafted, but nothing happened to it until 1705. Introduced to the House in November, action was postponed until the spring of 1706 when it underwent considerable debate during which the Council amended it several times before it passed.[73]

The act confirmed all lands of their current holders, and in a major concession to the great planters it absolved them of the expense of refiling their titles. For the future it prescribed four types of land grants. There were the traditional fifty-acre headrights. In a break with the past, only immigrants could claim them. Established colonists were entitled to grants of fifty acres for every 50 shillings current money they paid to the receiver general.

Apparently, this type of grant was designed to content lesser planters and to address abuses that Hartwell, Blair, and Chilton had identified. The third provided for the acquisition of lapsed land, and the fourth was meant for use whenever someone sought to procure land that had escheated to Queen Anne.[74] Each deed form was written in the act together with rather precise steps to suing out a patent. No patentee was allowed to take up more than 500 hundred acres in any one tract. If he owned fifty servants or slaves, however, he could claim an additional 250 acres per head. No one could have more than 4,000 acres in any one grant although there was no prohibition against claiming more than one grant at a time. (These two provisions were sops to the great planters, who were avid land speculators.) All grants were to be surveyed; if they were not occupied within three years they forfeited to the Crown. Grantees owed an annual quitrent of 50 shillings current money for every fifty acres they possessed. They also had to register certified copies of a written description of the metes and bounds of the property and a scale drawing, or plat, in the secretary's office, which also doubled as the land office. A corollary act was added to curtail shoddy surveys, sloppy record keeping, and inconsistent costs.[75] These reforms would be amended many times over after 1705 but they became the basis of Virginia land law for generations to come.[76]

"An act concerning Servants and Slaves" originated in the revisal commission, and it merged old laws with new ones. Sections 1 through 22 covered indentured servants. That part codified unwritten customs and set down contractual relationships between master and servant with greater certainty than in the past. So did its specifications of the rights and responsibilities of the contracting individuals and the rules for attending to sickly or aging servants. It softened some of the harsher features of former acts as a way of making bond service more tempting to highly prized, skilled white European craftsmen who were much in demand and in short supply. Even so, the law was no less stringent in its restraints on those whom the revisers regarded as troublesome, and in particular it retained the severe punishments of maidservants caught fornicating or who carried on secret liaisons or bore bastard children.

Sections 23 through 50 were all about restraint of another group of workers the revisers looked upon as disruptive but increasingly vital to their economic interests and threatening to planter safety—slaves. (Section 51 was the repealing clause.) These sections were little more than a lengthy list of banned behaviors, how they were dealt with, and by whom. Henceforth, intermarriage was forbidden, and not only were offenders subject to punishment, but any minister who married them was liable to hefty fines. Children of illicit unions would "be bond or free," according to the condition of their mothers, and the particular directions of this section were drawn from earlier legislation.[77] Baptism or conversion to Christianity were no escapes from enslavement; that rule was first enacted in 1667.[78] Servant women who bore bastards fathered by enslaved men had an additional time tacked on to their indentures and their children were bound to the use of parish churches until their thirty-first birthdays. Slaves could not have firearms or anything that might function as a weapon.[79] They could not resist a free white person for any reason. If they did they got whipped. So did anyone who was caught stealing livestock or hunting deer out of season. A master who killed a slave while disciplining her or him was innocent of murder. Similarly, killings that happened in the course of the authorities tracking down roving bands of escaped slaves or other runaways were regarded as justifiable homicide. In those instances, the owners were entitled to compensation by the provincial government. So that no one could ever pretend ignorance, the act concluded with a warning. Every parish clerk was required to obtain a certified copy and publish it annually in church on the first Sunday of February and March, and the local sheriff was to keep a copy and read it at the first meeting of court every March.[80]

Other statutes buttressed the act. Non-Christians, meaning Africans, were deemed slaves, and neither baptism nor having been in England altered their status. Mixed-race children inherited their mother's condition; along with Africans, adult mulattoes were classified as taxable property. Slaves "in all courts of judicature, and other places, within this dominion, shall be held, taken, and adjudged, to be real estate (and not chattels;) and shall descend unto heirs and widows of persons departing this life, according to the manner and custom of land of inheritance, held in fee simple." Furthermore, slaves could be considered as capital in debt litigation. They did not escheat or satisfy the franchise requirement, nor could they be witnesses in either the General or the county courts.[81] A special court was borrowed from the 1690s to try slaves accused of felonies as being "absolutely necessary." Felony convicts were executed, and their masters were compensated out of public funds approved by the General Assembly.[82]

Seen at the time as solutions to problems of the moment, and no more, "An Act concerning Servants and Slaves" and the others were the revisal committee's response to profound changes taking place in the workforce. African slaves had been around since 1619, and they were regarded as just another commodity for sale in the colony. Before mid-century, their numbers were small because only a few planters who had the wherewithal chose to invest in them. Unless whites lived near a slaveholder plantation, they were unlikely to encounter slaves on anything like a daily basis. Social distance minimized English suspicions and fears of the others whose color and folkways differed from their own, and it was one of the reasons why slavery escaped much statutory notice for as long as it did. That gap narrowed after imports of enslaved Africans took off in the 1670s and was passing the intake of white servants as the 1600s yielded to the eighteenth century. Increased numbers not only brought blacks and whites closer, they also magnified their owners' troubles. More slaves meant more slaves who pilfered, broke tools, killed livestock, ran off, assaulted masters or rebelled; more slaves meant more Africans cohabiting with English servants. In contrast to their West Indian cousins, English Virginians were rather more squeamish about bastardy, interracial marriage, or casual sexual relationships between whites and blacks. And so, slaveholders turned to the General Assembly seeking to invoke the power of the state to enforce their property rights and to protect them from unruly slaves.[83]

Incorporating these slave laws into the Revisal signaled something else. They validated the ongoing conversion of Virginia from a society with slaves into a race-based slave society. They were the basis for later additions to an emerging distinctly defined law of slavery. They foreshadowed the not-too-distant day when racial slavery outnumbered every other type of labor in the colony and became the norm not the exception in the eyes of white Virginians. And they are the one detail from the snapshot of the Revisal of 1705 that always catches the eye of modern scholars.

In the moment other changes mattered more. The Revisal may not have been entirely to the Crown's liking but it was the best that could be had for the time being, and it was always susceptible to royal amendments. Among leading Virginians there was relief that the deed was finally done even if the Revisal was a result of the Crown's success in restriking the balance between colony and mother country in the king's favor. A diminished General Assembly was to be regretted but the members could still come up with ways to outmaneuver the governors and frustrate the Crown. The streamlined acts modernized the legal order and eased judicial confusion, which had been the Virginians' goal. Had he lived to see it enacted, the Revisal would probably have pleased William Fitzhugh, although he would likely have bemoaned its four substantial flaws. Flaws and all, it was the *corpus juris* until 1748 when Sir William Gooch encouraged the General Assembly to take on the final recodification of the colonial era.

❦ 7 ❧

Sir William Gooch's Gift

The Revisal of 1748

From the opening of his administration to its conclusion twenty-two years later, William Gooch (1681–1751) was an immensely popular governor, and a highly successful one at that. He was born into a respectable Yarmouth family of modest means only to be orphaned as a teenager. His beloved elder brother Thomas, an Anglican bishop, looked after him into adulthood. He spent time at Queen's College, Oxford, before joining the army and receiving an officer's commission. During the War of Spanish Succession, he fought with John Churchill, 1st duke of Marlborough, at the battle of Blenheim. He campaigned against the Old Stuart Pretender in the Jacobite Rising of 1715 and gained the rank of major. Afterward he discovered that peacetime promotions came slowly, or not at all, and having a family to maintain, he resigned from the army hoping to trade his commission for some sort of civilian place in the government. Fortune ignored him until he became a client of Thomas Pelham-Holles, 1st duke of Newcastle. The duke was secretary of state for the Southern Department, which vested him with the gift of political offices in the colonies. In January 1726/27 he slid Gooch into place as lieutenant to Virginia's governor general, George Hamilton, 1st earl of Orkney.[1]

Months passed before Gooch found passage on a Chesapeake-bound merchant ship. What he did during the interval is obscure, though some of it can be guessed. He and the earl of Orkney agreed on the portion of the governor's salary he would receive. As Virginia was strange to him, he would have tried to learn as much about the place as he could. Consulting with Newcastle and members of the Board of Trade would have fleshed out the nature of his assignment and their expectations of him. He probably read through the board's collection of Virginia papers and sought information from London's principal tobacco merchants and anyone else with firsthand knowledge of the Old Dominion, especially Virginians who were in the capital. By whatever means Gooch familiarized himself with his new assignment, the ease and skill with which he assumed his government testify to his having subdued any trepidations about a situation where he would be met with suspicion and palpable resentment.

Virginia's great men were more than a trifle skittish about their new lieutenant governor. Except for a tranquil respite during the late Hugh Drysdale's short administration, their relations with Gooch's predecessors had been anything but cordial.[2] So it might be again with this new man, about whom they knew little, but they put on their good faces and sought to take his measure as soon as Gooch arrived in Williamsburg. On 11 September 1727, he and the councillors stood on the courthouse steps while Council clerk William Robertson read out Gooch's commission and a proclamation announcing the accession of King George II. Then everyone walked the short distance to the Council chamber in the Capitol where Robertson administered the oaths of office to Gooch, who in turn swore in the councillors. Gooch's first official deed was "an Act of mercy" that spared a condemned pirate from the hangman.[3]

Councillor William Byrd was soon to observe that "By a great Accident we have a very Worthy Man to represent Lord Orkney. It is Major Gooch, brother of an eminent Clergyman of that Name. He seems ... to Maintain the Character of a very just Man, and has a remarkable share of good Sense, good Nature, and good Breeding. How long he may hold his integrity I cannot warrant because Power and Flattery corrupt many a Hopeful Ruler."[4] Byrd and the others discovered that neither power not flattery corrupted Gooch. Personally charming and unfailingly friendly, Gooch easily drew people to him, and he was quick to make common cause with the gentry. No stranger to statecraft, Gooch knew the worth of stagecraft, which he often used to good effect. He respected the rights of representative government and the worth of electoral politics. That is why he usually acceded to the burgesses and councillors as he strove to sort through the colony's predicaments and tried to address them in ways that comported with imperial designs for the Old Dominion. Gooch was also astute enough to appreciate the necessity of mollifying the Virginians without arousing the censure of the Board of Trade or the duke of Newcastle. So, he and his General Assemblies spent much of their time attending to war, internal expansion, an unpredictable tobacco economy, and legal change.[5]

Gooch arrived in Williamsburg at a pivotal time for the status of the colony's statute law and its legal culture. Virginians no longer spurned trained barristers as they had in the previous century. Now the colony was fertile ground for immigrant lawyers who flocked into Virginia and vied for clients with local lawyers.[6] Increasingly, elite planters looked upon lawyering as a fit profession for gentlemen. Some packed their sons off to London to study at the Inns of Court, which automatically qualified the successful ones to litigate in any Virginia court. Most elite sons read law with local practitioners or taught themselves. Less well-heeled sons turned to the law too.[7]

More lawyers and a more complex imperial legal structure raised the demand for more law books, which fed the growth of private and court law libraries. English legal publishers tapped a steady market for case reports; statutory compilations, parliamentary debates, practice manuals, formularies, dictionaries, encyclopedias, and guides to conveyancing; commentaries on ecclesiastical, maritime, criminal, and foreign law; and books about the nature of English law, the rights of the subject, and the very idea of law itself. Gooch was probably quite surprised to find a Council library that was well stocked and that was already among Virginia's largest law libraries. That library was "public" in the sense that it was tax supported, as were those at the county courthouses, and as such its volumes were readily accessible. He would also have learned that the planters were a litigious bunch who owned or borrowed practice manuals, dictionaries, and English treatises or case reports.[8]

He was just as surprised by the existence of a nascent organization of lawyers who practiced in and about Williamsburg. It drew councillors, burgesses, advocates in the General Court, and other prominent lawyers who often came together socially in the town's taverns whenever the high court or the General Assembly were in session. Fretting about the poor condition of lawyering over drink and food led to organized meetings where discussions turned on influencing the General Assembly to legislate improvements. With Gooch's support, the Assembly passed an act in 1732 for that purpose. The act continued current "practisers" as advocates in the General Court and it effectively established a two-tier system of lawyers: those permitted to practice in the county courts only and those who could appear there and before the General Court. No one received his license from the governor until he passed an examination by someone from the Williamsburg bar. At first, the statute seemed satisfactory, but it eventually failed "to answer the good design and intention thereof." It was repealed in 1742, although the licensing requirement continued, the two-tier distinction remained, and members of the Williamsburg bar still examined applicants.[9]

Two other consequential changes that bear signs of Gooch's influence were the arrival of the printing press and the Revisal of 1748. A prohibition from King Charles II kept printing presses out of Virginia until Gooch ignored it and allowed William Parks to set up a print shop cum bindery on Williamsburg's Duke of Gloucester Street a few doors west of the Capitol.[10] Gooch embraced the idea of a printed compilation of the laws in force because, with Parks in town, a timely, authoritative Virginia edition was within reach. A meeting of the General Assembly in February 1727/28 gave Parks the opportunity to pitch his statutes project to the governor, the Council, and the House. Accepting his proposal, they named a select committee of Speaker John Holloway, burgesses John Clayton and Archibald Blair, House clerk (Sir) John Randolph, and Council clerk William Robertson, "or any three of them, . . . to agree with the s'd *Wm. Parks* for the printing a Complete Body of the Laws of this Colony, and to take a certain number of Books to be distributed at public charge among the Governor, Council Burgesses & Several Justices of the Peace of this Colony." In short order the select committee and the printer reached an agreement.[11]

No copy of the actual contract and its terms exists so there is no way of ascertaining how long Parks assumed he needed to complete the job, how much it would cost to produce, how to fund it, or how much he expected to earn. Evidently, the committee allowed Parks some leeway to finish moving into the Williamsburg shop because he was slow to start the statutes project. He tarried in Annapolis and continued publishing Maryland items well into 1730, which presumably would have provided working capital for the Williamsburg business. In the 13–20 October 1730 issue of the *Maryland Gazette* he went so far as to advertise copies of acts from the May session of the Virginia Assembly. At a distance of nearly three centuries, the advertisement seems disingenuous because no copy of that item exists, so it may have been a ploy to buy time. His first imprint from the Williamsburg press was Gooch's *Charge to the Grand Jury. At a General Court, held in the Capitol City of Williamsburg, in Virginia, on Monday the 19th Day of October 1730.*

(It also happens to be the sole example of a Gooch jury charge, which, as presiding judge, he was bound to give at every sitting of the General Court or the Court of Oyer and Terminer.)[12] The statutes project dragged on until there came a point where either Parks realized that it was beyond him and he could not finish the job without editorial help, or the select committee forced a knowledgeable assistant on him. Whatever the reason, he took on a planter called George Webb in June 1732, and it was Webb who undertook the editorial work.[13]

George Webb (d. 1758) stands in a brigade of obscure colonials whose influence on Virginia's early legal culture was deeply significant but whose importance is all but forgotten. A son of a London merchant, he settled in New Kent County early in the 1700s and established himself as a successful merchant planter. He took up the study of law and amassed a substantial law library that supported his legal interests.[14] Such was his reputation for legal scholarship and clerical abilities that he emerged as the choice to help Parks. Webb efficiently put together an accurate handwritten rendering of the Revisal of 1705 as well as all of its amendments and additions. He also roughed out an index, or "table" as he called it, which he perfected in the final stages of production. Given the size of the manuscript, Parks was compelled to set it in sections. Each was proofread, printed, and the sheets laid by. Its type was distributed for use in the next section, and so it went until all were completed. Parks then bound the sections into books and presented them to the select committee. No record of the press run survives, although it might have been around a thousand copies. That number would have been enough to hand one to Gooch, the justices of the peace, burgesses, councillors, the subscribers, and still leave copies to give away or sell privately.[15]

Parks was not only paid, but also appointed the public printer. As for Webb, he petitioned the House for his compensation, reminding the burgesses that "he was emploied to prepare a complete Copy of the Laws of this Colony, for the press . . . ; that he hath finished the same with great Care and Exactness, and has been at very great Expense in that Business; that he hath likewise composed a very comprehensive Table." The House, the Council, and Gooch approved a payment of £200 for his "Trouble and pains."[16]

A Collection of all the Acts of Assembly Now in Force in the Colony of Virginia finally came out in 1733.[17] It is a sizeable folio volume whose text is 622 pages in length. A striking title page with its bold type and its fancy depiction of the Virginia coat of arms catch the eye. George Webb's name is nowhere to be seen. The title page is followed by "A List of Subscribers to the Laws of Virginia." Subscriber lists were a form of advertising but they also acknowledged the individuals who put up the money for printing costs and received copies in return. Parks's list contains some 250 names. The names of lawyers predominate, but the others are those of clergymen, coffeehouse proprietors, merchants, government officials, ship captains, printers, and physicians. Not all of the subscribers were Virginians; a fifth were residents of Maryland, North Carolina, New York City, Philadelphia, Boston, Bristol, London, and Shropshire.[18]

Following the subscriber list are the statutes that were enacted at every legislative session between March 1661/62 and the third session of the General Assembly of 1727–1734 (May to July 1732). Sessions are identified by when and where they met and under whose reign they happened. The acts appear in the order of their adoption, and those that were repealed, disallowed, or obsolete Webb listed by title only while those that were retained are printed in full. Bounteous annotations are set as marginal glosses that comment learnedly on individual acts or give other pertinent information. Webb added a few footnotes that were usually discussions of instances where an act represented a variation upon English common law or a partial appropriation of an English statute. An occasional note hints at his frustration with his work. Remarking on a clause from a very long act about land titles, he tartly wrote "The Sense of this Part of the Clause is hard to be understood," and he caustically dismissed another part of the same act, saying "This Clause seems to be useless."[19] Finally, "A Catalogue, of the General Titles and Things, Contained in the Ensuing Table" precedes "A Table to the Laws of Virginia," which is a topical index.[20]

Publication of *A Collection of all the Acts* represents a turning point in the colony's statutory history. It was the first book about Virginia law written by Virginians and printed in Virginia. Webb's *Office and Authority of a Justice of Peace* and John Mercer's *An Exact Abridgment of all the Public Acts of Assembly in Force and Use* soon followed, as did Parks's regular issues of the Assembly journals and sessions laws.[21] Parks's founding of the *Virginia Gazette* in 1736 opened another conduit for the spread of law-related news and legal conversation. In effect the *Gazette*, the *Exact Abridgment*, the *Office of a Justice*, and *A Collection of All the Acts of Assembly* are the ancestors of a Virginia-specific line of legal literature that continues to this day. Their publication is also significant for another reason. None of them was possible without Parks and his press. But none of them could have happened at all without Gooch's encouragement and permission. His disapproval would have strangled them. So understated was his consent that the Board of Trade overlooked it, just as historians have missed this valuable exercise of his executive authority.

There was no rush to reform the statutes after publication of *A Collection of All the Acts of Assembly*. Complacency and more pressing issues like fixing the tobacco economy and grappling with explosive population growth and geographic expansion kept an overhaul off the legislative agenda. Gooch was away during the War of Jenkins' Ear (1739–1748) when he commanded colonial troops in the British expedition against the South American Spanish stronghold of Cartagena.[22] However, by the middle years of the 1740s, the choruses of complaints were difficult to ignore, all the more so after some appeared in the *Virginia Gazette*.[23] In his typically inconspicuous fashion this is how Gooch explained the situation to the Board of Trade in London: "The former impression of the Laws has been some Time ago distributed; and now a printed Copy can upon no Consideration be obtained, and the Counties are in the greatest need of them. The Printer could not find his Account in settling his Press for so voluminous a Work, on the private sales he might be able to make, without the assistance of the Public. The Assembly consider'd that of late many Acts had been intirely or partly repealed, others expired, altered, amended or explained; That a new Edition in the Order the Laws now Lie, would lead Men (not well experienced in them) into Errors and Mistakes."[24]

Although a thorough overhaul was in order, the records are silent about how and when Gooch and leaders in the General Assembly actually chose to embark on a renovation. The first apparent move started after Gooch unexpectedly recalled the Assembly on 20 February 1745/46. He opened the session with an apology. "I Should not have shorten'd my last Prorogation, to call you together so suddenly, and at this Season, if an Incident, of the most affecting Concern to us," had not happened. The "Incident" he revealed was the Jacobite uprising of 1745 when Charles Edward Stuart attempted to overthrow King George II and restore the House of Stuart to the English throne. Gooch proposed that Virginia form "an Association, obliging ourselves, with our Lives and Fortunes" to support King George as the "just Guardian of our sacred and civil Rights." Reminding his listeners that funding for the College of William & Mary was "now near expiring," he also urged that it be renewed. He particularly pressed the burgesses to make good a pledge of his to support the British naval forces who months earlier assisted in taking Fortress Louisburg from the French. Notably, he said nothing about revising the statutes, although the enabling legislation quietly emerged among the routine laws that the Assembly enacted.[25]

By 26 March 1746 most of the session was over. That morning the Speaker ordered "That Leave be given to bring in a Bill, for the Revisal of the Laws." He assigned the writing to William Beverley and four others who introduced their bill a week later. It received its second and third readings, and some changes were made before it passed. Then Benjamin Waller took the bill to the Council. Summarizing the contents, he called attention to its provision for a joint committee to draft the revisal, and he requested Gooch and his colleagues to name some of them to the committee. The bill went back and forth until it was acceptable to the two houses, and "several Blanks . . . [were] filled up." Gooch signed it into law on the 12th of April and sent everyone home.[26]

The "several Blanks" were the spaces for the names of the committeemen. John Blair, William Nelson, and John Robinson Sr. spoke for Gooch and the Council; William Beverley, Thomas Nelson, Richard Randolph, John Robinson Jr., Benjamin Waller, and Beverley Whiting represented the House.[27] Blood, political interest, and public experience knit the nine together; moreover, the House designees were the burgesses who carried the bill to enactment. Scion of the Beverley and Byrd families, William Beverley was educated in England as were the Nelson brothers. Thomas was the sitting secretary of the colony as well as a burgess. The Robinsons were father and son. Blair bore no relation to the late Commissary James Blair. He was a son of Archibald Blair, the politically influential Williamsburg merchant who had been on the select committee that oversaw the making of *A Complete Collection of All the Acts*. Randolph was a brother of the late Sir John Randolph, the one-time Speaker, attorney general, and House clerk. A prominent Williamsburg lawyer, Waller had served as the clerk of the Council before going to the House. Whiting was from a family that took root in Gloucester County around the middle of the seventeenth century and became part of its ruling establishment. Within a year, however, three appointees left. Overtaken by old age, Councillor John Robinson Sr. quit in favor of the newly minted councillor Thomas Nelson. Advancing years got the better of Richard Randolph, too. He was replaced by Philip Ludwell, the current chairman of the House Committee on Propositions and Grievances. John Robinson Jr. traded his committee seat for the Speaker's chair. Another Randolph, Peyton, the attorney general, took it.

Quite likely, "An Act, for the revisal of the Laws" came to life by prearrangement because, as Gooch remarked, it "was almost a Copy of an Act passed here in the Year 1699 on a like Occasion."[28] The number of revisers, the charge, and the duration were the same in both laws. Where there were differences, they tended to be refined variations on the old statute, such as where the committee would meet, meeting times, and the explicit choice of members from the Williamsburg area. Naming replacements was detailed with greater particularity. Instead of putting clerks on the committee, it was left to the members to find one. George Webb was coaxed into accepting the assignment. He would come to regret his decision because the House refused to pay his expenses.[29] Whether Gooch met privately with the committee as Governor Nicholson had done in 1699 cannot be said because there are no papers from the committee's deliberations. But given Nicholson's precedent it seems inconceivable that Gooch failed to speak with them before he administered their oaths and charged them. It is equally likely that the members petitioned him for the same freedom of speech and liberty of debate they enjoyed in the General Assembly, as was done in 1699.

Despite the loss of the commission records, it is still possible to sketch out some of who did what and when. An initial meeting took place on the fourth Monday of July 1746. It lasted several days while the committee was formally inaugurated, and the members worked out a method of proceeding. They adjourned to November. Although a fire destroyed the Capitol in January 1747, they reconvened as scheduled in March in Williamsburg. Thereafter they sat every fourth Monday for the next year and a half until they readied their report, which went to the General Assembly in October 1748.

With one exception, the basic choice faced by the committee was the same one that had confronted revisers ever since 1632: determining which laws to discard, which laws to reenact unchanged, which laws to amend or consolidate, and what new laws to add. The exception was the decision not to meddle with church law. Since George Webb was their clerk, the committee probably looked to him for initial recommendations about which laws fell into which category. Webb most likely turned to *A Collection of All the Acts of Assembly,* all the acts printed between 1733 and 1746, and the Council and House journals. Additionally, he would have taken note of the acts that had been repealed in the past or that the Crown had disallowed and put all of them aside. Webb's task by itself was incalculably time-consuming because of the sheer number of acts he plowed through and the length and complexity of a large percentage of the statutes. When he finished, he drew up a draft that the committee worked over. This is where things would have gotten sticky because the members' disagreements caused lengthy, probably heated, discussions before everyone came to a consensus. After they did, Webb drew up the committee report.[30]

When Gooch greeted the Assembly in October 1748, he warned the burgesses "The Committee for the Revisal of the Laws, having perform'd their laborious Task prepared a Work for you to finish, which, with the other Matters that must unavoidably fall under your Deliberations, will require a considerable Time to perfect." It did.[31]

The committee's report first went to the Council. Honoring lessons from the past, Gooch and the councillors decided that its disposition should initiate in the House, "it being the most proper for them to proceed upon." On the 1st of November 1748 Speaker Robinson ordered "That the said Report do lie on the Table" and named a committee led by William Beverley to bring in a bill.[32] A week later it was introduced as an omnibus bill in the form of three resolutions. The first recommended that twenty old laws were "obsolete, useless, or otherwise provided for; and therefore ought to be Repealed." A second called for the reenactment of three dozen statutes that were "fit to remain as they now stand." The last was a resolution to debate all the continuing acts the committee combined, altered, or amended and "reduced into severall Bills."[33]

The omnibus bill passed. Its adoption meant nothing more than that the committee bills would be lumped together with all the other pending legislation and debated piecemeal. Each would come to the floor, be vetted by a committee of the whole, have three readings. After being engrossed, it would go up to the Council for its say, and when it satisfied both bodies it would be prepared for Gooch's eventual signature. By mid-December Speaker Robinson succeeded in moving twenty-one committee bills to passage. Gooch assented to all of them and adjourned the Assembly "to *Thursday* the Second Day of *March* next ensuing." Reconvening on the appointed day, both houses picked up from where they left off. They labored for two and a half months before they finished and Gooch consented to the last batch of acts.[34]

Eighty-nine statutes comprised the new code, and they supplanted nearly 400 current laws. This revisal differed from the other six in two respects. It was the only one to be held in abeyance until it was thoroughly vetted by the Board of Trade for possible conflicts with the royal prerogative or violations of the trade laws, which is why its effective date was delayed until June 1751. (Five revisals were done before there was a Board of Trade, and the 1705 revisal only received the board's cursory inspection.) And it was neither a blueprint for sweeping structural reform nor a dictionary of a new statutory vocabulary. Instead, it was a modernizing codification of the status quo that was crafted in a familiar form and language.

Even so, there were changes, the nature of which are evident in the ensuing examples. Acts addressed Virginia's growth and expansion westward. Several called for establishing new towns or splitting overlarge counties and parishes into smaller, more manageable units; others specified ways to improve infrastructure.[35] A group remodeled laws about land titles and boundaries, fences and trespass, stray animals and livestock theft, all of which were perennial issues that first drew the Assembly's attention in the 1620s.[36] Gooch's signature piece of legislation, the tobacco inspection act of 1730, which addressed ways to reduce overproduction and elevate quality, was tightened considerably. So were the acts that regulated the inspection of beef, flour, pork, tar, pitch, and turpentine, which had become important items in the colony's mushrooming export economy.[37] "An act for the better support of the College of William and Mary" levied taxes on the export of animal skins and designated forfeitures of certain fines as a means of assuring a reliable source of funding for the college.[38]

The statutes that defined the courts were revamped in ways that ensured greater efficiency and openness. Councillors and justices of the peace were forbidden to represent clients in their courts, a rule that merely reiterated a decades-old prohibition. They were required to take new shorter, more pointed oaths of office that eliminated outdated verbiage. Jurisdictions were more tightly defined. Rules of civil procedure were specified at greater length and rearranged more logically. For the first time, too, how to bring suits in chancery and how to prosecute them were put in writing. Rules that governed the conduct of trials, summoning witnesses, issuing writs, and taking appeals were also retuned. Both courts were required to maintain their records in accessible places, which was one reason why there was a mandate in the county court act that the justices oversee the erection and upkeep of purpose-built courthouses. The secretary of the colony kept the General Court archives, and after the Capitol burned they were housed in a separate record office that still sits adjacent to the reconstructed Capitol.[39]

There was an important corollary to the county court act. It was a new statute that addressed an extraordinary situation in Brunswick, Fairfax, Frederick, Albemarle, and Augusta Counties. Those five counties were large frontier jurisdictions with widely scattered populations. Because of their size, the "the attendance of the inhabitants at monthly courts [was] grievous and burthensome, and it [was] impossible for the officers" to do their duty. The remedy in the statute looked a bit like an English court of quarter sessions. Each county would have a court that sat four times annually according to a table of prescribed meeting dates and times. Sittings would last for however long it took to clear the dockets. They operated under rules of procedure that were like those of a regular county court. The act represented a temporary remedy for a problem of the moment that would be revisited with an eye to its repeal at a future date.[40]

The rules for trying white colonists accused of felonies were spelled out more completely than before. If legally bailable, defendants were entitled to bail. There were guarantees of a trial before a jury of their peers and an attorney, if they could afford one. They might summon witnesses, although "no negro, mulatto or Indian" could testify for them. Witnesses called on the behalf of a defendant as well as anyone subpoenaed for the Crown were legally bound to appear. If convicted, defendants might plead benefit of clergy to escape punishment or they might seek the governor's clemency. If the prosecution succeeded, the convict's estate was liable for the costs associated with the trial.[41]

An act for trying slaves accused of capital crimes redefined a statute from the Revisal of 1705 and an act of 1723. Among other changes, it combined a section from a 1732 law that extended benefit of clergy[42] to capitally convicted slaves with an addition that permitted masters to defend their slaves in open court, but on the whole, this was by no means a gentler law. The full weight of the state was more vigorously invoked in support of the masters' rights of ownership and protection against recalcitrant slaves. Masters were strictly admonished to use any method necessary to control their workers and none of them was legally accountable for the death of a slave under punishment. They were compensated with public funds for runaways killed in the course of their apprehension. County courts could maim "incorrigible" slaves by branding them, cutting off body parts, or crippling them. The individuals who inflicted the dismemberments were held harmless, although if a slave died while being dismembered the owner could sue for damages.[43]

Other incorporated slave laws were altered more cosmetically than substantively but one changed the property definition of slaves. Slaves had been deemed to be chattels before an act in the Revisal of 1705 declared them to be real estate that descended to "the heirs and widows of persons departing this life, according to the manner and custom of land of [sic] inheritance." Twenty years later the General Assembly had amended that statute to eradicate "many mischiefs" that were the cause of an excess of lawsuits. Now the altered statute redefined slaves as personal property. The reason for that change is unclear, though it may have been merely change for change's sake, which is what Gooch believed.[44]

Another act filled the hole created by the failure of the bar law of 1732. The two-tier bar was revived. County court lawyers were allowed to practice only locally. General Court lawyers were barred from arguing in the counties, although this prohibition did not apply to barristers who lived in Williamsburg and the surrounding counties. In order to qualify for a license a would-be practitioner had to present evidence of good character and learning. Candidates were examined and certified by a committee drawn from General Court judges and the General Court bar. Appointed by the Council, examiners served unspecified tenures. Unless illness or some other incapacity befell them, they were expected to hold examinations with as little delay as possible; procrastination or refusal to administer a test without a reasonable excuse opened them to fines and censure.[45]

"An Act for repealing several acts of Assembly therein mentioned" codified a committee recommendation that eliminated nearly two dozen statutes that were now obsolete. One of those was a 1666 act that had required the courts to keep copies of Michael Dalton's *Countrey Justice* and Michael Swinburne's *Treatise of Testaments and Last Wills*. No one could question the centrality of these two venerable workhorses in fashioning Virginia law but they had been effectively replaced by George Webb's *Office and Authority of a Justice of Peace* after William Parks published it in 1736.[46]

After Gooch initialed all the bills, they were turned over to House clerk Peter Randolph who was to prepare two copies—one for the Board of Trade and another for southern secretary of state John Russell, 4th duke of Bedford. Speaker Robinson also instructed a select committee to gather up the acts "as they are now revised" and to engage "some Person to make a proper Index to them." They were to hire William Parks to print a thousand copies with the same type and paper that he had used in 1733. Parks was to bind them, stamp the arms of Virginia on their front covers, and he was to finish "by the 10th day of *June* in the Year 1751."[47]

When Gooch ended the session, he delivered his customary closing speech It was a speech unlike any from the past. As always, he began by congratulating members for their successful meeting. Their patience and judgment in adopting the Revisal afforded him the "fullest Satisfaction, and intitle you to my most hearty Thanks." Then he said the unexpected. He was resigning. Advancing years and worsening health forced him to seek permission to go home in search of "the Recovery of my Health," and "his Majesty has been graciously pleased to grant me" that request. He acknowledged "the real Pleasure" he had constantly derived from working with the General Assembly to enact laws that met the interests of the Crown and the welfare of Virginia. For that reason and others, it was with the greatest reluctance that he had soon to depart from the place where he had so long resided and for which he held "the sincerest Affection." He ended with the hope "That this Colony therefore, may forever flourish . . . with the Blessing of a lasting Peace, cordial Love and a good Understanding, may constantly subsist among yourselves; shall be always my fervent wish," and he prorogued the Assembly.[48]

Gooch remained in Williamsburg through the summer while he cleared his desk, packed, and arranged a passage to England. His ship sailed from Yorktown in September, but he left without the copies of the Revisal because Peter Randolph was not done making them. When Randolph finished them, he gave them to Council president Thomas Lee who sent them to London in November.[49] Gooch was back in London ahead of the copies, and in keeping with his instructions, he drew up a commentary, which he delivered in person to the colonial office on 3 May 1750.[50] A week later, the Revisal and Gooch's commentary were presented to the Board of Trade. A short hearing followed before the board ordered that "the said Acts, together with Sir William Gooch's observations thereupon, be referred to Mr. Lamb for his opinion thereupon in point of law as soon as conveniently may be."[51]

"Mr. Lamb" was Mathew Lamb,[52] a member of Parliament who was an attorney for the king and the board's legal counsel, and his opinions determined the fate of the Revisal. Lamb submitted his reports in January 1751, only to have the board set them aside while it attended to other business. In May the board, including its new president George Montagu Dunck, 2d earl of Halifax, returned to Virginia matters.[53] They debated the content of the Revisal, Gooch's commentary, and Lamb's reports ostensibly with an eye toward protecting the rights and privileges of the colonists, checking innovations, and upholding the royal prerogative. Halifax had more in mind. An authoritarian by nature, he was bent on using the board to diminish the General Assembly permanently. After a week's worth of deliberations, Halifax and the others concluded that ten acts should be disallowed *ab initio*, fifty-seven should be formally confirmed, and the rest should be assigned probationary status, and they sent those conclusions to the Privy Council.[54] The Privy Council accepted their recommendations and promulgated an order from the King-in-Council to that effect. In October 1751 the order was dispatched to Gooch's successor, Robert Dinwiddie. The order arrived in Williamsburg in April 1752 while Dinwiddie was meeting with his first General Assembly. He immediately summoned the burgesses to the Council chamber and read them the order.[55]

No member of the House or the Council expected such disturbing news. No one questioned the Crown's authority to examine the Revisal and to set aside those parts that the Board of Trade found contrary to English law or against the royal prerogative. But the issuance of this order seemed arbitrarily misplaced. Three years had passed since the Revisal had been enacted, and its effective date had come and gone. Once that date passed without a response from the King-in-Council the Revisal was taken to be the law of the colony. Moreover, William Hunter had printed copies of the Revisal, and they would need to be corrected.[56]

The repercussions of the king's order escaped no one's notice. This thorough vetting of the entire Revisal portended a major change in board policy that threatened constant interference in the General Assembly's ordinary legislative processes. Acts disallowed *ab initio* negated the Assembly's authority because they were held never to have existed, and they could never be reenacted. Furthermore, the board's choice of the ten acts it vacated had a random feel to it. It seemed capricious to void three laws that prevented constructing wooden chimneys and keeping hogs in several towns when the King-in-Council had approved such laws in the past. Negating the laws of servants and slaves and intestate estates seemed equally whimsical. Disallowing the General Court statute was perhaps the most alarming. Overturning it not only repealed a well-designed modern law, but also upset all of the court's actions between that law's implementation and its nullification, which bred confusion and the likelihood of endless litigation. No less annoying but a more ominous limitation for the future was the restraint imposed by the king's approval of the fifty-seven laws by formal confirmation. By its nature, formal confirmation required *all* legislation—new acts, amendments to existing laws, even the repeal of obsolete statutes—to include suspending clauses that prevented them from coming into force for at least two years, and that denied the General Assembly the freedom to make changes as time and circumstances dictated.[57]

Caught unawares, the General Assembly wasted no time in seeking ways to moderate the king's order. A joint committee of councillors and burgesses urged passage of a bill that legalized the actions of the General Court under the now disallowed statute.[58] It suggested soliciting support from the colony's London agents and appealing to King George for relief from the objectionable parts of his order. The appeal styled "The humble address and representation of the council and burgesses, of this your majesty's antient colony, and dominion of Virginia, now met in general assembly" came largely from the pen of Richard Bland (1710–1776). Prized for his knowledge of history and law, and the grace of his pen, this long-time member for Prince George County was one of the most effective defenders of Virginia's rights during the waning years of British rule. His work on "The humble address" was an early example of that steadfast commitment.

Bland argued that the acts the king disallowed *ab initio* benefitted the common good. They were by no means repugnant to laws and statutes of Great Britain, and they should be revived. The change in the form of the disallowance bred confusion and unduly circumscribed the General Assembly's legislative power. Because the Assembly could not believe the king meant to use the more restrictive formal confirmation, it pleaded for his declaration that such was not his intention. The Board of Trade rejected the appeal. Eventually, the outbreak of hostilities with the French in what became the Seven Years' War turned the board's attentions elsewhere and its oversight of the General Assembly's legislation abated for the time being.[59]

The timing of the Revisal of 1748 was unfortunate for the Virginians. Had they undertaken it a few years earlier, the result could have been different. For one thing, it would have been promoted by a vigorous, more effective Governor Gooch. He was sickly when he gave up his office, and his illnesses blunted his effectiveness in London as an advocate for the Revisal. His advocacy was clouded by forgetfulness and clamoring for moneys the government owed him. It was less compelling because he was an ex–lieutenant governor, a private citizen without the weight of influence that once was his. Done earlier, the Revisal could have passed muster after a cursory inspection by a somnolent Board of Trade. Instead, it was intensely vetted by a revivified board whose authoritarian president, the earl of Halifax, was intent on narrowing the scope of the General Assembly's legislative reach.

In the end, the significance of the Revisal of 1748 is this. It was the final summary of the revisals that forged the Old Dominion between 1632 and 1748. It differed from the other six because it did not fundamentally reorder Virginia's legal order. And its treatment by the Board of Trade was a stark lesson in the precariousness of the rights and privileges of the General Assembly, which showed how easily its ability to legislate for Virginia could be challenged and undercut by the Crown. Perceiving a threat to the independence of the General Assembly, the members pushed back. The threat receded, but they began to see the home government's unprecedented interference in their ordinary legislative routines in a new light that heightened their anxieties about future threats and foreshadowed the American Revolution.

※ 8 ※

Endings

For decades, Virginia's burgesses and councillors operated mainly without formal legal training, but they were far from legal illiterates. Their intellectual baggage included self-learned elements of that extraordinarily arcane collection of ancient wisdom, courts, rules, customs, and folkways that they knew as the common law.[1] Inspired by the peculiarities of frontier settlement, they fused their knowledge into a body of acts in a distinctly Virginia voice that they revised five times before that generation passed away. Native-born sons and grandsons and immigrant lawyers succeeded them and prepared the last two revisals in modernized versions that resembled acts of Parliament in form and language. The Board of Trade's challenge to the General Assembly's legislative authority broached the question of the relationship between the acts of assembly and the statutes of the realm.

In 1639, when King Charles I legitimated it, he authorized the still-fledgling General Assembly to make laws, but he said nothing about how its laws and those of Parliament should correspond to each other, if at all. Instead, he merely enjoined Sir Francis Wyatt to sign only bills that were "as near as may be to the laws of England."[2] Variations of his injunction routinely showed up in later gubernatorial instructions and imperial policy papers, but precisely what latitude it conferred on the General Assembly was never clarified. Twice during the Berkeley administration, however, there were hints that the Virginians presumed it bestowed an ill-defined equivalency between their statutes and acts of Parliament.

In June 1642, the General Assembly enacted "The Declaration against the Company." The act not only repudiated a parliamentary effort to revive the Virginia Company, but it also promised the direst of consequences for anyone who covertly or openly advocated returning the colony to the control of a resurrected company. It took effect in the colony as soon as Berkeley initialed it. Intriguingly, it was to become law in England within five days of its arrival there. Parliament did not acknowledge it. King Charles embraced it and vouchsafed it with his promise to preserve Virginia's existing government. His pledge came to nothing. He and Parliament were about to war on one another, and the act of a faraway primitive colonial legislature hardly seemed of great moment.[3] The second whisper came during the General Assembly of 1647–48. It passed a statute that contained a clause that claimed that "noe lawe should be established within the kingdome of England concerning us, without the consent of a grand Assemblye here." That contention derived from a good precedent the members took from Virginia's founding charter. It guaranteed to the original planters and their progeny "all liberties Franchises and Immunities within anie of our domynions to all intents and purposes as yf they had been abiding and borne within this our Realme of Englande or anie other of our saide Domynions." Parliament ignored the Assembly.[4]

The belief in some sort of an equivalency gathered currency in Virginia as the seventeenth century faded into the eighteenth. George Webb explained the relationship this way in his *Office and Authority of a Justice of Peace*: "Acts of Parliament made in *England,* expressly declaring, That they shall extend to *Virginia,* or to his Majesty's *American* Plantations, are of full force in this Dominion, tho' not Enacted here," whereas the General Assembly enacts "Divers other Statutes here, and [Declares them] to be of Force in this Colony, by our Acts of Assembly." Webb expressed the view that "law" in Virginia encompassed English and Virginia customs, parliamentary statutes, *and* acts of the General Assembly that stood on approximately equal footings and inferred a certain equality between English and colonial legislation. The matter was clearly unsettled in 1736, because that was a reading the Board of Trade was never quite willing to accept. Lacking a rational collection of imperial law to fall back on, the board refrained from facing down the Virginians. The earl of Halifax changed that and effectively ended the revisals that forged the Old Dominion.[5]

Even though they sprang from common legal origins, no two groups of early American legislators approached making written law in the same way. Their motives were as varied as the circumstances that contributed to the development of their colonies, and from that variety arose differing ways of converting the pluralities of English law and diverging ends to which their revisions should apply. Consequently, unique indigenous statutes existed everywhere the English settled. That property of uniqueness militates against crafting master narratives or overarching analyses on a grander scale. There is value, nevertheless, in seeing the centrality of statutes as a new means of comprehending early Virginia in the way its lawmakers saw it. In the end, that perspective invites the question of whether other colonial legislatures embarked on comparable quests and achieved similar results. That question awaits answers elsewhere.[6]

NOTES

SHORT TITLES

Billings, *Berkeley and the Forging of Colonial Virginia:* Warren M. Billings, *Sir William Berkeley and the Forging of Colonial Virginia* (Baton Rouge, La., 2004).

Billings, *Berkeley Papers:* Warren M. Billings, ed., *The Papers of Sir William Berkeley, 1605–1677* (Richmond, 2007).

Billings, *Effingham Papers:* Warren M. Billings, ed., *The Papers of Francis Howard, Baron Howard of Effingham, 1643–1695* (Richmond, 1989).

Billings, *A Little Parliament:* Warren M. Billings, *A Little Parliament: The Virginia General Assembly in the Seventeenth Century* (Richmond, 2004).

Billings, "Some Acts Not in Hening's *Statutes*": Warren M. Billings, ed., "Some Acts Not in Hening's *Statutes*: The Acts of Assembly, April 1652, November 1652, and July 1653," *Virginia Magazine of History and Biography* 83 (1975): 22–77.

Hartwell, Blair, and Chilton, *The Present State of Virginia:* Henry Hartwell, James Blair, and Edward Chilton, *The Present State of Virginia, and the College,* ed. Hunter Dickinson Farish (Princeton, N.J., 1940).

Hening, *Statutes at Large:* William Waller Hening, ed., *The Statutes at Large; Being a Collection of all the Laws of Virginia, From the First Session of the Legislature in the Year 1619 . . . ,* 13 vols. (Richmond, 1809–1823; facsimile edition Charlottesville, 1969).

Kennedy and McIlwaine, *Journals of the House of Burgesses:* John Pendleton Kennedy and H. R. McIlwaine, eds., *Journals of the House of Burgesses of Virginia, 1619–1776,* 13 unnumbered vols. (Richmond, 1905–1915).

Kukla, *Speakers and Clerks:* Jon Kukla, *Speakers and Clerks of the Virginia House of Burgesses, 1643–1776* (Richmond, 1981).

Leonard, *General Assembly Register:* Cynthia Miller Leonard, comp., *The General Assembly of Virginia, July 30, 1619–January 11, 1978: A Bicentennial Register of Members* (Richmond, 1978).

McIlwaine, *Legislative Journals of the Council:* H. R. McIlwaine, ed., *Legislative Journals of the Council of Colonial Virginia,* 2d ed. (Richmond, 1979).

McIlwaine, *Minutes of the Council:* H. R. McIlwaine, ed., *Minutes of the Council and General Court of Colonial Virginia, 1622–1632, 1670–1676,* 2d ed. (Richmond, 1979).

McIlwaine, Hall, and Hillman, *Executive Journals of the Council:* H. R. McIlwaine, Wilmer L. Hall, and Benjamin J. Hillman, eds., *Executive Journals of the Council of Colonial Virginia* (Richmond, 1925–1966).

ODNB: *Oxford Dictionary of National Biography Online* (Oxford, 2004–).

PRO: National Archives, Kew, United Kingdom.

Rastell, *A Collection of Statutes:* William Rastell, *A Collection of Statutes Now in Force, Continued from the Beginning of Magna Charta, Made in the 9. Yere of the Raigne of H.3. Untill the End of Parliament Holden in the 7. Yere of Our Soveraigne Lord King James. Under Titles Placed by Order of Alphabet* (London, 1615).

Robinson, "Notes": Conway Robinson, comp., "Notes and Excerpts from the Records of Colonial Virginia," Conway Robinson Papers, Virginia Historical Society.

VMHB: *Virginia Magazine of History and Biography.*

WMQ: *William & Mary Quarterly.*

PREFACE

1. Warren M. Billings, "Law in the Colonial South," *Journal of Southern History* 73 (2007): 602–16.
2. Warren M. Billings, "Needs and Opportunities in Virginia's Legal History and Culture," in *Magistrates and Pioneers: Essays in the History of American Law* (Clark, N.J., 2011), 417–40.
3. Joseph Priestley, *Lectures on History and General Policy,* 1st American ed., 2 vols. (Philadelphia, 1803), 1:148–49.
4. R. Neil Hening, "A Handbook for All: William Waller Hening's *The New Virginia Justice,*" in *"Esteemed Bookes of Lawe" and the Legal Culture of Early Virginia,* ed. Warren M. Billings and Brent Tarter (Charlottesville, 2017), 83–91.
5. Brent Tarter coined the phrase in his essay "The New Virginia Bookshelf," *VMHB* 104 (1996): 27. It is also the title to his book of the same name, which the University of Virginia Press issued in 2013.
6. The quotation comes from *Instructions to Sir George Yeardley* (sometimes called "The Great Charter"), 18 Nov. 1618, in Samuel M. Bemiss, ed., *The*

Three Charters of the Virginia Company of London, With Seven Related Documents, 1606–1621 (Williamsburg, 1957), 95.
7. On the point, see John Mercer Patton and Conway Robinson, comps., *The Code of Virginia* (Richmond, 1849), preface; and Kent C. Olson, "State Codes," in *Virginia Law Books: Essays and Bibliographies,* ed. W. Hamilton Bryson (Philadelphia, 2000), 1–11.

1. BEGINNINGS AND THE ACTS OF 1623/24

1. Wesley Frank Craven, *Dissolution of the Virginia Company of London: The Failure of a Colonial Experiment,* reprint ed. (Gloucester, Mass., 1964); William M. Kelso, *Jamestown, the Buried Truth* (Charlottesville, 2006); Karen Ordahl Kupperman, *The Jamestown Project* (Cambridge, Mass., 2009); Karen Ordahl Kupperman, *Pocahontas and the English Boys: Caught between Cultures in Early Virginia* (New York, 2019); Alexander B. Haskell, *For God, King, and People, Forging Commonwealth Bonds in Renaissance Virginia* (Chapel Hill, N.C., 2017); James Horn, *A Land as God Made It: Jamestown and the Birth of America* (New York, 2005); James Horn, *1619: Jamestown and the Forging of American Democracy* (New York, 2018); Paul Musselwhite, Peter C. Mancall, and James Horn, eds., *Virginia 1619: Slavery and Freedom in the Making of English America* (Chapel Hill, N.C., 2019); Jennifer Potter, *The Jamestown Brides: England's "Maids for Virginia"* (Oxford, 2019).
2. Promulgated in 1609, William Strachey compiled a printed edition that appeared in London in 1612 under the title *For the Colony in Virginea Britannia Lawes Divine, Morall and Martiall, etc.* A modern rendition, prepared by David H. Flaherty, was issued by the University Press of Virginia in 1969.
3. Craven, *Dissolution,* 47–81, 99–103, 187–89; Samuel M. Bemiss, ed., *The Three Charters of the Virginia Company of London, With Seven Related Documents, 1606–1621* (Williamsburg, 1957), 95–108.
4. No text of Yeardley's writ exists, but the likely wording, quoted here, survives in a later example. See Susan Myra Kingsbury, ed., *Records of the Virginia Company of London,* 4 vols. (Washington, D.C., 1906–1935), 4:448–49.
5. The other priests were the Rev. Dr. James Blair, founder of the College of William & Mary, and the Rev. William Dawson, a pre-Revolutionary professor of moral philosophy at the college.
6. Alison Games, *The Web of Empire: English Cosmopolitans in an Age of Expansion* (Oxford, 2008), 14.

7. William S. Powell, *John Pory, 1572–1636: The Life and Letters of a Man of Many Parts* (Chapel Hill, N.C., 1977); Charlotte Fell-Smith, "John Pory," ODNB.
8. Nora Miller Turman, *George Yeardley: Governor of Virginia and Organizer of the General Assembly in 1619* (Richmond, 1959); R.C.D. Baldwin, "Sir George Yeardley," ODNB; John Chamberlain to Sir Dudley Carleton, 28 Nov. 1618, in Norman Egbert McClure, ed., *The Letters of John Chamberlain*, 2 vols. (Philadelphia, 1939), 2:188, 186.
9. On the provenance of the "reporte," see Billings, *A Little Parliament*, 227–28n6. The best rendering from the manuscript is William J. Van Schreeven and George H. Reese, eds., *Proceedings of the General Assembly, July 30–August 4, 1619. Written & Sent from Virginia to England by Mr. John Pory Speaker of the First Representative Assembly in the New World* (Jamestown, 1969), which is the source for the quotations here.
10. Van Schreeven and Reese, *Proceedings of the General Assembly*, 19–25.
11. Sir Thomas Elyot, *The Boke named the Governour, devised by Sr. Thomas Elyot* (London, 1531), fols. 83–98, 102–106; Craven, *Dissolution*, 149–75; Kingsbury, *Records of the Virginia Company*, 1:440; Alexander B. Haskell, "Deference, Defiance, and the Language of Office in Seventeenth-Century Virginia," in *Early Modern Virginia: Reconsidering the Old Dominion*, ed. Douglas Bradburn and John C. Coombs (Charlottesville, 2011), 158–85.
12. Audrey Horning, *Ireland in the Virginian Sea: Colonialism in the British Atlantic* (Chapel Hill, N.C., 2013), 69–70; Virginia Bernhard, "Sir Francis Wyatt (1588–1644)," ODNB.
13. Commission to Sir Francis Wyatt and the Council of State, 26 Aug. 1624, Patent Rolls, C/66 2340, pt. 17, no. 2, PRO; Craven, *Dissolution*, 148–337; Warren M. Billings, John E. Selby, and Thad W. Tate, *Colonial Virginia: A History* (White Plains, N.Y., 1986), 41–45; Theodore Rabb, *Jacobean Gentleman: Sir Edwin Sandys, 1561–1629* (Princeton, N.J., 1998), 353–89; Thomas Cary Johnson, ed., *A Proclamation for setling the Plantation of Virginia, 1625* (Charlottesville, 1946).
14. Billings, *A Little Parliament*, 1–16.
15. Election writ, 26 Jan. 1623/24, in Kingsbury, *Records of the Virginia Company of London*, 4:448–49. The writ, which is the earliest example of an election writ on record, reads "Whereas the Governor and Councell of State are determined to call a generall Assemblie for the better setling of the affairs of this Cuntrie. These are to will & require you [blank] to assemble all the freemen and Tenants inhabiting those Plantations and by pluralitie of voices to make ellections of two sufficient men. Willing &

requireing the persons so chosen to give their attendance at James Cittie the 14th day of February next comeing." It probably replicated the one Governor Yeardley circulated when he summoned the General Assembly of July 1619. It is remarkable because it established who could vote for burgesses. Those qualifications persisted until they were changed by statute in 1670. See Hening, *Statutes at Large*, 2:280. The wording of the writ itself seems to have remained unaltered but it had fallen out of fashion by the 1670s, after which time it took on a nearer likeness to its English counterpart. See Billings, *A Little Parliament*, 174–76.

16. Joshua Eckhardt, "Ralph Hamor," *Encyclopedia Virginia*, Web, 9 June 2020.
17. "The Medical Men of Virginia," *WMQ*, 1st. ser., 19 (1911): 146–49; McIlwaine, *Minutes of the Council*, 46, 479; Martha W. McCartney, *Documentary History of Jamestown Island*, 4 vols. (Williamsburg, 2000), 3:287.
18. McCartney, *Documentary History of Jamestown Island*, 3:283.
19. Richard Beale Davis, *George Sandys, Poet-Adventurer: A Study in Anglo-American Culture in the Seventeenth Century* (London and New York, 1955).
20. Virginia M. Meyer and John Frederick Dorman, eds., *Adventurers of Purse and Person, Virginia 1607–1624/5*, rev. ed. (Richmond, 1987), 656; David R. Ransome, "Francis West (1586–1633/4)," *ODNB*.
21. The most accurate modern list of the burgesses is in Cynthia Miller Leonard, comp., *The General Assembly of Virginia, July 30, 1619–January 11, 1978: A Bicentennial Register of Members* (Richmond, 1978), 5. McCartney, *Documentary History of Jamestown Island* and Meyer and Dorman, *Adventurers of Purse and Person* have biographical information on the burgesses noted here. Additional details may also be gleaned from annotations in Billings, *Berkeley Papers* and several sketches in *Encyclopedia Virginia*.
22. Robert Johnson, "The humble Petition of Sundry Adventurers and Planters of the Virginia and Summer Ilands Plantations," in Kingsbury, *Records of the Virginia Company*, 2:372–76; Nathaniel Butler, *The Unmasked Face of Our Colony in Virginia as it was in the winter of the Yeare 1622* (London, 1622?); Kennedy and McIlwaine, *Journals of the House of Burgesses, 1619–1658/59*, 21–42; Privy Council to Sir Francis Wyatt and the Council of State, 31 Aug. 1626, Privy Council Register 2/34, fol. 82, PRO.
23. Kingsbury, *Records of the Virginia Company*, 2:253.
24. Hening, *Statutes at Large*, 1:122–28. Hening's source text was an eighteenth-century transcript that belonged to the Randolph family, which was acquired by Thomas Jefferson who lent it to Hening. See ibid., 1:121. In

March 1624 Sharples prepared a copy that Wyatt sent to London, which now resides in the Colonial Office Papers housed at the National Archives of the United Kingdom, Kew, Surrey. Neither Jefferson nor Hening knew of its existence.

25. A close observer of the *Statutes at Large* will notice that from time to time Hening commented on inconsistencies in the numbers he found in his sources. Though he did not say so, those irregularities resulted from clerical errors and his not having the enrolled texts, the official versions of the statutes, which were lost long before his day.
26. Billings, *A Little Parliament*, 115.
27. Hening, *Statutes at Large*, 1:127.
28. Sir Thomas Smith, *De Republica Anglorum: The maner of Gouvernement or policie of the Realme of England* (London, 1583), 34–43.
29. Edward L. Bond and Joan R. Gunderson, "The Episcopal Church in Virginia, 1607–2007," *VMHB* 115 (2007): 167–74. For a map showing the geographic locations of the early parishes see Warren M. Billings, ed., *The Old Dominion in the Seventeenth Century: A Documentary History of Virginia, 1606–1700*, rev. ed. (Chapel Hill, N.C., 2007), 85.
30. Hening, *Statutes at Large*, 1:122–23.
31. To the English the word "corn" referred to grains such as barley, rye, oats, or wheat rather than maize. Sometimes they called the latter Turkey wheat; at other times Indian corn. See John Gerard, *The Herball or Generall Historie of Plantes. Gathered by John Gerarde of London Master in Chirurgerie* (London, 1597), 58, 77.
32. Hening, *Statutes at Large*, 1:123–24.
33. Ibid., 1:124.
34. Ibid., 1:125.
35. Warren M. Billings, "William Claiborne (bap. Aug. 10, 1600–d. by Aug. 25, 1679)," in *Dictionary of Virginia Biography*, ed. John T. Kneebone et al. (Richmond, 1998), 3:255–57.
36. Hening, *Statutes at Large*, 1:126, 125.
37. Ibid., 1:125–26.
38. Ibid., 1:127–28.
39. Ibid., 1:126, 128, 127.
40. Code of Virginia, tit. 30, §30–6.
41. Hening, *Statutes at Large*, 1:125, 124, 128, 125 (quotation at 125).

2. SIR JOHN HARVEY AND THE REVISAL OF 1632

1. Brent Tarter, "Sir John Harvey: Royal Governor of Virginia, 1628–1639," *VMHB* 125 (2017): 2–37; Billings, *A Little Parliament*, 20–22, 71–73, 142–43, 198–99.
2. Capt. John Smith, *A Sea Grammar* (London, 1627), in *The Complete Works of Captain John Smith (1580–1631) in Three Volumes*, ed. Philip L. Barbour (Chapel Hill, N.C., 1986), 3:82–83.
3. Audrey Horning, *Ireland in the Virginian Sea: Colonialism in the English Atlantic* (Chapel Hill, N.C., 2013), 330–33, 336–38, 339–40; Alexander B. Haskell, *For God, King, and People: Forging Bonds in Renaissance Virginia* (Chapel Hill, N.C., 2017), 199–272.
4. McIlwaine, *Minutes of the Council*, 104–106.
5. Hening, *Statutes at Large*, 1:140–44.
6. Ibid., 1:139–44, 149–53.
7. Agreement between Harvey and the councillors, 20 Dec. 1631, C.O. 1/6, fols. 92–93, PRO.
8. John West (1590–1659) was the brother of Lord De La Warr and Francis West.
9. In General Assembly of March 1627/28, thirty-five burgesses represented twenty-five constituencies. The General Assembly of October 1629 consisted of forty-four burgesses who sat for twenty-four constituencies. There were forty-two burgesses for twenty-four constituencies in the General Assembly of March 1630. See Leonard, *General Assembly Register*, 6–10.
10. Hening, *Statutes at Large*, 1:154.
11. Ibid., 1:177.
12. That supposition is suggested by two acts that bear the dates of their passage, ibid., 1:171, 174.
13. Ibid., 1:155.
14. Ibid., 1:156–57.
15. Ibid., 1:156.
16. Ibid., 1:166, 172.
17. Ibid., 1:173.
18. Ibid., 1:162–65.
19. Stat. 1 Jac. I. c. 6, Rastell, *A Collection of Statutes*, fol. 242c; Hening, *Statutes at Large*, 1:167. Artificers were skilled craftsmen.
20. Stat. 4 Jac. I. c. 5, Rastell, *A Collection of Statutes*, fol. 132d; Hening, *Statutes at Large*, 1:167.

21. Stat. 6 Edw. VI. c. 14; Stat. 13 Eliz. I. c. 25, Rastell, *A Collection of Statutes*, fols. 182b; 218d; Hening, *Statutes at Large*, 1:172.
22. The Council began sitting quarterly in January 1627. McIlwaine, *Minutes of the Council*, 128.
23. Hening, *Statutes at Large*, 1:172, 173, 177.
24. Ibid., 1:177, 168–70; Billings, *A Little Parliament*, 149–51. The wording of the commission was apparently drawn up while Pott was acting governor. Hening, *Statutes at Large*, 1:132–33.
25. Leonard, *General Assembly Register*, 11.
26. Hening, *Statutes at Large*, 1:178–209.
27. Ibid., 1:179.
28. Ibid., 1:153, 178.
29. Compare Acts XIV and XV of Feb. 1632 with Acts XV and XVI of Sept. 1632; Acts XVI and XIX of Feb. 1632, which related to French vinedressers and assemblymen's attendance at church services during meetings, were dropped. Hening, *Statutes at Large*, 1:159–61, 184, 161, 162.
30. Ibid., 1:185–87.
31. Ibid., 1:188–90.
32. Ibid., 1:193, 194–95.
33. Ibid., 1:193.
34. Ibid., 1:179–80.
35. Billings, *Berkeley and the Forging of Colonial Virginia*, 98–99.
36. Arthur P. Scott, *Criminal Law in Colonial Virginia* (Chicago, 1930); Warren M. Billings, "Pleading, Procedure, and Practice: The Meaning of Due Process of Law in Seventeenth-Century Virginia," *Journal of Southern History* 46 (1981): 569–84.
37. Hening, *Statutes at Large*, 1:204–24.

3. SIR WILLIAM BERKELEY AND THE REVISAL OF 1643

1. Billings, *Berkeley and the Forging of Colonial Virginia*, 1–38.
2. The population stood at 1210 in 1625, whereas it was 4914 a decade later, and by 1639, it surpassed 10,000. See Edmund S. Morgan, *American Slavery, American Freedom: The Ordeal of Colonial Virginia* (New York, 1975), 412; Warren M. Billings, ed., *The Old Dominion in the Seventeenth Century: A Documentary History of Virginia, 1606–1700*, rev. ed. (Chapel Hill, N.C., 2007), 131–32.
3. Charles M. Andrews, *British Committees, Commissions, and Councils of Trade and Plantations, 1622–1675* (Baltimore, 1908), 14; Hening, *Statutes*

at Large, 1:224; Warren M. Billings, "The Growth of Political Institutions in Virginia, 1634 to 1676," *WMQ,* 3d ser., 31 (1974): 225–42; Billings, *A Little Parliament,* 16, 25–49.
4. Kemp (1600?–1649) arrived in Virginia about the year 1634 and settled at Rich Neck in James City County. He displaced Claiborne as secretary of the colony and was acting governor while Berkeley was in England in 1644 and 1645.
5. Brent Tarter, "Sir John Harvey: Royal Governor of Virginia, 1628–1639," *VMHB* 125 (2017): 2–37; Billings, *Berkeley and the Forging of Colonial Virginia,* 40, 50–52.
6. Billings, *A Little Parliament,* 24; Billings, *Berkeley and the Forging of Colonial Virginia,* 35.
7. Billings, *Berkeley Papers,* 29.
8. Richard Beale Davis, *George Sandys: Poet-Adventurer* (London, 1955), 257–64.
9. Billings, *Berkeley Papers,* 40–44, 43. The Declaration reached the king at York. He replied to it on 5 July 1642, saying in part, "Your so earnest desire to continue under our immediate Protection is very acceptable to Us; And that as Wee had not before the least intention to consent to the Introduction of any Company over that Our Colony, So wee are by it much confirmed in our former resolutions as thinking it unfitt to change a forme of Government wherein . . . Our Subjects there (having had so long experience of it) receive so much contentment and satisfaction." That promise meant nothing in reality. The House of Commons had abandoned the scheme to revive the company. Roundheads and cavaliers were soon to take the field against one another, which pushed aside immediate concerns about faraway Virginia. As a result, the nature of the relationship between Virginia and the statutes was not addressed in 1642. See Billings, *Berkeley Papers,* 52.
10. Hening, *Statutes at Large,* 1:267.
11. Berkeley's successors were not so indulgent. Their unwillingness to share became a source of political tension, especially with the burgesses, after 1676.
12. Billings, *Berkeley and the Forging of Colonial Virginia,* 91–93.
13. Kukla, *Speakers and Clerks,* 35–37.
14. Hening, *Statutes at Large,* 1:179.
15. Kukla, *Speakers and Clerks,* 137, 139.
16. Warren M. Billings, "'Send us . . . what other Lawe books you shall thinke fitt': Books That Shaped the Law in Virginia, 1600–1860," *VMHB* 120

(2013): 315–38; Brent Tarter, "The Library of Colonial Virginia," in *"Esteemed Bookes of Lawe" and the Legal Culture of Early Virginia*, ed. Warren M. Billings and Brent Tarter (Charlottesville, 2017), 37–42.
17. Hening, *Statutes at Large*, 1:240–41.
18. Hening's compilation contained seventy-three laws. However, there were more because a reference in the Revisal of 1652 mentions an eighty-fourth statute in a lost text that differed from Hening's source. See Warren M. Billings, ed., "Some Acts Not in Hening's *Statutes*: Acts of Assembly April 1652, July 1653, and November 1653," *VMHB* 73 (1975): 47–48.
19. "Acts of the General Assembly, Jan. 6, 1639–40," *WMQ*, 2d ser., 4 (1924): 17–34. Because he was unaware of the existence of a full text of these acts, Hening published an abridged version of them that he borrowed from Thomas Jefferson. See Hening, *Statutes at Large*, 1:224–25. Conway Robinson found an original of the full text among the records of the General Court before it burned in 1865. He copied it, and that copy now rests at the Library of Virginia. See also Governor Sir Francis Wyatt's proclamation implementing the restrictions, 16 Oct. 1640, in Susie M. Ames, ed., *County Court Records of Accomack-Northampton, Virginia 1640–1645* (Charlottesville, 1973), 106–108.
20. Louis Cecil Gray, *History of Agriculture in the Southern United States to 1860*, 2 vols., repr. ed. (Gloucester, Mass., 1958), 1:260–64; Russell R. Menard, "A Note on Chesapeake Tobacco Prices, 1618–1660," *VMHB* 84 (1976): 401–10.
21. In the 1640s, the county magistrates were statutorily designated "commanders" or "commissioners of the peace" instead of "justices of the peace" in the apparent belief that their office carried fewer responsibilities than an English justice of the peace. Even so, colonists used "commander," "commissioner," and "justice" indiscriminately.
22. Billings, *Berkeley Papers*, 30, 47–48.
23. Hening, *Statutes at Large*, 1:272–73.
24. Ibid., 1:273.
25. Ibid., 1:264, 257–58.
26. Ibid., 1: 259–60.
27. Ibid., 1:264–65.
28. Ibid., 1:270.
29. Ibid., 1:270–72.
30. A letter of procuration granted an attorney-in-fact the power to act for someone that he or she represented in legal proceedings. See John Cowell, comp., *A Law Dictionary: Or the Interpreter of Words and Terms Used*

either in the Common or Statute Laws of Great Britain, and in Tenures and Jocular Customs (London, 1727; first published at Oxford in 1607), s.v. "Procurator."
31. Hening, *Statutes at Large*, 1:275–76.
32. Ibid., 1:263, 264.
33. Ibid., 1:267.
34. Ibid., 1:274–75.
35. Ibid., 1:257.
36. Ibid., 1:252–53.
37. Stat. 7 Jas. I. c. 16, Rastell, *A Collection of Statutes*, fol. 132b.
38. Hening, *Statutes at Large*, 1:254–55.
39. Ibid., 1:244.
40. Ibid., 1:258.
41. Ibid., 1:248, 256, 260; Billings, *Berkeley Papers*, 170–71.
42. Hening, *Statutes at Large*, 1:268–69. The law incorporated the English recusancy act 3 Stat. Jas. 1, c. 4–5, Rastell, *A Collections of Statutes*, fol. 90b, fol. 92b.
43. Hening, *Statutes at Large*, 1:277.
44. Billings, *Berkeley and the Forging of Colonial Virginia*, 103–105; Edward L. Bond, *Damned Souls in a Tobacco Colony: Religion in Seventeenth-Century Virginia* (Macon, Ga., 2000), 153–54.
45. Billings, *Berkeley Papers*, 29.
46. Hening, *Statutes at Large*, 1:261, 277–79, 240–43.
47. Warren M. Billings, "William Claiborne (bap. 10 Aug. 1600–d. by 25 Aug. 1679)," in *Dictionary of Virginia Biography*, ed. Sara B. Bearss et al. (Richmond, 2006), 3:255–57.
48. Hening, *Statutes at Large*, 1:282–338; "Acts, Orders and Resolutions of the General Assembly of Virginia at Sessions of 1643–1646," *VMHB* 23 (1915): 229–40; Billings, *A Little Parliament*, 208–209; Billings, *Berkeley and the Forging of Colonial Virginia*, 96–99; Billings, *Berkeley Papers*, 61, 62, 71–73; William L. Shea, *The Virginia Militia in the Seventeenth Century* (Baton Rouge, La., 1983), 56–72.
49. Jon Kukla, *Political Institutions in Virginia, 1619–1660* (New York, 1989), 132–37; Billings, *Berkeley and the Forging of Colonial Virginia*, 104–106.

4. A NEW CONSTITUTIONAL ORDER

1. Billings, *Berkeley Papers*, 84, 95–97; Hening, *Statutes at Large*, 1:359–61, 65; order-in-council, 14 Dec. 1649, State Papers Class 25, vol. 3, PRO;

order-in-council, 10 Aug. 1650, SP 25/8, PRO; An Act for prohibiting Trade with the Barbadoes, Virginia, Bermuda and Antego, 3 Oct. 1650, in C. F. Firth and R. S. Rait, eds., *Acts and Ordinances of the Interregnum, 1642–1660*, 3 vols. (London, 1911), 2:425–29.
2. J. Frederick Fausz, "Richard Bennett (bap. 6 August 1609–d. by 12 April 1675)," *Dictionary of Virginia Biography*, 1:445–47.
3. "Surrender of Virginia to the Parliamentary Commissioners, March 1651/52," *VMHB* 11 (1903–1904): 32–41.
4. Billings, *Berkeley Papers*, 102–05.
5. Lower Norfolk County, Deeds, Wills, and Orders, 1646–1656 (microfilm copy, Library of Virginia, Richmond), 7.
6. Leonard, *General Assembly Register*, 26–29; Jon Kukla, *Political Institutions in Virginia, 1619–1660* (New York, 1989), 148–57; Steven D. Crow, "'Your Majesty's Good Subjects': A Reconsideration of Royalism in Virginia, 1642–1652," *VMHB* 87 (1979): 158–73; Jason McElligott, "Atlantic Royalism: Polemic, Censorship, and the 'Declaration and Protestation of the Governour and Inhabitants of Virginia,'" in *Royalists and Royalism during the Interregnum*, ed. Jason McElligott and David L. Smith (Manchester, 2010).
7. Kukla, *Speakers and Clerks*, 46–47.
8. Billings, "Some Acts Not in Hening's *Statutes*," 31. The "book of the Acts" contained the enrolled texts of the statutes.
9. Surry County Deeds and Wills Book 1, 1652–57, following p. 405; Billings, "Some Acts Not in Hening's *Statutes*," 22n5. Now the volume is housed at the Library of Virginia in Richmond.
10. Billings, "Some Acts Not in Hening's *Statutes*," 45, 50, 58, 59, 61.
11. The sixteenth new act was interposed between the saved acts: Billings, "Some Acts Not in Hening's *Statutes*," 45.
12. Ibid., 31.
13. Ibid., 31–32, 66–69; Sir William Blackstone, *Commentaries on the Laws of England in Four Books*, 5th ed. (Dublin, 1773), 4:64.
14. Billings, "Some Acts Not in Hening's *Statutes*," 34–35.
15. Ibid., 32–34, 71.
16. Ibid., 71.
17. Hening, *Statutes at Large*, 1:367–68.
18. Billings, "Some Acts Not in Hening's *Statutes*," 34.
19. Hening, *Statutes at Large*, 1:199.
20. Billings, "Some Acts Not in Hening's *Statutes*," 28–30, 33; Commission of the Peace for Northumberland County, 28 May 1652, Northumberland

County Order Book, 1650–52 (microfilm copy, Library of Virginia), fol. 76.
21. Northumberland County Order Book, 1650–52, 71.
22. Billings, "Some Acts Not in Hening's *Statutes*," 70; Paul Musselwhite, *Urban Dreams, Rural Commonwealth: The Rise of Plantation Society in the Chesapeake* (Chicago, 2019).
23. Billings, *Berkeley Papers*, 104.
24. Kennedy and McIlwaine, *Journals of the House of Burgesses, 1619–1659/60*, 83.
25. Hening, *Statutes at Large*, 1:390–428.
26. Brent Tarter, "Edward Digges (1621–1675)," *Encyclopedia Virginia*, Web, 28 Jan. 2018.
27. Minnie G. Cook, "Governor Samuel Mathews, Jr.," *WMQ*, 2d ser., 14 (1934): 105–14.
28. Kukla, *Speakers and Clerks*, 49–52; Menna Prestwich, "Diplomacy and Trade in the Protectorate," *Journal of Modern History* 22 (1950): 103–21.
29. Kukla, *Speakers and Clerks*, 57–59.
30. Kennedy and McIlwaine, *Journals of the House of Burgesses, 1619–1659/60*, 99, 101, 106–13 (quotation at 111); Hening, *Statutes at Large*, 1:495.
31. Hening, *Statutes at Large*, 1:428. An online version is available via http://hdl.loc.gov/loc.mss/mtj.mtjbib026588.
32. It is classified as Sloane MS 1378 Laws of Virginia, 1657. I relied on a digital image that the British Library provided. Another copy is in the Virginia Colonial Records Project microfilm housed at the Library of Virginia and described in VCRP Survey Report 00007.
33. On the transcript is the notation "Examined and compared with the Originall and according thereto corrected. Per Peter Beverley Clerke of the House of Burgesses." See Jefferson Papers, Series 8, Virginia Records, 1606–1737, 7:312. The entry in the collection guide is misleading because it incorrectly identifies the volume as being a journal of the Council and General Assembly.
34. Hening, *Statutes at Large*, 1:414–95.
35. Ibid., 1:444, 450, 459, 460.
36. Ibid., 1:472; Billings, "Acts Not in Hening's *Statutes*," 34.
37. Hening, *Statutes at Large*, 1:475.
38. Ibid., 1:419.
39. Ibid., 1:486–87.
40. Ibid., 1:448–49, 480, 469.
41. Ibid., 1:454.

42. Ibid., 1:486; Blackstone, *Commentaries on the Laws of England*, 1:374–75.
43. Kennedy and McIlwaine, *Journals of the House of Burgesses, 1619–1659/60*, 115–16.
44. Hening, *Statutes at Large*, 1:477, 519–20, 520, 521, 523.
45. Ibid., 1:516–17.
46. The session laws are printed in ibid., 1:530–43.
47. Billings, *Berkeley and the Forging of Colonial Virginia*, 120–30.
48. Billings, *Berkeley Papers*, 91–95, 122, 124–27, 129.

5. SAFEGUARDING VIRGINIA'S AUTONOMY

1. Hening, *Statutes at Large*, 1:531–32, 542; Billings, *Berkeley Papers*, 130.
2. Jon Kukla, ed., "Some Acts Not in Hening's *Statutes*: The Acts of Assembly, October 1660," *VMHB* 65 (1975): 86–87.
3. This Nathaniel Bacon is not to be confused with the leader of Bacon's Rebellion. The latter was a thirteen-year-old child in 1660. The two Bacons were cousins though they were apparently unacquainted until the younger Nathaniel Bacon emigrated to Virginia in 1674.
4. Kukla, "Some Acts Not in Hening's *Statutes*," 90–93.
5. Billings, *Berkeley and the Forging of Colonial Virginia*, 68–78, 126–27, 140–62; Alexander B. Haskell, *For God, King, and People: Forging Commonwealth Bonds in Renaissance Virginia* (Chapel Hill, N.C., 2018), 272–353.
6. Billings, *Berkeley Papers*, 150.
7. Hening, *Statutes at Large*, 2:17.
8. Billings, *Berkeley Papers*, 139–41, 142–44, 143; Hening, *Statutes at Large*, 2:34; Billings, *Berkeley and the Forging of Colonial Virginia*, 132–36.
9. Kenneth B. Murdoch, *The Sun at Noon: Three Biographical Sketches* (New York, 1939), 65–66; Kukla, *Speakers and Clerks*, 54–57; Hening, *Statutes at Large*, 1:403, 424, 426, 428, 525; Billings, *Berkeley Papers*, 157.
10. Kukla, *Speakers and Clerks*, 140; Kennedy and McIlwaine, *Journals of the House of Burgesses, 1619–1659/60*, 100.
11. Kukla, *Speakers and Clerks*, 61–62.
12. Ibid., 63–64.
13. Edmund Plowden, *Les Commentaires, ou les Reportes de Edmunde Plowden vn apprentice de le Ley, de dyuers cases esteantes matters en ley & de les Argumentes sur yceaux, en les temps des Raygne, le Roye Edwarde le sizele Roigne Mary, le Roy & Roigne Phillipp & Mary, le Roigne Elizabeth* (London, 1571, 1579). That Wynne owned Plowden, now in a private library, is clearly established by his signature on leaf ¶ ii and various notations about the

Wynne family that appear on the front and back paste-downs and flyleaves of the two volumes. Still in the original boards and leather bindings, the set is in remarkably good condition, considering its antiquity.

14. "Epistle Dedicatory," in Francis Moryson, *The Lawes of Virginia Now in Force Collected Out of the Assembly Records and Digested into One Volume* (London, 1662), 14–17; William L. Shea, *The Virginia Militia in the Seventeenth Century* (Baton Rouge, La., 1983), 73–83; Billings, *Berkeley and the Forging of Colonial Virginia*, 199–200.

15. Warren M. Billings, "A Quaker in Seventeenth-Century Virginia: Four Remonstrances by George Wilson," *WMQ*, 3d ser., 33 (1976): 127–40; Edward L. Bond, *Damned Souls in a Tobacco Colony: Religion in Seventeenth-Century Virginia* (Macon, Ga., 2000), 160–74.

16. An "interstitium" is a long interval of time between two events. The reference here is obscure because copies of the draft revisal have all disappeared so there is no way to determine the events or the time between them. The loss of the House journals also precludes a deeper understanding of the information this cryptic order was meant to convey.

17. Kennedy and McIlwaine, *Journals of the House of Burgesses, 1659/60–1693*, 16.

18. Hening, *Statutes at Large*, 2:136–38.

19. Billings, *Berkeley Papers*, 142–44.

20. Hening, *Statutes at Large*, 1:240–43, 2:41–43.

21. Ibid., 2:44–55.

22. 23 Elizabeth 1, c. 1, Rastell, *A Collection of the Statutes*, fol. 82c.

23. Hening, *Statutes at Large*, 2:49.

24. Ibid., 2:49–55.

25. Ibid., 2:56–57, 25.

26. Lothrop Withington, "Virginia Gleanings in England," *VMHB* 12 (1903): 396–99; Richard L. Morton, *Colonial Virginia: A History*, 2 vols. (Chapel Hill, N.C., 1960), 1:189–90; Billings, *Berkeley and the Forging of Colonial Virginia*, 147.

27. Bond, *Damned Souls in a Tobacco Colony*, 185–95; Edward L. Bond and Joan R. Gundersen, "The Episcopal Church in Virginia, 1607–2007," *VMHB* 115 (2007): 174; Warren M. Billings, ed., *The Old Dominion in the Seventeenth Century: A Documentary History of Virginia, 1606–1700*, rev. ed. (Chapel Hill, N.C., 2007), maps between 83–84.

28. Hening, *Statutes at Large*, 2:58–89, esp. 58–69; Warren M. Billings, "Pleading, Procedure, and Practice: The Meaning of Due Process of Law

in Seventeenth-Century Virginia," *Journal of Southern History* 46 (1981): 569–84.
29. John Cowell, comp., *A Law Dictionary: Or the Interpreter of Words and Terms Used either in the Common or Statute Laws of Great Britain, and in Tenures and Jocular Customs* (London, 1727; originally published at Oxford in 1607), s.v. "tales."
30. Hening, *Statutes at Large*, 1:397–98, 461, 524, 2:65–66; Billings, *A Little Parliament*, 155–56.
31. "Acts of the General Assembly, Jan. 6, 1639–40," 151; Hening, *Statutes at Large*, 2:90–91.
32. Hening, *Statutes at Large*, 1:304, 463, 2:69–71, 73–74, 74.
33. Ibid., 2:78–84.
34. Cowell, *A Law Dictionary*, s.v. "clerk of the peace" and "custos rotularum."
35. Hening, *Statutes at Large*, 2:107, 106; Billings, *A Little Parliament*, 19, 72.
36. Hening, *Statutes at Large*, 2:94–103, 136–38.
37. Ibid., 2:113–19, 26, 116–17.
38. Ibid., 2:138–43, 106–25, 130–32, 133–34.
39. Ibid., 2:147. The act also gave Randolph a ten-year exclusive right to contract for and sell additional copies in Virginia.
40. The little information that exists about Cotes and Seile was assembled by Henry R. Plomer, *A Dictionary of the Booksellers and Printers Who Were at Work in England, Scotland, and Ireland from 1641 to 1667* (London, 1907), 52, 162.
41. The Privy Council ordered Berkeley back to Virginia on 2 Sept. 1662, and he received new instructions and a batch of additional papers over the course of the next three weeks before he set sail for Jamestown. See Billings, *Berkeley Papers*, 175–81; and Billings, *Berkeley and the Forging of Colonial Virginia*, 159–62.
42. The license reads "September 3[d.] 1662/ Imprimatur,/ Jo. Berkenhead" (the royal licenser of printed works). Rows of acorns enclose the wording of the title page. The title itself is a moderately long one for a law book of that time: "The/Lawes of/ Virginia/Now in Force./Collected out of the *Assembly Records*, and/Digested into one Volume./Revised and Confirmed by the *Grand Assembly/held at James-City* by Prorogation, the 2d of/*March* 1661. in the 13th Year of the Reign/of our Soveraign Lord/King Charles the II." A narrow rule separates an image of the royal crown, which is centered on the page, and below the crown, set off by another narrow rule, sit the publication data. Acts are numbered with roman numerals, their titles are in italics, and they are separated by narrow rules. Surviving copies of

The Lawes are readily available in digital versions via the Early English Books Online data base. I used a digital text from the copy that belongs to the Henry E. Huntington Library and Art Gallery (Wing/468:01).

43. Moryson, "The Epistle Dedicatory."
44. Billings, *Berkeley and the Forging of Colonial Virginia*, 142–62.
45. Billings, "Sir William Berkeley's *Discourse and View of Virginia:* A Note on Its Authorship," *Documentary Editing* 24 (2002): 33–36.
46. "An Inventory of the Goods Chattells and Merchandizes belonging to the Estate of Arthur Spicer," 8 Feb. 1701/02, Richmond County Deeds, Wills, and Inventories, 1699–1701 (Library of Virginia, Richmond), fols. 36–41; John Stuart Bryan, "Report of Committee on Library and Legal Literature," in *Report of the Tenth Annual Meeting of the Virginia State Bar Association*, ed. Eugene C. Massie (Richmond, 1898), 60–62; W. H. Bryson, "Private Law Libraries before 1776," in *Virginia Law Books: Essays and Bibliographies*, ed. W. Hamilton Bryson (Philadelphia, 2000), 489–90. Hening relied primarily on manuscripts copied in 1662 for the clerks of the Northumberland County and Charles City County courts but he also consulted John Purvis's corrupt *A Complete Collection of All the Laws of Virginia Now in Force*, William Parks's *A Collection of all the Acts of Assembly now in Force in the Colony of Virginia* (Williamsburg, 1733); and William Hunter's *The Acts of Assembly, Now in Force, in the Colony of Virginia* (Williamsburg, 1752). Comparing Hening with Moryson demonstrates a lack of a connection between them. In Hening, as noted above, there are 142 acts whereas in Moryson there are only 138. That discrepancy can be explained this way. In Hening, Acts CXL, CXLI, and CXLII related respectively to the effective date of the Revisal, a procedural matter in the General Assembly, and the order to send a transcript of the acts to London. Understandably, given their local character, Randolph may not have included them in the manuscript that he sent to Berkeley, and Seile used when she set type. Alternatively, Berkeley or Seile may have dropped them. Less certain is why Act CXXXVI was omitted. It concerned escheats, but it is absent from the Charles City manuscript too, although in a footnote Hening commented, "The subject matter of this act is improperly placed in Purvis, under chap. XVIII of this session (see *ante* page 56 and notes) and it is not given as a distinct act. In the Northumberland MS it is arranged as act (136) with the above title." See *Statutes at Large*, 2:136n. All that said, Hening suspected that a printed collection might have existed before the Purvis edition. He acknowledged his suspicion in a footnote to Act V of the General Assembly of April 1684, which referred

to two statutes in "the printed laws." "It is not probable," he wrote, "that Purvis's collection was printed at this time. Had it been the case, there certainly would have been some reference more distinct, than merely to the *printed laws*. This furnishes additional evidence that the revisal of 1661–2 was printed long before Purvis, and is the collection so often referred to, by 'the printed laws.'" See Hening, *Statutes at Large*, 3:13–14n.
47. Billings, *A Little Parliament*, 25–49.

6. THE LONG ROAD TO THE REVISAL OF 1705

1. Speech to the General Assembly, 22 June 1706, McIlwaine, *Legislative Journals of the Council*, 1:487.
2. Charles M. Andrews, *The Colonial Period in American History*, 4 vols. (New Haven, Conn., 1934–1938), 4:50–85; Stephen Saunders Webb, *The Governors-General: The English Army and the Definition of the Empire, 1569–1681* (Chapel Hill, N.C., 1979), 57–101; J. M. Sosin, *The Restoration Monarchy of Charles II: Transatlantic Politics, Commerce, and Kinship* (Lincoln, Neb., 1980), 5–91; Jack P. Greene, *Peripheries and Centers: Constitutional Development in the Extended Politics of the British Empire and the United States, 1607–1788* (Athens, Ga., 1986), 7–19.
3. Wilcomb E. Washburn, *The Governor and the Rebel: A History of Bacon's Rebellion in Virginia* (Chapel Hill, N.C., 1957); Billings, *Berkeley and the Forging of Colonial Virginia*, 136–63, 174–267; Brent Tarter, "Bacon's Rebellion, the Grievances of the People, and the Political Culture of Seventeenth-Century Virginia," *VMHB* 119 (2001): 2–41.
4. Billings, *Berkeley and the Forging of Colonial Virginia*, 131–32; Kukla, *Speakers and Clerks*, 89–94.
5. Kukla, *Speakers and Clerks*, 141–43; Emory G. Evans, "Robert Beverley (bap. 1635–1687)," *Encyclopedia Virginia*, Web, 30 Oct. 2018; Commission of the peace for Middlesex County, 16 Apr. 1669, in Billings, *Berkeley Papers*, 354–55; Hening, *Statutes at Large*, 3:541–71; McIlwaine, Hall, and Hillman, *Executive Journals of the Council*, 1:20–23, 55, 489, 490, 491, 494, 498, 499, 509.
6. Moryson died around the year 1680. Effingham to William Blathwayt, 6–24 Feb. 1685/86; Effingham to the Privy Council, 10 Feb. 1685/86; Effingham to James II, 20 Feb. 1685/86; James II to Effingham, 1 Aug. 1686, in Billings, *Effingham Papers*, 234–35, 237–42, 241–42, 263–64.
7. Billings, *Berkeley and the Forging of Colonial Virginia*, 250–51.

8. An indication of the influx of lawyers is the list of licensed attorneys in 1680, C.O. 1/46, fol. 187, PRO. Some were also native-born Virginians. See also J. Leo Lemay, "Robert Beverley's *History and Present State of Virginia* and the Emerging Political Ideology," in *American Letters and the Historical Consciousness: Essays in Honor of Lewis P. Simpson*, ed. J. Gerald Kennedy and Daniel Mark Fogel (Baton Rouge, La., 1987), 67–112; Alan McKinley Smith, "Virginia Lawyers, 1680–1776: The Birth of an American Profession" (Ph.D. diss., Johns Hopkins University, 1968); Anton-Hermann Chroust, *The Rise of the Legal Profession in America*, 2 vols. (Norman, Okla., 1965), 1:278–84.
9. Warren M. Billings, John E. Selby, and Thad W. Tate, *Colonial Virginia: A History* (White Plains, N.Y., 1986), 97–139; Emory G. Evans, *"A Topping People": The Rise and Decline of Virginia's Old Elite, 1680–1790* (Charlottesville, 2009), 5–23; Billings, *A Little Parliament*, 49–63, 115–31; John C. Rainbolt, "A New Look at Stuart 'Tyranny': The Crown's Attack on the Virginia Assembly, 1676–1689," *VMHB* 75 (1967): 387–406; Stephen Saunders Webb, "'Brave Men and Servants to His Royal Highness': The Household of James Stuart in the Evolution of English Imperialism," in *Perspectives in American History* 8 (1974): 55–83; Webb, *The Governors-General*, 3–57.
10. Lyon G. Tyler, ed., *Encyclopedia of Virginia Biography*, 5 vols. (New York, 1915), 1:49–50. Webb, *Governors-General*, 122–37; Jeffreys to Francis Moryson, 10 July 1678, C.O. 1/42, fol. 294, PRO; Sherwood to Sir Joseph Williamson, 8 Aug. 1678, ibid., fols. 304–305; Susanna Jeffreys letters in Henry Coventry Papers, 78, fols. 295, 297, 329, 331, Longleat House, Wiltshire; "Abstract of Acts made in Virginia Transmitted by Capt. Jeffries . . . ," ca. Aug. 1678, C.O. 5/1377, fols. 1–30, PRO. The captain was Jeffreys's son; Webb, *The Governors-General*, 510.
11. Warren M. Billings, "Thomas Culpeper, second baron Culpeper," *ODNB*.
12. Hartwell, Blair, and Chilton, *The Present State of Virginia and the College*, 32.
13. Billings, *Berkeley and the Forging of Virginia*, 215–19.
14. The style was broadened with the addition of the words "and by the authority thereof, and it is hereby enacted . . ." The entire clause replaced the older one because of the Privy Council's objection to its reference to the Assembly as "the grand assembly."
15. Instruction from Charles II, 27 Jan. 1681, C.O. 1/48, fol. 30, PRO. It reiterated an earlier order.

16. Additional Instructions from Charles II, 23 Dec. 1683, in Billings, *Effingham Papers*, 44.
17. Address to the House of Burgesses, 17 Apr. 1684, 251–52; exchanges between Effingham and the burgesses, Apr.–May 1684, Kennedy and McIlwaine, *Journals of the House of Burgesses, 1659/60–1693*, 206, 210, 216; the burgesses to Effingham, 27 Oct. 1685 and Effingham's reply, 3 Nov. 1685, McIlwaine, *Legislative Journals of the Council*, 78, 85; Warren M. Billings, *Virginia's Viceroy: Their Majesties' Governor General Francis Howard, Baron Howard of Effingham* (Fairfax, Va., 1991), 42–46, 60–70.
18. The burgesses to Effingham, 29 Oct. 1686 and Effingham's reply, 6 Nov. 1686, Kennedy and McIlwaine, *Journals of the House of Burgesses, 1659/60–1693*, 267, 272.
19. McIlwaine, Hall, and Hillman, *Executive Journals of the Council*, 1:87; Kennedy and McIlwaine, *Journals of the House of Burgesses, 1659/60–1693*, 201, 202, 203; to Robert Spencer, 2d earl of Sunderland, 22 Feb. 1687, in Billings, *Effingham Papers*, 279.
20. McIlwaine, Hall, and Hillman, *Executive Journals of the Council*, 1:101–102; Kennedy and McIlwaine, *Journals of the House of Burgesses, 1659/60–1693*, 302, 304, 328; Billings, *Virginia's Viceroy*, 82–99.
21. To Robert Spencer, 2d earl of Sunderland, 22 May 1688; to William Blathwayt, 23 May and 23 June 1688, in Billings, *Effingham Papers*, 379–83, 383–86, 387–88; Nicholas Spencer to Sunderland, 17 May 1688, C.O. 1/64, fols. 321–24, PRO.
22. Billings, *Virginia's Viceroy*, 97–98.
23. Bruce T. McCully, "From the North Riding to Morocco: The Early Years of Governor Francis Nicholson, 1655–1686," *WMQ*, 3d ser., 19 (1962): 534–37; Stephen Saunders Webb, "The Strange Career of Francis Nicholson," *WMQ*, 3d ser., 23 (1966): 513–49.
24. James Edward Scanlon, "Sir Edmund Andros (1637–ca. 1714)," *Encyclopedia Virginia*, Web, 2 Nov. 2018; Edith F. Carey, "Amias Andros and Sir Edmund, His Son," Guernsey Society of Natural Science and Local Research *Transactions* 7 (1913): 38–66; Stephen Saunders Webb, "The Trials of Sir Edmund Andros," in *The Human Dimensions of Nation Making: Essays on Colonial and Revolutionary America*, ed. James Kirby Martin (Madison, Wisc., 1976), 23–53; Stephen Saunders Webb, *1676: The End of American Independence* (New York, 1984), 303–04; Jeanne Gould Bloom, "Sir Edmund Andros: A Study in Seventeenth-Century Colonial Administration" (Ph.D. diss., Yale University, 1962), 159–83, 199–226.

25. Order-in-council for a general assembly, 13 Jan. 1692/93, McIlwaine, Hall, and Hillman, *Executive Journals of the Council*, 1:275; advice from the Council, 2 Mar. 1692/93, McIlwaine, Hall, and Hillman, *Executive Journals of the Council*, 1:277; the burgesses to Andros, 15 Mar. 1692/93; Andros to the burgesses, 16 Mar. 1692/93, Kennedy and McIlwaine, *Journals of the House of Burgesses, 1659/60–1693*, 425, 426; the journal did not list the other eight members by name, Kennedy and McIlwaine, *Journals of the House of Burgesses, 1659/60–1693*, 428, 433–34, 435–36, 437–39.
26. Kennedy and McIlwaine, *Journals of the House of Burgesses, 1659/60–1693*, 450, 457, 458, 459.
27. Richard Beale Davis, ed., *William Fitzhugh and His Chesapeake World, 1676–1701: The Fitzhugh Letters and Other Documents* (Chapel Hill, N.C., 1963), 1–57.
28. Kennedy and McIlwaine, *Journals of the House of Burgesses, 1659/60–1693*, 460–93; Milner to Andros, 10 Nov. 1693, ibid., 486; Andros to Milner, 10 Nov. 1693, ibid., 486–87; 495.
29. To Nicholas Haywood, 19 Dec. 1694, in Davis, *Fitzhugh and His Chesapeake World*, 321.
30. To Nicholas Haywood, 25 July 1694, ibid., 330.
31. Both copies are in the Virginia Historical Society. Neither is in Fitzhugh's hand. The Ludwell copy eventually wound up in the papers of the Lee family before Cassius F. Lee (1808–1890) gifted it to the VHS. It was printed in the *VMHB* 9 (1902): 273–88, 369–84; 10 (1902): 49–64, 145–60, 241–54. In 1903, the VHS issued it as booklet under the title *An Abridgment of the Laws of Virginia, Compiled in 1694*. The introduction mis-attributed the authorship to Ludwell solely on the basis of a Ludwell signature that appears on the manuscript. The signature is that of Philip Ludwell Jr. Ludwell Jr. could not have written the "Alphabeticall Abridgement" in 1694 because he was in England, meaning that his endorsement was added at a later date.
32. [Fitzhugh,] "An Alphabeticall Abridgment of the Laws Under certaine heads . . ."
33. Alison G. Olson, "The Board of Trade and Colonial Virginia," *Encyclopedia Virginia*, Web, 23 Nov. 2019.
34. Kennedy and McIlwaine, *Journals of the House of Burgesses, 1695–1702*, 21–22, 34, 41–42; Hening, *Statutes at Large*, 3:229–481; council minute, 8 Mar. 1697/98; council minute, 13 Apr. 1698; council minute, 1 June 1698; council minute, 7 Oct. 1698; council minutes, 21–25 Oct. 1698, McIlwaine, Hall, and Hillman, *Executive Journals of the Council*, 1:378–79,

381, 385, 390, 392–95; "The Laws of Virginia now in Force," C.O. 5/1378, fols. 1–163, PRO.

35. Warren M. Billings, John E. Selby, and Thad W. Tate, *Colonial Virginia: A History* (White Plains, N.Y., 1986), 139–86; Parke Rouse Jr., *James Blair of Virginia* (Chapel Hill, N.C., 1971), chaps. 5–6; Hartwell, Blair, and Chilton, *The Present State of Virginia*, 16–20, 25–26, 39.

36. Kennedy and McIlwaine, *Journals of the House of Burgesses, 1695–1702*, 136, 164, 176, 182, 190, 191, 195; warrant for the commission to Francis Nicholson as governor of Virginia, 26 June 1698, C.O. 324/26, 71–87, PRO; McIlwaine, *Legislative Journals of the Council*, 1:271; Hening, *Statutes at Large*, 3:181–85.

37. The Council suspended Taylor in Feb. 1697/98 after he was charged with perjury in Charles City. He was acquitted at trial, and the Council restored him to his clerkship. See McIlwaine, Hall, and Hillman, *Executive Journals of the Council*, 1:439.

38. An act directing the building the Capitall and City of Williamsburg, Hening, *Statutes at Large*, 3:197. Hening noted, "This act, together with the title, is repeated verbatim in the revisal of 1705. Chap XLII. And declared to be in force; and several clauses added for the better execution thereof—It is therefore unnecessary to print it here." The text of the clause that assigned oversight to the committee is at page 421.

39. Instructions from the Lord Justices, 13 Sept. 1698, C.O. 324/26, 103–45, PRO. They are recapitulated in the House journal entry for 2 June along with explanations for how the burgesses intended to address them. See Kennedy and McIlwaine, *Journals of the House of Burgesses, 1695–1702*, 186–88. The revisal committee's response is in their journal. See McIlwaine, *Legislative Journals of the Council*, 3:1519.

40. Pounce was a fine sand or finely ground bone powder that was used to blot ink on paper.

41. Committee journal, 7 July 1699, McIlwaine, *Legislative Journals of the Council*, 3:1518–20. The titles were Ralph de Hengham and Simon Theolall's *Registrum Brevium Tam Originalium, Quam Judicialum* (London, 1687); William Rastell's *Entries of Declarations, Bars, Replications, Rejoynders, Issues, Verdicts, Judgments, Executions, Process, Continuances, Essoyns, and Divers Other Matters* . . . (London, 1670); the anonymously authored *A Book of Entries of Declaration, Pleas, Replications, Rejoinders, Issues, Demurrers, and other Parts of Pleadings, . . . With Divers other Material Points of Clerkship, necessary to be known by the Attornies, Entring Clerks, and Sollicitors, as well in the Courts of Record at Westminster, as other inferiour Jurisdictions*

(London, 1694); and Richard Garnet's *The Book of Oaths, and the severall forms thereof, both Antient and Modern* ... (London, 1649). Several were in print as early as 1530s, and they went through various impressions thereafter. See Joseph Worrall, *Bibliotheca Legum: or, A Catalogue of the Common and Statute Law Books of this Realm* (London, 1777), 81–89.

42. E.g., committee journal, n.d., McIlwaine, *Legislative Journals of the Council,* 3:1529.
43. Committee journal, 8 July, Aug. 2–10, 4–9 Oct., 1–11 Nov. 1699, McIlwaine, *Legislative Journals of the Council,* 3:1520–27; Samuel Clyde McCulloch, ed., "James Blair's Plan of 1699 to Reform the Clergy of Virginia," *WMQ,* 3d ser., 4 (1947): 70–86.
44. Tracking developments after April 1700 is difficult owing to the loss of the committee journal thereafter.
45. Kennedy and McIlwaine, *Journals of the House of Burgesses, 1702/03–1712,* 22; An act for the more effectual and speedy carrying on the revisal of the laws, Hening, *Statutes at Large,* 3:201–02.
46. Kennedy and McIlwaine, *Journals of the House of Burgesses, 1702/03–1712,* 3–127, passim.
47. Webb, *The Governors-General,* 512. Commission and instructions from Queen Anne, 25 Apr. and 23 Apr. 1705, Crown Docquet Book, 1700–1721, 125, IND 426, PRO; and Board of Trade Correspondence, 1704–1705, 120–95, C.O. 5/1361, PRO. Scholars frequently misidentify Nott as Orkney's lieutenant governor. That distinction belonged to Alexander Spotswood. Orkney, who remained in England, became governor in 1710. See commission from Queen Anne, 19 Jan. 1710, Crown Docquet Book, 1700–1721, 199, IND 4216, PRO. The mistake seems to have originated with the nineteenth-century Virginian Charles Campbell in his *History of the Colony and Ancient Dominion of Virginia* (Philadelphia, 1860), 375–76.
48. Blair to Archbishop Thomas Tenison, 2 Sept. 1706, in William Stevens Perry, ed., *Historical Collections Relating to the American Colonial Church,* 5 vols. (Hartford, Conn., 1870), 1:183.
49. McIlwaine, Hall, and Hillman, *Executive Journals of the Council,* 3:27; Leonard, *General Assembly Register,* 62–64.
50. Thomas Daniel Knight, "Edmund Jenings (1659–1727)," *Encyclopedia Virginia,* Web, 23 Nov. 2018.
51. H. C. Maxwell Lyte, ed., *Journal of the Commissioners for Trade and Plantations from April 1704, To February 1708-9* (London, 1920), 3ff; Edmund Jenings, "Observations upon the Laws of Virginia relating to the church, courts, Revenue, liberty of the subjects, militia, seating of lands,

appointing sheriffs, electing Burgesses, Officers, and rates of money," *Calendar of State Papers, Colonial, 1704–05*, 129.

52. Kennedy and McIlwaine, *Journals of the House of Burgesses, 1702/03–1712*, 135, 137–235.

53. Revisals and other acts were dated by the day and year when a General Assembly began, not when a session ended. Even though Nott and Speaker Harrison signed the enrolled text in June 1706, it would have been dated 23 Oct. 1705. See Hening, *Statutes at Large*, 3:229.

54. Hening noted that "In the present collection, such of the acts of this session as are printed in the revisal of 1733, will be taken from the printed volume, but where the title only is given in that revisal, the act itself will be printed from MS," *Statutes at Large*, 3:229n. What Hening called "the revisal of 1733" is not a revisal but a printed up-to-date compilation of the statutes that the Williamsburg printer William Parks issued in 1733 under the title *A Collection of All the Acts of Assembly, Now in Force in the Colony of Virginia* (see chapter 7). It was Parks who began the practice of designating the acts as "chapters" and numbering their sections with uppercase roman numerals, a habit that Hening retained. The manuscript to which Hening referred belonged the second William Byrd before it passed into the possession of Judge William Nelson (ca. 1754–1813) who lent it to Hening. Now it is in the Library of Virginia. House clerk William Randolph Jr. sent the revisal to the Board of Trade in a series of stand-alone documents, each of which he certified and sealed with the great seal of the colony (C.O. 5/1385, PRO).

55. The House journal differentiated between the two. It recorded that each of the thirty-six was introduced in these words: "A Bill Prepared by the Comittee for the Revisal of the Laws Entituled a Bill . . . was Read the First Time and Comitted to a Committee of the whole house." By contrast each of the other twenty-two was presented this way: "Resolved That a Bill for . . . be prepared . . . [, and it is] Ordered that it be referred to The Committee of propositions and Greivances to prepare and bring in The Said Bill."

56. Kennedy and McIlwaine, *Journals of the House of Burgesses, 1702/03–1712*, 137; McCullough, "James Blair's Plan of 1699," 76–85; McIlwaine, *Legislative Journals of the Council*, 1:467–72.

57. Kennedy and McIlwaine, *Journals of the House of Burgesses, 1702/03–1712*, 176; McIlwaine, Hall, and Hillman, *Executive Journals of the Council*, 3:109; Queen Anne extended the act to Virginia in 1710 by royal proclamation.

58. Kennedy and McIlwaine, *Journals of the House of Burgesses, 1702/03–1712*, 142, 194, 198, 204, 229, 230, 233; McIlwaine, Hall, and Hillman, *Executive Journals of the Council*, 3:109; McIlwaine, *Legislative Journals of the Council*, 1:482, 487; R. A. Brock, ed., *The Official Letters of Alexander Spotswood, Lieutenant-Governor of the Colony of Virginia, 1710–1722*, 2 vols. (Richmond, 1882), 1:53–54.
59. An act for establishing County Courts, and for regulating and establishing procedures therein, Hening, *Statutes at Large*, 3:504–16. Robert Hunter was selected to succeed Major Nott but he never served. Consequently, Council president Edmund Jenings declined to summon the General Assembly without the queen's order, which never came owing to the French war.
60. Kennedy and McIlwaine, *Journals of the House of Burgesses, 1702/03–1712*, 221, 224, 225, 227, 228, 229; McIlwaine, *Legislative Journals of the Council*, 484, 485; An act for settling the Fees of the Secretary's, County Court Clerks, Sherifs, Coroners, and Constables; and for ascertaining the Fees of Attornies allowed in a bill of Costs, Hening, *Statutes at Large*, 4:59–74.
61. An act for the continuing of General Assemblies, in case of the death or demise of her majesty, her heirs and successors; and for making valid all acts of the governor and council, and all judgments and proceedings at law, which shall happen between the death of any king or queen of England, and the notification in this country, Hening, *Statutes at Large*, 3:355–56.
62. Ibid., 3:287–302.
63. An act for limitation of actions, and avoiding of suits, ibid., 3:381–84; An act declaring how long judgments, bonds, obligations, and accounts shall be in force, for the assignment of bonds and obligations, directing what proof shall be sufficient in such cases; and ascertaining the damage upon protested bills of exchange, ibid., 3:377–81; An act for the distribution of intestates estates, declaring widows rights to their deceased husbands estates; and for securing orphans' estates, ibid., 371–76; An act for attorneys prosecuting suits on behalf of persons out of the country to give security for the payment of such costs and damages as shall be awarded against them, ibid., 3:384.
64. An act prescribing the method of appointment of sheriffs; and for limiting the time of their continuance in office, and directing their duty therein, ibid., 3:246–50.
65. Ibid., 3:367–71.

66. An act for regulating the Elections of Burgesses; for settling their Privileges; and for ascertaining their fees, ibid., 3:236–46. Clarification came in 1736 in An Act to declare who shall have a right to vote in the election of Burgesses in the General Assembly . . . , ibid., 4:475–80.
67. Ibid., 3:250–52; An act for regulateing officers and offices, ibid., 2:354.
68. Kennedy and McIlwaine, *Journals of the House of Burgesses, 1702/03–1712*, 137–38; An act for the effectual suppression of vice, and the restraint and punishment of blasphemous, wicked, and dissolute persons; An act concerning Marriages, Hening, *Statutes at Large*, 3:358–62, 441–46.
69. An Act concerning the Granting, Seating, and Planting, and for Settling the Titles and bounds of Lands . . . , Hening, *Statutes at Large*, 3:304–32.
70. The operative clause in the Charter of 1606 reads "all lands tenements and hereditaments which shalbe within the precincts limitted for that Colonie . . . to be houlden of us, our heires and successors as of our manor of Eastgreenwich in the countie of Kente, in free and common soccage and not in capite." It was reiterated in the charter of 1609. See Samuel M. Bemiss, ed., *The Three Charters of the Virginia Company of London, with Seven Related Documents, 1606–1621* (Williamsburg, 1957), 11.
71. Susan Myra Kingsbury, ed., *Records of the Virginia Company of London*, 4 vols. (Washington, D.C., 1906–1935), 3:99–108, 314; Beverley W. Bond Jr., *The Quit-Rent System in the American Colonies* (New Haven, Conn., 1919), 25–35, 219–30.
72. Fairfax Harrison, *Virginia Land Grants: A Study of Conveyancing in Relation to Colonial Politics* (Richmond, 1925); Manning C. Voorhis, "Crown versus Council in Virginia Land Policy," *WMQ*, 3d ser., 3 (1946): 499–506.
73. Gertrude Anne Jacobsen, *William Blathwayt, a Late Seventeenth-Century English Administrator* (New Haven, Conn., 1931), 150, 355ff; Hartwell, Blair, and Chilton, *The Present State of Virginia*, 16–20; Kennedy and McIlwaine, *Journals of the House of Burgesses, 1702/03–1712*, 151, 184, 185, 187, 192, 193–94, 202, 212, 215; McIlwaine, *Legislative Journals of the Council*, 1:460, 463, 464, 472.
74. The four deed forms each contained a recitation of the clause from the Charter of 1606.
75. An act directing the duty of Surveyors of Land, and ascertaining their fees, Hening, *Statutes at Large*, 3:329–33.
76. Benjamin Watkins Leigh, comp., *The Revised Code of the Laws of Virginia: Being A Collection of All Such Acts of the General Assembly, of a Public and Permanent Nature, as are Now in Force*, 2 vols. (Richmond, 1819), 2:334–37.

77. This clause came from Act III of Dec. 1662, which is the first statutory definition of the status of illegitimate children of interracial parentage. See Hening, *Statutes at Large*, 2:170.
78. Hening, *Statutes at Large*, 2:260.
79. That provision revived a law from 1640 that was dropped from the Revisals of 1643, 1652, 1658, and 1662. See "Acts of the General Assembly, Jan. 6, 1639–40," *WMQ*, 2d ser., 4 (1924): 147.
80. Hening, *Statutes at Large*, 3:447–62.
81. Ibid., 3:448, 252, 333–34. Slave merchants and factors were exempted from the act, ibid., 3:298.
82. Ibid., 3:269–70; An act for the more speedy prosecution of slaves committing Capital Crimes, ibid., 3:301–02.
83. Lawrence J. Friedman and Arthur H. Schaffer, "The Conway Robinson Notes and Seventeenth-Century Virginia," *VMHB* 78 (1970): 259–67, esp. 262–67; Warren M. Billings, "The Law of Servants and Slaves in Seventeenth-Century Virginia," *VMHB* 99 (1991): 45–62; David Galenson, "White Servitude and the Growth of Black Slavery in Colonial America," *Journal of Economic History* 41 (1981): 39–47; Susan Westbury, "Slaves of Colonial Virginia: Where They Came From," *WMQ*, 3d ser., 42 (1985): 228–37; Mary Sarah Bilder, "The Struggle over Immigration: Indentured Servants, Slaves, and Articles of Commerce," *Missouri Law Review* 61 (1996): 745–66; Gregory E. O'Malley, "Beyond the Middle Passage: Slave Migration from the Caribbean to North America, 1619–1807," *WMQ*, 3d ser., 66 (2009): 125–39; John C. Coombs, "The Phases of Conversion: A New Chronology for the Rise of Slavery in Early Virginia," *WMQ*, 3d ser., 68 (2011): 332–60; William A. Pettigrew, "Transatlantic Politics and the Africanization of Virginia's Labor Force, 1688–1712," in *Early Modern Virginia: Reconsidering the Old Dominion*, ed. Douglas Bradburn and John C. Coombs (Charlottesville, 2011), 279–300; James Horn, *1619: Jamestown and the Forging of American Democracy* (New York, 2018), 85–119; Winthrop D. Jordan, "American Chiaroscuro: The Status and Definition of Mulattoes in the British Colonies," *WMQ*, 3d ser., 19 (1962): 183–200; Daniel Livesay, *Children of Uncertain Fortune: Mixed-Race Jamaicans in Britain and the Atlantic Family, 1733–1833* (Chapel Hill, N.C., 2018), 1–90.

7. SIR WILLIAM GOOCH'S GIFT

1. Paul David Nelson, "Sir William Gooch, first baronet (1681-1751)," *ODNB*; Edward M. Riley, "Governor William Gooch, A Faithful Trustee for the

Public Good," Colonial Williamsburg Foundation Library Research Report Series–0092 (1960?), Edward M. Riley Papers, John D. Rockefeller Library, Williamsburg; Brent Tarter, "Sir William Gooch (1681–1751)," *Encyclopedia Virginia*, Web, 17 Mar. 2019.

2. Madeleine Curcio Kaduboski, "The Administration of Lieutenant Governor Hugh Drysdale, 1722–1727" (M.A. thesis, College of William & Mary, 1969).

3. McIlwaine, Hall, and Hillman, *Executive Journals of the Council*, 4:148.

4. Byrd to Charles Boyle, 4th earl of Orrery, 5 Feb. 1727/28, in Marion Tinling, ed., *The Correspondence of The Three William Byrds of Westover Virginia, 1684–1776*, 3 vols. (Charlottesville, 1977), 1:371; commission from King George I, 23 Jan. 1726/27, C.O. 5/1365, 308–309, PRO.

5. Warren M. Billings, John E. Selby, and Thad W. Tate, *Colonial Virginia: A History* (Port Washington, N.Y., 1984), 231–85; David Alan Williams, "Political Alignments in Colonial Virginia Politics, 1690–1750" (Ph.D. diss., Northwestern University, 1959), 224–47.

6. A contemporary traveler remarked, "Lawyers have an excellent Time here, and if a Man is a clever Fellow, that Way, 'tis a sure way to an Estate," *London Magazine, or, Gentleman's Monthly Chronologer*, July 1746, 323.

7. Alan McKinley Smith, "Virginia Lawyers, 1680–1776: The Birth of An American Profession" (Ph.D. diss., Johns Hopkins University, 1967), ii–iv, 342–54; A. G. Roeber, *Faithful Magistrates and Republican Lawyers: Creators of Virginia Legal Culture, 1680–1810* (Chapel Hill, N.C., 1981), chap. 2; Anton-Hermann Chroust, *The Rise of the Legal Profession in America*, 2 vols. (Norman, Okla., 1965), 1:263–85.

8. Warren M. Billings, "'Send us . . . what other Lawe books you shall thinke fitt': Books That Shaped the Law in Virginia, 1600–1860," *VMHB* 120 (2013): 319–20; Brent Tarter, "The Library of the Council of Colonial Virginia," in *"Esteemed Bookes of Lawe" and the Legal Culture of Early Virginia*, ed. Warren M. Billings and Brent Tarter (Charlottesville, 2017), 37–57; W. Hamilton Bryson, "Law Books in the Libraries of Colonial Virginians," in *"Esteemed Bookes of Lawe,"* ed. Billings and Tarter, 27–37; and his classic *Census of Law Books in Colonial Virginia* (Charlottesville, 1978).

9. Hening, *Statutes at Large*, 4:360–62; 5:171.

10. Lawrence C. Wroth, *William Parks: Printer and Journalist of England and Colonial America* (Richmond, 1926); David Rawson, "William Parks (d. 1750)," *Encyclopedia Virginia*, Web, 29 Jan. 2019.

11. McIlwaine, *Legislative Journals of the Council*, 2:730; Kennedy and McIlwaine, *Journals of the House of Burgesses, 1727–1734*, 25.

12. An exhaustive chronological list of Parks imprints is included in Wroth, *William Parks,* 36–70. Only a single copy of the *Charge to the Grand Jury* is known to exist, and it is in the Fulham Palace Library in London. Seeking advice on composing grand jury charges Gooch probably sent it to his brother who passed it on to Edmund Gibson, bishop of London. Lawrence C. Wroth reproduced a facsimile in the 1920s that lies between the notes and the list of imprints in *Parks.* McIlwaine, *Legislative Journals of the Council,* 2:80.
13. Ibid.
14. John Ruston Pagan, "English Statutes in Virginia, 1660–1714," in *"Esteemed Bookes of Lawe,"* ed. Billings and Tarter, 59–61; Kennedy and McIlwaine, *Journals of the House of Burgesses, 1727–1734,* 141.
15. The estimate is based on a similar number that the House ordered for a printing of the Revisal of 1748.
16. Kennedy and McIlwaine, *Journals of the House of Burgesses, 1727–1734,* 141; McIlwaine, *Legislative Journals of the Council,* 2:80.
17. It is now quite rare. Witnesses are in the Library of Virginia, Swem Library and the Wolf Law Library, William & Mary Law School; the Huntington Library, Art Collections & Botanical Gardens; and the University of Virginia Law Library. It is also available in various digital formats. The Virginia State Bar underwrote the publication of a facsimile that was issued in 1976 by Gateway Press of Baltimore, which is the source used here.
18. Parks printed the book on leaves of off-white paper that measure 12 by 8 inches and set it in an imported Dutch pica font. He bound it in unadorned calfskin, but the text is generously graced with a variety of decorative embellishments. Book publishing depended on a printer raising the necessary capital by rounding up subscribers who received a copy of the book in return for their investment.
19. Parks, *A Collection of All the Acts of Assembly,* 112, 242, 258, 360, 361.
20. Ibid., 511–622.
21. Bennie Brown, "John Mercer: Merchant, Lawyer, Author, Book Collector" and Warren M. Billings, "A Virginia Original: George Webb's *Office and Authority of a Justice of Peace,*" in *"Esteemed Bookes of Lawe,"* ed. Billings and Tarter, 95–113, 157–79.
22. Billings, Selby, and Tate, *Colonial Virginia: A History,* 204–15.
23. "Common Sense," *Virginia Gazette,* 10 Oct. 1745 (Parks), 1, Digital Library, John D. Rockefeller Library, Colonial Williamsburg.
24. Gooch to the Board of Trade, 4 July 1746, C.O. 5/1326, fol. 200–02, PRO.

25. Kennedy and McIlwaine, *Journals of the House of Burgesses, 1742–1747,* xxii–xxvi, 153–55.
26. Ibid., 202–19; Hening, *Statutes at Large,* 4:321–24.
27. Kennedy and McIlwaine, *Journals of the House of Burgesses, 1742–1747,* 217, 267; McIlwaine, *Legislative Journals of the Council,* 2:983.
28. Gooch to the Board of Trade, 4 July 1746, C.O. 5/1326, fol. 200–202, PRO; Hening, *Statutes at Large,* 3:180–84.
29. Kennedy and McIlwaine, *Journals of the House of Burgesses, 1748–1749,* 354.
30. Benjamin Waller's grandson Littleton Waller Tazewell claimed in 1823 that Waller did most of the work. See Tazewell, "A Sketch of his own family," Tazewell Family Papers, Series 3, Library of Virginia. No doubt Waller worked with Webb, but he figured more prominently in 1752 when the General Assembly was debating a response to the Crown's voiding a number of acts in the Revisal. At that point Webb no longer had any connection with the Revisal or the Assembly.
31. Kennedy and McIlwaine, *Journals of the House of Burgesses, 1748–1749,* 257.
32. Ibid., 267
33. Ibid., 277–81.
34. Ibid., 282, 287, 289, 290, 297, 300, 301, 303, 304, 305, 311, 327–29.
35. Hening, *Statutes at Large,* 6:13, 60, 62, 64–69, 69–71, 210–12, 214–15.
36. Ibid., 5:408–32, 6:36–41, 118–21, 133–35, 121–24.
37. Ibid., 3:247–71, 6:154–93, 51–54, 146–52; Stacy L. Lorenz, "'To Do Justice to His Majesty, the Merchant, and the Planter': Governor William Gooch and the Virginia Tobacco Inspection Act of 1730," *VMHB* 108 (2000): 345–92.
38. Hening, *Statutes at Large,* 6:91–94.
39. Ibid., 3:288–303, 5:467–89, 3:504–16, 5:489–509, 4:182–97, 327.
40. Ibid., 6:201–10.
41. Ibid., 4:32–27, 5:541–47, 523–25, 4:327; Hugh F. Rankin, "Criminal Trial Proceedings in the General Court of Colonial Virginia," *VMHB* 72 (1954): 50–74.
42. A custom that originated in medieval English legal procedure, benefit of clergy was devised to shield clerks in religious orders and ecclesiastical jurisdictions from secular interference. In time it allowed any convict to escape capital punishment who could read or recite the so-called "neck verse," Psalm 51:1. See Jeffrey K. Sawyer, "'Benefit of Clergy' in Maryland and Virginia," *American Journal of Legal History* 34 (1990): 49–68, esp. 62–63.

43. Hening, *Statutes at Large*, 3:269–70, 6:104–12, 4:126–34, 323–27.
44. Ibid, 3:447–62, 4:222–28, 5:547–58, 3:333–35, 5:432–44.
45. Ibid., 6:140–43.
46. Ibid., 2:146, 6:131–33.
47. Kennedy and McIlwaine, *Journals of the House of Burgesses, 1748–1749*, 255–406.
48. Ibid., 406.
49. Gooch received £300 from the Council to cover the cost of his passage on 12 July. The date of his departure fell within day or two of Thomas Lee's formal assumption of the Council's presidency on 4 Sept. See McIlwaine, Hall, and Hillman, *Executive Journals of the Council*, 5:295, 300. Thomas Lee sent two copies to London on 6 Nov, one to the Board of Trade, the other for the duke of Bedford, C.O. 5/1327, 64–66, PRO; Lee to Bedford, 6 Nov. 1749, C.O. 5/389, 132–33, PRO. There is a notation on the back of Lee's letter to the Board of Trade "Letter from Colo. Lee, Presid.^{t} of Council & Commander in Chief of Virginia, to the Board, dated at Williamsburg, the 6th of Nov.^{br} 1749, transmitting a Box of Papers, vizt Minutes of Council, Journals of Assembly & Laws passed there between Dec.^{br} 1748, & May 1749." The Board of Trade copy is in C.O. 5/1394, fols. 1–171, PRO.
50. The commentary is endorsed "Delivered by Governor Gooch," C.O. 5/1327, fol. 77, PRO.
51. A. E. Stamp, ed., *Journal of the Commissioners for Trade and Plantations from January 1749–1750 to December 1753* (London, 1932), 67.
52. Roger Turner, "Sir Matthew Lamb (1705?–1768)," *ODNB*.
53. W. A. Speck, "George Montagu Dunk, second earl of Halifax," *ODNB*; Andrew D. M. Beaumont, *Colonial America and the Earl of Halifax, 1748–1761* (Oxford, 2005).
54. Stamp, *Journal of the Commissioners*, 195–202.
55. James Munro and Almeric W. Fitzroy, eds., *Acts of the Privy Council of England. Colonial Series*, vol. 4, (1745–1766) (London, 1911), 131–38; Kennedy and McIlwaine, *Journals of the House of Burgesses, 1752–1755*, 78; "A Proclamation Repealing Certain Acts of Assembly Passed at the Revisal of 1748," 8 Apr. 1752, Hening, *Statutes at Large*, 5:567–68; *Virginia Gazette*, 24 Apr. 1752 (Hunter), 10, 17; Gwenda Morgan, "'Privilege of Making Laws': The Board of Trade, the Virginia Assembly, and Legislative Review, 1748–1754," *Journal of American Studies* 10 (1976): 1–15.
56. After William Parks died in April 1750, his shop foreman William Hunter (d. 1761) took over the printing business, and it was he who completed the

contract for a printed book of the revisal that Parks had undertaken with the General Assembly in 1749.
57. Munro and Fitzroy, *Acts of the Privy Council*, 138–41; Morgan, "'The Privilege of Making Laws,'" 8–10.
58. The committee consisted of burgesses Richard Bland, Charles Carter, Landon Carter, Peyton Randolph, Benjamin Waller, and Beverley Whiting, and councillors John Blair, Thomas Nelson, and William Nelson.
59. Kennedy and McIlwaine, *Journals of the House of Burgesses, 1752–1758*, 78; McIlwaine, *Legislative Journals of the Council*, 2:1075; Brent Tarter, "Richard Bland (1710–1776)," *Encyclopedia Virginia*, Web, 18 Apr. 2019; Hening, *Statutes at Large*, 5:432–43.

8. ENDINGS

1. Sir Edward Coke remarked on the plural nature of English law, and he classified the variety of its species. See Coke, *The First Part of the Institutes of the Laws of England, Or, A Commentary upon Littleton, not the name of the Author, but of the Law it self* (London, 1664), fols. 11b, 114b.
2. Abstract of Instructions from Charles I to Sir Francis Wyatt, 11 Jan. 1638/39, *VMHB* 11 (1903): 54. A full text is replicated in Instructions from Charles I to Sir William Berkeley, 10 Aug. 1641, in Billings, *Berkeley Papers*, 29.
3. "The Declaration against the Company," June 1642, in Billings, *Berkeley Papers*, 46.
4. Acts of Assembly, 5 Apr. 1647, in Billings, *Berkeley Papers*, 75–77; letters patent to Sir Thomas Gates and others, 10 Apr. 1606, in Philip L. Barbour, ed., *The Jamestown Voyages under the First Charter, 1606–1609*, 2 vols. (Cambridge, 1969), 1:31–32. See also Jack P. Greene, "Law and the Origins of the American Revolution," in *The Cambridge History of Law in America*, ed. Michael Grossberg and Christopher Tomlins, 3 vols. (Cambridge, 2008), 1:447–53.
5. George Webb, *The Office and Authority of a Justice of Peace* (Williamsburg, 1736), 18, 115, 324; Daniel J. Hulsebosch, "English Liberties outside England: Floors, Doors, Windows, and Ceilings in the Legal Architecture of Empire," in *The Oxford Handbook of Literature and Law*, ed. Lorna Hutson (Oxford, 2017), 747–73.
6. Erwin C. Surrency, "Revision of Colonial Laws," *American Journal of Legal History* 9 (1965): 189–202; Joseph H. Smith, "The Foundations of Law in Maryland, 1634–1715," in *Selected Essays in Law and Authority in Colonial*

America, ed. George Athan Billias (Barre, Mass., 1965), 92–116; Barbara Shapiro, "Law Reform in Seventeenth Century England," *American Journal of Legal History* 19 (1975): 280–312; G. B. Warden, "Law Reform in England and New England, 1620 to 1660," *WMQ*, 3d ser., 35 (1978): 668–90; Scott D. Gerber, "Law and Catholicism in Colonial Maryland," *Catholic Historical Review* 103 (2017): 465–90; Scott D. Gerber, "Law and Religion in Colonial Connecticut," *American Journal of Legal History* 55 (2015): 149–93; Robert Gerard Smith, "Toward a System of Law: Law Revision and Codification in Colonial America" (Ph.D. diss., Cornell University, 1977); Mary Sarah Bilder, *The Transatlantic Constitution: Colonial Legal Culture and the Empire* (Cambridge, Mass., 2004); Mary Sarah Bilder, "Charter Constitutionalism: The Myth of Edward Coke and the Virginia Charter," *North Carolina Law Review* 94 (2016): 1545–98.

❦ BIBLIOGRAPHIC ESSAY ❦

Of all the statutes that have come to light since William Waller Hening published *The Statutes at Large,* the largest accumulations are these: Waverly K. Winfree, comp., *The Laws of Virginia, Being a Supplement to Hening's Statutes at Large, 1700–1750* (Richmond, 1971); Warren M. Billings, ed., "Some Acts Not in Hening's *Statutes:* The Acts of Assembly, April 1652, November 1652, and July 1653," *VMHB* 83 (1975): 22–77; and Jon Kukla, ed., "Some Acts Not in Hening's *Statutes:* The Acts of Assembly, October 1660," *VMHB* 83 (1975): 77–98. Smaller collections include "Acts of the General Assembly, January 6, 1639/40," *WMQ,* 2d ser., 4 (1924): 16–35, 145–62; Jon Kukla, ed., "Nine Acts of the Grand Assembly of Virginia, 1641" (typescript, Library of Virginia, Richmond); and "The General Assembly of 1641–42: A List of Members and Some of the Acts," *VMHB* 9 (1901): 50–59.

The Virginia Colonial Records Project (VCRP) consists of 963 reels of microfilmed manuscripts that relate to Virginia in the period between 1607 and 1783. Those films reproduce duplicate texts of lost Virginia items that are housed mainly in the British Library, the National Archives of the United Kingdom, and other British depositories. Record groups range from public documents to private papers. A searchable digital guide to the collection is available on the Library of Virginia website.

At the Library of Virginia is a record group denominated "Virginia Colonial Records, 1652–1775," which is a collection of remnants salvaged from the 1865 fire. Individual items are mainly petitions, judgments, or other showings that attached to suit files from the General Court. The documents have been microfilmed, and Reel #1 has a calendar that serves as a definitive guide to the collection.

County court records contain miscellaneous legislative papers, correspondence, fugitive statutes, orders-in-council, General Court judgments, and similar items. Records for seven counties no longer exist. Others span the seventeenth and eighteenth centuries in more or less unbroken series, beginning with the year when each of the counties came into existence. Still others go from a few fragmentary files to runs that cover years or even decades. Microfilm copies are housed at the Library of Virginia. For further details, consult Morgan P. Robinson, "Virginia Counties: Those Resulting from Virginia Legislation," *Bulletin of the Virginia State Library* 9 (1916) and Library of Virginia Research Notes Number 6, which is available on line.

Series 8 of the Thomas Jefferson Papers, 1606–1827, at the Library of Congress includes papers relative to the General Assembly, the General Court, and the governors general that Jefferson assembled over the course of a lifetime. Digital copies are accessible via the Library of Congress website.

A portion of William Blathwayt's papers housed at the John D. Rockefeller Library in Williamsburg contains exchanges between Blathwayt and Virginia officials from the 1660s to the end of the seventeenth century.

Henry and William Coventry held high places at the court of King Charles II after the Restoration, and they accumulated a mammoth quantity of manuscripts. Their collection now belongs to their descendant, the incumbent Marquess of Bath, and it resides in the library of his great seat, Longleat House, which lies near Warminster in Wiltshire. Volumes 76–78 of the Coventry Papers incorporate many items that relate to Virginia, especially in the time of Bacon's Rebellion, but volumes 2, 3, and 12 are useful as well. The entire collection is available on microfilm that may be borrowed from the Library of Congress. Lester K. Born, comp., *British Manuscripts Project: A Checklist of the Microfilms Prepared in England and Wales for the American Council of Learned Societies, 1941–1945* (Washington, D.C., 1955), provides a complete list of reels and short descriptions of their contents.

The Ferrar family papers, which are in the library at Magdalene College, Cambridge, bear mainly on the period when the Virginia Company of London controlled the colony. Portions of the collection were microfilmed for the VCRP, but it is filmed in its entirety in David Ransome, ed., *The Ferrar Papers 1590–1790 in Magdalene College Cambridge* (East Ardsley, Wakefield, West Yorkshire, 1992). Ransome did a most helpful introduction and finding aid, both of which appear on Reel #1.

Samuel Hartlib (1600–1662) maintained a broad circle of international correspondents in his mature years, and his surviving papers amount to some twenty-five thousand manuscripts that are housed at the University of Sheffield. An online digital version is available from that university. Hartlib maintained close ties to Parliament during the Interregnum through Benjamin Worsley (1618–1677), the surveyor-general for Ireland under Cromwell. Consequently, the Worsley correspondence file contains especially pertinent insight into the parliamentary takeover of Virginia in 1652.

The Conway Robinson Papers at the Virginia Historical Society (a.k.a. the Virginia Museum of History and Culture) in Richmond proved highly useful. When Robinson inventoried the provincial archives in the 1820s, he took copious notes, and in more than a few instances, he also made verbatim transcripts of individual documents that later burned in 1865. Significant portions of his compilations appeared in early issues of the *VMHB,* and some are in McIlwaine, ed., *Minutes of the Council,* but the file "Notes and Excerpts from the Records of Colonial Virginia" includes items that never made it into print or into the historical literature.

Various sections of the Lee Family Papers, also at the Virginia Historical Society, include pertinent records relating to the Lees, Ludwells, Carters, Byrds, and Fitzhughs, among others, as well as items from the General Assembly, the General Court, and certain governors general.

Susan Myra Kingsbury, ed., *The Records of the Virginia Company of London* (Washington, D.C., 1904–1936) documents the company years. William J. Van Schreeven and George H. Reese, eds., *Proceedings of the General Assembly of Virginia, July 30–August 4, 1619, Written & Sent from Virginia to England by Mr. John Pory Speaker of the First Representative Assembly in the New World* (Jamestown, 1969) is the best printed rendition of that important document, the original of which is in the British National Archives.

Henry Read McIlwaine was chiefly responsible for gathering up and publishing the majority of the extant legislative and higher judicial records. Those renditions appear in his *Journals of the House of Burgesses of Colonial Virginia, 1619–1776* (Richmond, 1905–1915); *Legislative Journals of the Council of Colonial Virginia* (Richmond, 1918–1919); *Executive Journals of the Council of Colonial Virginia, 1680–1776* (Richmond, 1925–1945); and *Minutes of the Council and General Court of Colonial Virginia* (Richmond, 1924). Despite an occasional misapprehension of the nature or purpose of what he printed, McIlwaine was a scrupulous scholar; consequently, his editions retain the usefulness he intended for them. Equally noteworthy, his work testifies to the persistence of a dedicated historian who labored under conditions and financial constraints unknown today.

As for papers of the seventeenth-century governors general, only those of Sir William Berkeley; Thomas Culpeper, 2d baron Culpeper of Thoresway; Francis Howard, 5th baron Howard of Effingham; and Francis Nicholson exist in sufficient quantity to have merited scholarly editions. I edited the Berkeley and Effingham papers, which the Library of Virginia published in 2007 and 1989, respectively. The Culpeper and Nicholson papers await their editors. Robert A. Brock, ed., *The Official Letters of Alexander Spotswood*, 2 vols. (Richmond, 1882–1885); Robert A. Brock, ed., *The Official Records of Robert Dinwiddie, Lieutenant Governor of the Colony of Virginia, 1751–1758* (Richmond, 1883); and George Reese, ed., *The Official Papers of Francis Fauquier, Lieutenant Governor of Virginia, 1758–1768*, 3 vols. (Charlottesville, 1980–1983) are the only printed collections of eighteenth-century lieutenant governors.

Richard Beale Davis, ed., *William Fitzhugh and His Chesapeake World, 1676–1701: The Fitzhugh Letters and Other Documents* (Chapel Hill, N.C., 1963) and Marion Tingling, ed., *The Correspondence of the Three William Byrds of Westover, Virginia, 1684–1776* (Charlottesville, 1977) provide glimpses into the political activities of Fitzhugh and William Byrd (1652–1704) who loomed prominently in the activities of the General Assembly.

Not to be overlooked are books about English law that circulated in the colony, which are discussed in Warren M. Billings, "'Send us . . . what other Lawe books you shall thinke fitt': Books That Shaped the Law in Virginia, 1600–1860," *VMHB* 120 (2013): 319–20 and Warren M. Billings and Brent Tarter, *"Esteemed Bookes of Lawe" and the Legal Culture of Early Virginia* (Charlottesville, 2017).

Books, articles, dissertations, theses, and other secondary literature are identified throughout the endnotes and need not be rehearsed here.

INDEX

Page numbers with an "n" appended indicate a page number in the notes section. Titles of authored works are located under the author's name. Women are listed under their maiden names.

Acts of 1623/24, 8–16, 21, 30
Acts of Assembly, Now in Force, in the Colony of Virginia, The (1752), 115, 137n46
Africans, free, 95
African slaves. *See* slaves and slavery
agriculture, in Acts and Revisals, 14, 21, 42, 51. *See also* tobacco
Allerton, Isaac, 74
American Revolution, 117
Andros, Sir Edward, 75, 80–85
Anglican Church. *See* religion and the church
Anglo-Powhatan Treaty (1646), 38, 44, 50
Anglo-Powhatan War (1622–32), 7, 10, 13
Anglo-Powhatan War (1644–46), 24, 37–38, 67
Anne (queen of England), 88, 89, 97
Arlington, Henry Bennett, 1st earl of, 76
Armistead, Anthony, 86, 88
Armistead, John, 74
artificers, statute of, 21, 23
attorneys. *See* law and lawyers

Bacon, Nathaniel (1620–92), 56, 74, 77, 134n4
Bacon, Nathaniel (1647–76), and Bacon's Rebellion, 71, 72, 74, 76, 134n4

Basse, Nathaniel, 10
beginnings of Virginia statutes, 1–16; Acts of 1623/24, 8–16, 21, 30; downfall of Virginia Company and proclamation of Virginia as royal dominion, xv, 1, 7–8; initial meeting of General Assembly (1619), 1, 2–6; Jamestown, early attempts to develop and manage, 1–2; Wyatt's administration and, 7; Yeardley's administration and, 6–7
benefit of clergy, 112, 150n42
Bennett, Henry, 1st earl of Arlington, 76
Bennett, Richard, 40, 41, 42, 43, 46
Berkeley, John, 2d baron Berkeley of Stratton, 72–73
Berkeley, Sir William: background, education, and early career, 26; Bacon's Rebellion and, 71; chosen as governor by General Assembly (1659/60), 53–54; Civil War and removal as governor, 38, 39–40; *A Discourse and View of Virginia*, 68; in England as agent for Virginia, 57–58, 62, 68, 71, 136n41; General Assembly as "little Parliament" and, 118, 119; Indian policy devised by, 24, 37–38, 67; Moryson's *Lawes of Virginia* (1662) and, 67–69, 136–37n42, 137–38n46; papers of,

Berkeley, Sir William (*continued*) 158; relations with Virginia statesmen after 1643, 72–74, 76; republican-era governors compared, 46; Revisal of 1643 and, xvi, 26–32, 34–37, 119; Revisal of 1662 and, xvi, 55–60, 62–63, 66–69; royal instructions shared with Council of State by, 29, 129n11; royal view of, 75; as urban developer, 51, 68; wife of, 10, 73, 77

Beverley, Peter, 49, 86, 87, 88, 89, 133n33

Beverley, Robert (1635–87), 72, 73–74, 75–76, 78

Beverley, Robert (1673–1722), 86, 89

Beverley, William, 108

bicameral entity, General Assembly as, xvi, 30, 36–37, 45

Bishops' Wars (against Scotland, 1639 and 1640), 26

Blackstone, William, *Commentaries on the Laws of England* (1773), 132n13, 134n42

Blair, Archibald, 104, 108

Blair, James, 85–92, 95–97, 108, 123n5

Blair, John, 108

Bland, Richard, 116, 152n58

Bland, Theodoric, 53–54, 56

blasphemy/swearing, prohibition of, 15, 95, 146n68

Blathwayt, William, 77, 79, 80, 96, 156

Blenheim, battle of, 101

Board of Trade, London: equivalency between General Assembly and Parliament not accepted by, 119; Revisal of 1705 and, 84, 85, 89–92, 96, 144n54; Revisal of 1748 and, xvii, 101–2, 103, 107, 111, 114–17, 118

Bolton, Francis, 20

bonded labor. *See* indentured servants; slaves and slavery

Book of Common Prayer, 63

Book of Entries of Declaration . . . , A (1694), 142–43n41

branding, 34, 67, 113

Brewster, Thomas, 49

British Civil War, 27, 38, 59, 75, 129n9

British Parliament: Acts of 1623/24 and, 12; commercial policy of, 44, 46; first General Assembly proceedings compared to, 5; General Assembly as "little Parliament" resembling, xvi, 1, 8, 24–25, 27, 29, 36, 69, 118–19; Pory's legislative experience with, 3, 5–6; republican governance of Virginia and, 44–45; restoration of Charles II and, 56; Revisal of 1632 borrowing from legislation of, 21–22

Buck, Richard, 4, 5

Buckner, William, 86

Butler, Nathaniel, 11

Byrd, William, 74, 84–85, 102, 144n54, 158

Campbell, Charles, 143n47

Carter, Charles, 152n58

Carter, John, 47

Carter, Landon, 152n58

Cary, Lucius, 2d viscount Falkland, 59

Cary, Miles, 56, 86, 89

Catholic recusants, 35, 131n42

Charles I (king of England): beginnings of Virginia statutes and, 1, 4, 8; British Civil War and, 27, 38, 59, 75, 129n9; "Declaration against the Company" and, 119, 129n9; execution of, xvi, 39, 63; General Assembly and, 1, 8, 27, 118; Revisal of 1632 and, 17, 18; Revisal of 1643 and, 26, 27, 31, 32, 35, 38, 129n9; royal dominion, proclamation of Virginia as (1625), xv, 1, 8, 18, 118

Charles II (king of England): printing press in Virginia, prohibition of, 104; Revisal of 1705, events leading up to, 70–72, 75–78; Revisals of 1652/1658 and, 39–40, 53, 54; Revisals of 1662 and, 56–58, 63, 67, 68

Chiles, Walter, 46

Chilton, Edward, 96, 97

Churchill, John, 1st duke of Marlborough, 101

Church of England. *See* religion and the church

civil procedure, rules of, 94, 111
Civil War, British, 27, 38, 59, 75, 129n9
Claiborne, William: Acts of 1623/24 and, 14; republican government in Virginia and Revisals of 1652/58, 40, 41, 42, 43, 46, 48; Revisal of 1632 and, 18, 19, 20; Revisal of 1643 and, 27, 28, 29, 37, 129n4
Clayton, John, 104
clerks and clerkship, 66, 92–93
Coke, Sir Edward, 152n1
Collection of All the Acts of Assembly, Now in Force in the Colony of Virginia, A (1733), 104, 105–7, 108, 110, 137n46, 144n54
College of William & Mary, 82, 85, 86, 87, 94, 108, 111, 123n5
colonial Virginia. *See* Virginia
common law in colonial Virginia, 2, 12, 87, 106, 118
Compton, Henry, 87, 95
Corker, John, 31, 41
corn, as term, 126n31
Cotes, Anna, 67
Council of State, London, 39, 52
Council of State, Virginia: beginnings of Virginia statutes and Acts of 1623/24, 2, 9, 10; Berkeley, Sir William, and Revisal of 1643, 27–28, 30–31, 34, 129n11; *Collection of Acts* (1733) project approved by, 104; death of monarch, effects of, 93; election of Berkeley as governor (1659/60) and, 54; as General Court, 93; Harvey, Sir John, and Revisal of 1632, 18, 19; House of Burgesses regulating powers of, 52–53; Revisals of 1652/1658 and, 48, 52; Revisal of 1662 and, 58, 59, 61, 62; Revisal of 1705 and prior events, 72, 73, 74, 78, 79–81, 83, 84, 85, 93, 142n37; Revisal of 1748 and, 108, 110; ruling by proclamation, 72
county magistrates, designations for, 130n21
courts. *See* judicial and court statutes
Coventry, Henry, 76, 156

Coventry, Sir Thomas, 7
Coventry, William, 156
Cowell, John, *A Law Dictionary* (1607/1727), 130–31n30
criminal statutes. *See* public order/criminal law
Cromwell, Oliver, 39–40, 47, 52, 157
Cromwell, Richard, 52
Culpeper, Frances (later Stephens, later Berkeley, later Ludwell), 10, 73, 77
Culpeper, Thomas, 2d baron Culpeper of Thoresway, 75, 76–77, 78, 158
Curtis, Edmond, 43

Dade, Francis (John Smith), 47
Dalton, Michael, *Countrey Justice*, 113
Dawson, William, 123n5
"Declaration against the Company," 28, 119, 129n9
De La Warr, Thomas West, 12th baron, 10
Digges, Edward, 46
Dinwiddie, Robert, 115
drunkenness/public intoxication, statutes on, 15, 21–22, 23, 43, 95
Drysdale, Hugh, 102
Duke, Henry, 86, 89
Dunck, George Montagu, 2d earl of Halifax, 115, 117, 119
Dutch, trade with, 34, 40, 44, 46, 57, 71

ecclesiastical governance. *See* religion and the church
economic/trade statutes: in Acts of 1623/24, 14; republican government in Britain and, 39; in Revisal of 1632, 21; in Revisal of 1643, 34–35; in Revisal of 1652, 42, 44; in Revisal of 1662, 67; in Revisal of 1748, 111
education: College of William & Mary, 82, 85, 86, 87, 94, 108, 111, 123n5; Revisal of 1662, provisions for Virginia college in, 63
Effingham, Charles Howard, 3d earl of Nottingham and 4th baron Howard of, 77

162 INDEX

Effingham, Francis Howard, 5th baron Howard of (governor), 73–74, 75, 77–80, 82, 86, 158
Ellyson, Robert, 56
Elyot, Sir Thomas, *The Boke named the Governour* (1531), 124n11
English, as vocabulary of Virginia law, 12
engrossers and forestallers, 21–22, 23

Falkland, Lucius Cary, 2d viscount, 59
farming, in Acts and Revisals, 14, 21, 42, 51. *See also* tobacco
Ferrar family papers, 156
First Anglo-Dutch War, 46
Fitzhugh, William, 74, 82–84, 100, 158; digest or abridgement manuscript of, 83–84, 141n31
Flowerdew, Temperance (later Yeardley), 4
food shortages and famine, 8, 14, 18, 21
Foreign Plantations, Committee/Council for, 57–58, 62, 68, 76
forestallers and engrossers, 21–22, 23
Fortress Louisburg, 108
Fowler, Bartholomew, 86–87, 88

Games, Alison, 3
Garnett, Richard, *Book of Oaths* (1649), 93
Gates, Sir Thomas, 3, 13
General Assembly: Acts of 1623/24 and, 8–16; as bicameral entity, xvi, 30, 36–37, 45; burgesses, as title for representatives in, 2; *Collection of Acts* (1733) project approved by, 104; consent required for any English law concerning Virginia, statute on, 119; death of monarch, effects of, 93; diminished by Revisal of 1705, 70, 71–72, 99–100, 139n14; election writ for 1623/24, 124–25n15; governor's and council's powers, legislation affecting, 50, 52–54; increasing number of representatives in, 127n9; initial meeting (1619), 1, 2–6; legislation added 1625–29 by, 18–19; legislation regarding burgesses of, 15, 33, 44, 50, 66, 94–95; as "little Parliament," xvi, 1, 8, 24–25, 27, 29, 36, 69, 118–19; modern list of burgesses serving in, 125n21; orders to convene, 2, 8; petition to crown over Smythe-Warwick faction, 11; proclamation of Virginia as royal dominion affecting, 8; prorogation and recall of, 28; qualifications for representatives in, 2, 5, 50, 95; under republican government, 39–41, 44–45; as unicameral entity until 1643, 5, 27. *See also specific Revisals*
General Court, 7, 62–65, 73, 87, 93, 94, 103–5, 112, 113, 116
George II (king of England), 102, 107–8, 116
Gibson, Edmund, 148n12
Glorious Revolution, 81
Gooch, Thomas, 101, 102
Gooch, Sir William, xvii, 100, 101–5, 107–11, 113–14, 117, 151n49; *Charge to the Grand Jury . . .* (1730), 104–5, 148n12
governors: lieutenant governor, problem of not having, 53; papers of, 158; political factions leading up to Revisal of 1705 and, 72–81, 89; Revisals of 1652/58 affecting powers of, 50, 52–54. *See also specific governors by name*
grand juries, 52, 65, 94, 104–5, 149n12
Great Charter, 2, 5–6, 8, 122–23n6

habeas corpus, 92
Hakluyt, Richard, the Younger, 3
Halifax, George Montagu Dunck, 2d earl of, 115, 117, 119
Ham, Jerome, 47
Hamilton, George, 1st earl of Orkney, 89, 101, 143n47
Hamor, Richard, 9
Harrison, Benjamin (1645–1712), 86, 87, 88, 89, 92
Harrison, Benjamin (1673–1710), 86, 87, 88

Harrison, Nathaniel, 89
Hartlib, Samuel, 157
Hartwell, Henry, 74, 96, 97
Harvey, Sir John, xv, 9, 10, 17–20, 22, 27–28, 65
Haywood, Nicholas, 83
headright system, 96–97
Hengham, Ralph de, and Simon Theolall, *Registrum Brevium* . . . (1687), 142n41
Hening, William Waller, *Statutes at Large* (1809), iv, xiv–xv, 41, 48, 69, 125–26nn24–25, 130nn18–19, 137–38n46, 142n38, 144n54
Hill, Edward, 85, 86, 88, 93
Holloway, Sir John, 104
Horsemanden, Wareham, 47
House of Burgesses: bicameral General Assembly, introduction of, xvi, 30; *Collection of Acts* (1733) project approved by, 104; conflation with General Assembly, 5; governor's and council's powers, regulation of, 50, 52–53; under republican government, 40, 45, 47–48; restoration of crown and diminished authority of, 72; Revisal of 1652 and, xvi
Howard, Sir Charles (d.1673), 77
Howard, Charles (d.1681), 3d earl of Nottingham and 4th baron Howard of Effingham, 77
Howard, Francis, 5th baron Howard of Effingham (governor), 73–74, 75, 77–80, 82, 86, 158
Howard, Henry, 6th duke of Norfolk, 77
Hunter, Robert, 145n59
Hunter, William, 115, 137n46, 151–52n56

immigration law and policy, 19, 35, 51, 74, 96, 103, 118
indentured servants: Revisal of 1632 not addressing, 23; Revisal of 1643 on, 33–34; Revisal of 1658 on, 50–51; Revisal of 1662 on, 67, 68; Revisal of 1705 on, 97; as runaways, 34, 67, 98
Indian relations: Anglo-Powhatan Treaty (1646), 38, 44, 50; Anglo-Powhatan War (1622–32), 7, 10, 13, 50; Anglo-Powhatan War (1644–46), 24, 37–38, 50, 67; beginnings of Virginia statutes and, 1, 3, 6–10, 13, 14–15; burgesses, Indians barred from serving as, 95; King William's War, 84; Queen Anne's War, 88; Revisal of 1632 and, 18, 21, 23, 24; Revisal of 1643 and, 27, 37–38; Revisal of 1652 and, 43; Revisal of 1658 and, 50; Revisal of 1662 and, 61; Revisal of 1705 and, 88, 95; witnesses, Indians barred from serving as, 112
interstitium, 61, 135n16

Jacobite Rising of 1715, 101
Jacobite Rising of 1745, 107
James I (king of England), 4, 7–8, 11, 17, 96
James II (king of England; formerly duke of York), 71, 73–74, 75, 77, 80, 81
Jamestown: Berkeley's urban development plans for, 51, 68; Church, General Assembly meetings in, 2–3, 4, 6, 20; early attempts to develop and manage, 1–2
Jefferson, Thomas, 48, 125–26n24, 130n19, 156
Jeffreys, Herbert, 73, 75–76, 78
Jenings, Edmund, 85, 90, 143–44n51, 145n59
Jenkins' Ear, War of, 107
Johnson, Robert, 11
Journal of Southern History, xiii
judicial and court statutes: in Acts of 1623/24, 15; church court, rejection of proposal for, 91–92; grand juries, 52, 65, 94, 104–5, 149n12; habeas corpus, 92; republican government, colonies under, 41; in Revisal of 1632, 22, 23, 24, 43; in Revisal of 1643, 32–33; in Revisal of 1652, 42–44; in Revisal of 1658, 50; in Revisal of 1662, 63–66; in Revisal of 1705, 91–94; in Revisal of 1748, 111–13; substitution of county courts for monthly courts, 24, 27
jury trials, 32, 64, 65, 94, 112

Kemp, Matthew, 74
Kemp, Richard, 28, 30, 129n4
Kent Island, 37
Kingsbury, Susan Myra, 157
King William's War, 84

Lamb, Matthew, 115
land. *See* property and land
law and lawyers: English, as vocabulary of Virginia law, 12; law libraries, 31, 49, 62, 87, 103, 105, 158; statutes on attorneys and lawyers, 33, 50, 94, 103–4, 113, 130–31n30, 139n8; Virginia legal culture, xiii–xiv, 103–4, 118, 148n6
Lawes Divine, Morall and Martiall (1612), 2
Lawrence, Henry, 52
Lee, Cassius F., 141n31
Lee, Thomas, 114, 151n49
Lee family papers, 157
legal profession. *See* law and lawyers
liberties: habeas corpus, 92; of speech and debate, 87, 109
lieutenant governor, problem of not having, 53
Ludwell, Philip, 72–73, 74, 77, 78–79, 80, 83, 109, 141n31
Ludwell, Thomas, 67, 72

Major, Edward, 41
Mallory, Phillip, 63
maritime matters, in Revisal of 1652, 44
Marlborough, John Churchill, 1st duke of, 101
marriage laws, 21, 34, 88, 95, 98
Martiau, Nicholas, 10
Mary II (queen of England), 79, 80
Maryland Gazette, 104
Mathews, Samuel (ca. 1629–60), xvi, 46–48, 50–53
Mathews, Samuel (d. 1657), 10, 14, 18, 19, 27, 28, 29, 43, 46
Maycock, Samuel, 3
McIlwaine, Henry Read, 157–58
Meade, John, 31

Mercer, John, *An Exact Abridgment of all the Public Acts of Assembly in Force and Use*, 106
Middle Plantation (later Williamsburg), settlement of, 24
Milner, Thomas, 81, 82, 83
miscegenation, prohibition of, 98
Mitchell, William, 47
mixed-race persons/mulattos, 95, 98, 112
morals act, 95
Mordaunt, Henry, earl of Peterborough, 77
Moryson, Francis, xvi, 46, 58–62, 65–69, 74, 91, 137n46; *Lawes of Virginia Now in Force* (1662), 67–69, 79, 84, 136–37n42, 137–38n46
Moryson, Lettice, 59
Moryson, Richard, 59
mulattos/mixed-race persons, 95, 98, 112

Navigation Act (1696), 84
neck verse (Psalm 51:1), 150n42
Necotowance (Indian leader), 37–38
Nelson, Thomas, 108, 109, 152n48
Nelson, William, 108, 144n54, 152n58
Newcastle, Thomas Pelham-Holles, 1st duke of, 101, 103
Newell, Jonathan, 49
Nicholas, Sir Edward, 54
Nicholson, Francis, 75, 80, 85, 87–90, 109, 158
Norfolk, Henry Howard, 6th duke of, 77
Norwood, Charles, 60
Nott, Edward, 70, 75, 89–92, 143n47, 145n59

oaths, swearing, 21, 40, 45, 48, 63, 94
"old planters," as protected class, 13, 22, 50
Old Point Comfort, fort at, 19, 59
Old Pretender (James Stuart), 101
Opechancanough (Indian leader), 37–38
Orkney, George Hamilton, 1st earl of, 89, 101, 143n47

Page, John, 78–79
Page, Matthew, 86, 88

Parks, William, 104–7, 114, 144n54, 148n12, 149n18, 151–52n56
Parliament. *See* British Parliament
Peirce, William, 10, 13
Pelham, Philadelphia (later Howard of Effingham), 77, 78
Pelham-Holles, Thomas, 1st duke of Newcastle, 101, 103
Peterborough, Henry Mordaunt, earl of, 77
Plowden, Sir Edmund, *Commentaries* (1571/79), 60, 134–35n13
Pocahontas, 3
population of Virginia (1625–1635), 128n2
Pory, John, 3–6
Pott, John, 9, 10, 19, 128n24
Pountis, John, 9, 11
Powell, Nathaniel, 3
Powhatans. *See* Indian relations
Priestley, Joseph, iv, xiv
printing press and print shop in Williamsburg, 104–7, 151–52n56
property and land: in Acts of 1623/24, 13–14; headright system, 96–97; Revisal of 1632 not addressing, 23; in Revisal of 1652, 43; in Revisal of 1658, 50; in Revisal of 1662, 67; in Revisal of 1705, 92, 94, 146n70; slaves, as property, 98, 99, 113
public intoxication/drunkenness, statutes on, 15, 21–22, 23, 43, 95
public order/criminal law: in Acts of 1623/24, 15; in Revisal of 1632, 21–22, 23, 24; in Revisal of 1652, 43; in Revisal of 1662, 64; in Revisal of 1705, 95, 96–97; in Revisal of 1748, 112
Puritans, 14, 35, 42–43
Purvis, John, *A Complete Collection of All the Laws of Virginia Now in Force* (1684), 79, 137n46

Quakers and Quakerism, 61, 63, 68
Quarter Court, 22, 24, 32–33, 44, 50, 52, 64
Queen Anne's War, 88

race: miscegenation, prohibition of, 98; mixed-race persons/mulattos, 95, 98, 112. *See also* Indian relations; slaves and slavery
Randolph, Henry, xvi, 48, 58–62, 65–69, 91
Randolph, Sir John, 48, 49, 104, 108
Randolph, Peter, 114
Randolph, Peyton, 48, 109, 152n58
Randolph, Richard, 108, 109
Randolph, William (1681–1742), 85, 89
Randolph, William (1723–1761), 144n54
Randolph manuscript of 1658 Revisal, 48–49, 125–26n24, 133n33
Rastell, William: *A Collection of Statutes Now in Force* (1615), 21, 62; *Entries of Declarations . . .* (1670), 21, 62
Reade, George, 46–47
religion and the church: in Acts of 1623/24, 12–13; Andros (governor) and, 85; benefit of clergy, 112, 150n42; Catholic recusants, 35, 131n42; church court, rejection of proposal for, 91–92; legislation enacted after 1623/24 Acts, 19; Quakers and Quakerism, 61, 63, 68; in Revisal of 1632, 21; in Revisal of 1643, 35–36; in Revisal of 1652, 42–43; in Revisal of 1662, 61, 62–63; in Revisal of 1705, 87, 88, 91–92, 95–96; slaves/slavery and, 98
republican government, Virginia under, xvi, 38, 39–41, 44–45, 53. *See also* Revisals of 1652 and 1658
restoration of crown, 54, 55–57, 62, 70–71, 75
Revisal of 1632, xv, 17–25; Acts of 1623/24, patterned on, 21; amendments of and additions to, xvi, 24; authority of General Assembly extended by, 20, 24–25; British Parliament, borrowing from legislation of, 21–22; February Assembly statutes, passage and withdrawal of, 19–23; Harvey, Sir John, and, xv, 17–20, 22; preambles, introduction of, 22–23; review and purging pf existing statutes, 20;

Revisal of 1632 (*continued*)
road maintenance in, 43; September Assembly and statutes, 22–24

Revisal of 1643, xvi, 26–38; Berkeley, Sir William, and, xvi, 26–32, 34–37; bicameral General Assembly, institution of, xvi, 30, 36–37; legislative recodification by, 30–36; new General Assembly called for 1642/43, 30; preamble, 31; recall of General Assembly in 1642, 28–29; Speaker, creation of office of, 30

Revisals of 1652 and 1658, xvi, 39–54; Berkeley chosen as governor by burgesses and, 53–54; General Assembly of 1652, activities of, 41–46; General Assembly of 1658, activities of, 47–51; General Assembly of 1658/59, activities of, 49, 52–53; governor's and council's powers, regulation of, 50, 52–54; Moryson, Francis, and, 59; preambles, 42, 49; Randolph manuscript of 1658 Revisal, 48–49, 125–26n24, 133n33; rediscovery of 1652 Revisal in 1970s, 41–42; republican government, Virginia under, xvi, 38, 39–41, 44–45, 53; review committee (1656–57), 46–47; Revisal of 1662 and, 57; Sloane Manuscript of 1658 Revisal, 48–49, 133n32

Revisal of 1662, xvi, 55–69; autonomy of Virginia, ensuring, 57–59, 62, 68–69; Berkeley and, xvi, 55–60, 62–63, 66–69; Foreign Plantations, Committee/Council for, 57–58, 62, 68; General Assembly of 1661/62, called by Berkeley, 58–59; legislation of, 60–67; Francis Moryson/Henry Randolph and, 58–62, 65–69; other Revisals compared, 57, 91; preamble, 56, 62; printing of (Berkeley, *Lawes of Virginia Now in Force,* 1662), 67–69, 136–37n42, 137–38n46; recall of General Assembly in 1660/61 and, 55–56; restoration of crown, constitutional implications of, 55–57, 62

Revisal of 1705, xvi, 70–100; committee/commission on law reform (1698–1703), 84–89; diminishment of authority of General Assembly and autonomy of Virginia by, 70, 71–72, 99–100, 139n14; law reform efforts (1692–1698) under Andros, 81–85; passage of, 90–91; political factions and rivalries leading up to, 72–81, 89; provisions of, 91–100, 113; restoration of crown and, 70–71, 75; Revisal of 1662 compared, 91

"Revisal of 1733" (Hening), 144n54

Revisal of 1748, xvii, 101–17; Board of Trade and, xvii, 101–2, 103, 107, 111, 114–17, 118; committee for, 108–10; compared to earlier Revisals, 111; General Assembly of 1745/46 approving act for, 107–9; General Assembly of 1748 adopting, 110–11, 114; Gooch and, xvii, 100, 101–5, 107–11, 113–14, 117; indexing and printing of, 114; printing press and *Collection of Acts* (1733) project, 104–7; provisions of, 111–13; significance of, 117; vetting and revision of, 111, 114–17

Revolutionary War, 117

Rich, Robert, 2d earl of Warwick, 2, 7, 10, 11, 15

Richmond fire of April 1865, loss of documents in, xiv, xv, 49, 56

road maintenance, 43

Robertson, William, 102, 104

Robinson, Conway, 130n19, 157

Robinson, John (1683–1749), 108–9

Robinson, John (1705–66), 108, 109, 110, 114

Rolfe, John, 3

royal dominion, proclamation of Virginia as (1625), xv, 1, 7–8, 18, 118

royal government, return to, 54, 55–57, 62, 70–72. *See also* Revisal of 1662

runaways, legislation on, 34, 67, 98, 113

Russell, John, 4th duke of Bedford, 114

Sandys, Sir Edwin, 2, 3, 4, 7, 9–11

Sandys, George, 9, 28, 29

Sea Venture, 4
Second Anglo-Dutch War, 71
Seile, Ellen, 67
sericulture (silkworms), encouragement of, 51
Seven Years' War, 117
Sharples, Edward, 12, 126n24
Shelley, Walter, 6
sheriffs: in Revisal of 1632, 19, 24; in Revisal of 1643, 30, 32; in Revisals of 1652/58, 41, 43, 44, 50, 52; in Revisal of 1662, 64–65; in Revisal of 1705, 93, 94, 98, 145n64
Sidney, John, 47
slaves and slavery: increase in numbers of, 99; property, slaves as, 98, 99, 113; religion/the church and, 98; Revisal of 1632 not addressing, 23; Revisal of 1658 on, 50–51; Revisal of 1662 on, 67; Revisal of 1705 on, 97–99, 113; Revisal of 1748 on, 112–13; runaway slaves, 98, 113; Virginia as slave-owning culture, 99
Sloane, Sir Hans, and Sloane Manuscript, 48–49, 133n32
smallpox epidemic, 84
Smith, John (Francis Dade), 47
Smith, Sir Thomas, *De Republica Anglorum* (1583), 126n28
Smythe, Sir Thomas, 2, 7, 10, 11, 15
Soane, Henry, 56, 60
Southampton, 17
Spanish Succession, War of the, 101
Speaker: Acts of 1623/24, no Speaker for, 11; creation of office of, 30; at first meeting of General Assembly (1619), 4–5; Revisal of 1632, no Speaker for, 20. *See also specific Speakers by name*
Spencer, Nicholas, 74, 78–79
Spencer, Robert, 2d earl of Sunderland, 79
Spotswood, Alexander, 92, 143n47
statute law in colonial Virginia, xiii–xvii, 118–20; Acts of 1623/24 (*see also* Acts of 1623/24); beginnings of, 1–16 (*see also* beginnings of Virginia statutes); consent of General Assembly required for any English law concerning Virginia, 119; dates and dating, xix, 144n53; legal culture of settler society, importance to, xiii–xiv; other colonial legislatures and, 120; Revisals of, xv–xvii (*see also specific entries at* Revisal); Richmond fire of April 1865, loss of documents in, xiv, xv, 49, 56; source materials for, xiv–xv; sources for, xiv–xv, 155–58 (*see also* Hening, William Waller)
statute of limitations, 94
Stegge, Thomas, 30, 40
Stephens, Richard, 10, 19
Stephens, Samuel, 10
stint act, 31–32
Strachey, William, *A True Discourse of the True Estate of Virginia* (1615), 9, 123n2
Stuart, Charles Edward (the Young Pretender), 107–8
Stuart, James (the Old Pretender), 101
Sunderland, Robert Spencer, 2d earl of, 79
Swann, Samuel, 81
Swann, Thomas, 47
swearing/blasphemy, prohibition of, 15, 95, 146n68
Swinburne, Michael, *Treatise of Testaments and Last Wills*, 113

tales de circumstantibus, 64, 94
Tarter, Brent, 122n5
taxation: in Acts of 1623/24, 15; for burgesses' costs, 33; in Revisal of 1643, 33, 34; in Revisal of 1658, 50–51; in Revisal of 1748, 111
Taylor, John, 86, 88, 142n37
Tazewell, Littleton Waller, 150n30
Tenison, Thomas, 95
Theolall, Simon, and Ralph de Gingham, *Registrum Brevity* . . . (1687), 142n41
Third Anglo-Dutch War, 71
Thirty Years' War, 17
tobacco: in Revisal of 1632, 21; in Revisal of 1643, 31–32; in Revisal of 1658, 51;

tobacco (*continued*)
  in Revisal of 1662, 67; in Revisal of 1748, 111; rioting over price of, 77; royal interest in, 2, 18; Virginia society based on, xvi, 27
Tucker, Sarah (later Fitzhugh), 82
Tucker, William, 10, 13
Twine, John, 4

urban development, 24, 44, 51, 68, 111
Utie, John, 10–11, 19

VCRP (Virginia Colonial Records Project), 155, 156
vestries and vestrymen, 36, 63
Virginia: common law in, 2, 12, 87, 106, 118; designated as royal dominion, xv, 1, 7–8, 18, 118; founding charter, 119; growth and expansion westward of, 111; legal culture in, 103–4, 118, 148n6; population (1625–1635), 128n2; Richmond fire of April 1865, loss of documents in, xiv, xv, 49, 56; as slave-owning culture, 99; tobacco, Virginia society based on, xvi, 27. *See also* Council of State, Virginia; General Assembly; House of Burgesses; statute law in colonial Virginia
Virginia Colonial Records Project (VCRP), 155, 156
Virginia Company of London: beginnings of statute law in Virginia and, 1, 6–7, 14; Berkeley, Sir William, and, 28; "Declaration against the Company," 28, 119, 129n9; downfall and dissolution of, xv, 7–8, 11, 18, 63; Harvey, Sir John, and, 17, 18; land policy, lack of, 96; possible revivals of, 8, 9, 18, 27, 28, 29, 57, 58; sources for, 156, 157
Virginia Gazette, 106, 107
voter qualifications, 94–95

Waller, Benjamin, 108, 150n30, 152n58
Warner, Augustine, 74
wars. *See specific wars by name, e.g.* Jenkins' Ear, War of
Warwick, Robert Rich, 2d earl of, 2, 7, 10, 11, 15
Webb, George, 105–6, 109–10, 150n30; *Office and Authority of a Justice of Peace* (1736), 106, 113, 119
Webster, Richard, 47
West, Francis, 3, 9–10, 13, 19
West, John, 19
West, Thomas, twelfth baron De La Warr, 10
Whiting, Beverley, 108, 152n58
Wickham, William, 3
Wilcox, John, 46–47
William III (king of England), 79, 80, 88, 96
Williamsburg: building of capitol and city of, 87, 88, 89, 142n38; burning of capitol building (1747), 109, 112; Middle Plantation (later Williamsburg), settlement of, 24; printing press and print shop in, 104–7, 151–52n56
Willis, Francis, 46–47
Wood, Abraham, 46–47
Wormeley, Ralph, 84–85
Worrall, Joseph, *Bibliotheca Legum* (1777), 143n41
Worsley, Benjamin, 157
Wroth, Lawrence C., 148n12
Wyatt, Sir Francis: beginnings of Virginia statutes and, 1, 7, 8, 10–13, 15–16, 126n24; replaced by Berkeley as governor, 26, 27, 28, 29; Revisal of 1632 and, 17, 18, 130n19
Wynne, Robert, 56, 60, 61, 134–35n13

Yeardley, Sir George, 1–7, 9, 10, 123n4
Young Pretender (Charles Edward Stuart), 107–8

Recent books in the series
EARLY AMERICAN HISTORIES

Against Popery: Britain, Empire, and Anti-Catholicism
Evan Haefeli, editor

Conceived in Crisis: The Revolutionary Creation of an American State
Christopher R. Pearl

Redemption from Tyranny: Herman Husband's American Revolution
Bruce E. Stewart

Experiencing Empire: Power, People, and Revolution in Early America
Patrick Griffin, editor

Citizens of Convenience: The Imperial Origins of American Nationhood on the U.S.-Canadian Border
Lawrence B. A. Hatter

"Esteemed Bookes of Lawe" and the Legal Culture of Early Virginia
Warren M. Billings and Brent Tarter, editors

Settler Jamaica in the 1750s: A Social Portrait
Jack P. Greene

Loyal Protestants and Dangerous Papists: Maryland and the Politics of Religion in the English Atlantic, 1630–1690
Antoinette Sutto

The Road to Black Ned's Forge: A Story of Race, Sex, and Trade on the Colonial American Frontier
Turk McCleskey

Dunmore's New World: The Extraordinary Life of a Royal Governor in Revolutionary America—with Jacobites, Counterfeiters, Land Schemes, Shipwrecks, Scalping, Indian Politics, Runaway Slaves, and Two Illegal Royal Weddings
James Corbett David